NO ONE LOVES
YOUR MONEY
LIKE YOU DO

NO ONE LOVES YOUR MONEY LIKE YOU DO

THE ULTIMATE RETIREMENT PLANNING GUIDE FOR BUSINESS OWNERS AND PRIVATE PRACTITIONERS

James B. Jackson, DDS, CFP

New York   Chicago   San Francisco   Athens   London
Madrid   Mexico City   Milan   New Delhi
Singapore   Sydney   Toronto

1 2 3 4 5 6 7 8 9 0   DOC/DOC   1 2 0 9 8 7 6 5 4

ISBN   978-0-07-183936-5
MHID   0-07-183936-4

e-ISBN   978-0-07-183939-6
e-MHID   0-07-183939-9

This publication is designed to provide accurate and authoritative information in regard to the subject matter covered. It is sold with the understanding that neither the author nor the publisher is engaged in rendering legal, accounting, securities trading, or other professional services. If legal advice or other expert assistance is required, the services of a competent professional person should be sought.
> —*From a Declaration of Principles Jointly Adopted by a Committee of the American Bar Association and a Committee of Publishers and Associations*

Library of Congress Cataloging-in-Publication Data

Jackson, James B.
   No one loves your money like you do : the ultimate retirement planning guide for business owners and private practitioners / James Jackson.
       pages cm
    ISBN 978-0-07-183936-5 (hardback)—ISBN 0-07-183936-4 (hardback)
1. Retirement income—Planning.   2. Retirement—Planning.
3. Businesspeople—Retirement.   4. Professional employees—Retirement.
5. Finance, Personal.   I. Title.
    HG179.J235 2015
    332.024'014—dc23

                                                                2014023637

McGraw-Hill Education books are available at special quantity discounts to use as premiums and sales promotions or for use in corporate training programs. To contact a representative, please visit the Contact Us pages at www.mhprofessional.com.

To my wife, Dee, who has heard me say "I've got to finish this book" a bit too often. Thanks for your patience, understanding, and above all, for putting up with me.

Contents

Preface   ix

Acknowledgments   xi

PART ONE

INTRODUCTION

1   If You Love Your Money, It's Time to Get Started   3

2   You Can Do This   13

PART TWO

GOALS AND SELF-ASSESSMENT

3   Establishing Your Goals   27

4   Assessing What You Have   49

5   Your Business and Your Retirement   59

PART THREE

RETIREMENT TOOLS AND RESOURCES

6   Understanding the Market and Your Investments   71

7   Understanding Mutual Funds, Exchange-Traded
     Funds (ETFs), and Index Funds   93

8   Selecting and Managing Your Mutual Funds   121

9   Stocks and Bonds   135

10   Other Investment Options   155

11   Social Security   171

12   Finding the Right Financial Adviser and Investment
     Manager   177

     PART FOUR

     LIVING THE GOOD LIFE: LIFE AFTER RETIREMENT

13   Using Your Savings for the Rest of Your Life   193

14   The Three Pots   209

15   Long-Term Care, Healthcare, and Other Needs   219

16   Emergency Alternatives   231

17   Life After Retirement for Professionals and Business
     Owners   237

     CONCLUSION: Putting It All Together   243

     INDEX   245

     ABOUT THE AUTHOR   255

Preface

Why did I write this book? In the late 1980s, I began making my transition from dentistry to financial planning. I had already written one book and coauthored another. But back then, I was principally a financial and retirement planning *teacher*—simply giving advice to my fellow health professionals on "how to retire."

There is a big difference between telling someone how to do something and doing it yourself. In 1989, I left private practice at the urging of some of my colleagues from around the country, and I started Jackson Financial Co., Inc., a financial planning firm geared to health professionals—busy, hard-working people who are incredibly well trained in their fields but who get absolutely no training in how to save and invest while they are in school. Today, at my new firm, JBJ Investment Partners, we no longer limit ourselves to only health professionals. We now have a big enough team to help anyone who needs guidance and advice.

Through the years, my clients, who are also my friends and colleagues, shared their stories of how they had been "bamboozled" by too many in the financial industry. Physicians, dentists, professionals, and business owners are very susceptible to being the scapegoat in the investment world because they have an attractive income level—and they generally have had no investment courses or advice along the way. I wanted to put an end to that, and my approach became, and it still is, to help my clients—and now, you, dear reader—invest wisely today and for retirement.

I've already passed retirement age, so I thought the most important thing I could do is to show you how to do it from the perspective of someone who has experienced the things that you will experience in the future. This is one time that I can tell you I am practicing what I preach, and I am enjoying helping others at the same time. My goal is to die with my boots on because helping others realize their dreams is a wonderful occupation that has no age limit to it.

You **can** do this! Yes, it may take a little work and organization, but I am ready to answer any questions you might have and to help you in any way I can.

I have named some mutual funds and stocks in the book but not named others. Funds come and go, and while many funds have been good investments longer than you could imagine, things change. I don't want to prescribe a fund to people if, over time, it is no longer a valid choice.

There is no reason that any of us cannot retire comfortably and successfully—all we have to do is to put one foot down and then the other on the road to getting you there. I sincerely hope you will enjoy reading this, and if you need any help or suggestions of where to get this or that, you can find me at http://www.940financialconsulting.com. All you have to do is ask.

Acknowledgments

Thanks go to Ken Beacham, who asked me to speak on financial and retirement planning for the American Dental Association in the 1980s. His insistence that I share my knowledge with my profession has allowed me to have two careers—pediatric dentistry and financial and retirement planning. I am a very lucky guy!

Besides the "usual suspects," my hat is off to the clients who have been with me all the way and are still enthusiastic about investing and to the investment managers who have been wonderful to our clients, helping our clients see their dreams come true. You can hardly ask for more in our business. If I started naming names, it would take several pages, so I'll only say that "you know who you are," and my gratitude for your help is immeasurable.

I can never thank Mathew, my business partner, enough for caring about our work as much as I do, and that's saying something. It's good to know the office is in such good hands.

And last, but not least, thanks go to Mark Butler, of Butler Beyond Books. He has been a great editor—especially prodding me to finish the book and get it to the publisher.

PART ONE

INTRODUCTION

1

If You Love Your Money, It's Time to Get Started

Wake-Up Call: The gap between what Americans have saved for retirement and what they will likely need is $6.6 trillion. That's almost half of the gross domestic product of the United States.

Every investor and saver needs to remember: no one loves your money the way you do, and it is up to you to make sure it is well tended at all times.

You've spent a large part of your life working hard, building a practice or a business. You've worked long hours and made sacrifices—and you've enjoyed the rewards of your hard work. So let's keep it that way!

If you love your money, you need to care about it. You need a good plan to grow and maintain your money, and you need to make sure that the people who interact with it are concerned about its well-being and are responsible people. If it sounds like I am comparing money to a child, it is not too far from the truth. You would not place your young children with complete strangers without very careful research and references. You should treat your money with the same concern.

> *Wake-Up Call: Many people spend more time planning a two-week vacation to Europe than they do planning their future. Folks who will study* Consumer Reports *for a month before buying a TV will buy a mutual fund after just two minutes of scanning through a Morningstar report or a 30-second conversation with a broker.*

When your retirement begins, you will have a certain amount of money, and it will have to last. You might consider this your starting point. In other words, you can't just save *for* retirement. You need to formulate your plan *through* retirement. You need to think about your goals, your wishes, and the expenses that will be a big part of your post-work life.

> *Wake-Up Call: If you are a man and make it to 65, your odds are better than 50/50 that you will live to reach 85 and about 1 in 4 that you will see age 91. (The odds are better still for women.) That means the average retiree needs to plan for a retirement period of not less than 20 years.*

As the world continues to change, the old rules about retirement continue to be rewritten. The lessons about your parents' retirement may not teach you much about your own.

Retirement is something of a new phenomenon. Prior to the twentieth century, most people basically worked as long as they were able and then relied upon family members or charitable groups to care for them for a relatively brief period before dying.

Thinking about retirement means thinking about a time period bracketed by the end of your working life and your death. Healthy, well-adjusted people generally don't set a target date for their end. However, some planning is necessary. Unfortunately, people come up with a host of excuses for their lack of preparation for retirement.

One inescapable trend in retirement is that workers are being saddled with a great deal more of the responsibility to plan and provide for their retirement needs.

And this group includes you—whether you are a dentist, a physician, an attorney, or an entrepreneur and whether you are an independent practioner, own your business, or are in a partnership. You are in charge of your destiny—so take charge. This book will guide you through creating a plan, selecting advisers, investing wisely, and managing your money after you retire. There's a lot of common ground between you and everyone else reaching retirement age. But there are unique challenges specific to professionals—and I'll address those throughout the book.

Chapters 5 and 17 will tackle the complexities you will likely face: dealing with partners, having a large part of your wealth tied up in your business, and selling your business or practice, just to name a few. You can skip ahead to these parts or read them as a part of the whole book.

In this book, I want to help you:

- Take control of your retirement.
- Plan for the kind of retirement you've always wanted.
- Have the best chance possible for the best retirement.

When you have finished this book, you should be able to:

- Set goals for your retirement—and match an investment strategy to your goals.
- Assess what you have to start.
- Understand the basics of investing.
- Build and manage a solid portfolio of risk-appropriate investments, or find qualified people to help you.
- Set up a drawdown plan that will meet your day-to-day spending needs and preserve the capital you need for the longer term.
- Feel more comfortable and confident about how to handle the financial decisions that go with retirement.

Are You Ready to Get Started?

Luckily, you **can** tackle this yourself. It is not as complicated as it might seem. At a bare minimum, even if you choose not to handle the day-to-day affairs of your financial future, you should be able to create a plan of your own.

> *Wake-Up Call: The financial services industry has worked hard to convince the public that what its advisers do is mysterious and difficult and that it requires years of training. It clearly makes financial sense for the industry to convince us all that we ought not try this ourselves. The reality is quite the opposite. Put in a little time and effort, and you can do it as well!*

If you do not actively involve yourself in the process, you risk being a passenger—and a statistic. Every planner has tools that will craft a financial plan of action for the "average" person of your age. Unfortunately, financial planning is just too important for such an off-the-rack sort of approach. Do you have off-the-rack needs and dreams? Do you want to live out everybody else's (or the "average person's") retirement?

Advisers are not the gatekeepers to a successful retirement. You are.

> *Wake-Up Call: Every day you delay planning—and saving—for retirement is a lost opportunity. If you spend $4 each workday at Starbucks instead of investing it in an 8 percent average-yield mutual fund over 30 years, your daily caffeine fix will cost you just over $130,000 if you compound weekly.*

There's still time to catch up once you establish a plan. The government may allow you to make larger-than-normal tax-deductible contributions to retirement accounts. If you are 50 years of age or older, you can contribute up to $5,500 (for the 2014 calendar year) to a traditional or Roth individual retirement account (IRA), and if you are over 50, you can use the catch-up exemption with an extra $1,000 so your total contribution can be $6,500. On top of that, you can add $5,500 more per year to a 401(k) plan (up to $23,000) or a 403(b) or 457(b) plan. These numbers change over time, so check the IRS website (http://www.irs.gov) for accurate amounts.

Isn't Retirement Living Cheaper Than Regular Living?

The idea that retirement means a sudden reduction in living expenses is one of the most dangerous ideas about retirement. Retirement may actually end up being even more expensive than regular work-a-day living. However, the idea that it's cheaper is a common misconception that often leads people to undersaving and overestimating how long their resources will last. The truth is that retirement is not cheaper unless you are willing to accept a significant drop in your standard of living.

You might get a few more perks beyond your senior citizen discount on movies or coffee. For example, property tax exemptions to homeowners over 65 years of age are common in many states. However, a comfortable and enjoyable quality of life still has a price tag, so while you'll get some breaks, there will be a number of continuing and/or new expenses such as supplemental insurance for your Medicare coverage, as well as some of these:

- Mortgage payments or rent
- Ongoing expenses like home maintenance and repairs, income taxes, and property taxes
- Car expenses
- Personal expenses (Are you going to eat any less just because you are retired, and are you going to stop turning on your lights?)

Wake-Up Call: There are hundreds of resources that tell you how to set up an IRA or how to build a nest-egg. But when it comes to how to actually live off that nest egg, things get suddenly quiet in advice land.

The advice many people get about how to draw down their savings is shockingly shallow and generic. Oftentimes, you will not hear much more than "Do not take out more than 4 percent of your savings in a year." In the meantime, are you supposed to keep all of it in bonds? Should you still own stocks? Do certificates of deposit (CDs) have a useful role to play? Instead of answering these questions in any detail, a lot of advisers will simply push a pamphlet about annuities across the desk.

Part Four of the book is devoted to living off what you have, but this is not just about making do with your savings. It's about dreaming big—and investing accordingly to match your life's goals with your money.

Wake-Up Call: There are risks involved in saving for retirement, but the biggest risk is in doing nothing.

Mistakes Will Happen—and You Can Still Retire If You Make One!

Making a mistake is one of the biggest fears that people have about investing their own money—after all, money that you worked hard to earn can be lost. But if you follow some very basic rules, then a single investment mistake *will not* ruin your retirement. And I have some very good news . . .

My approach helps protect you from big mistakes because it requires you to have a diversified array of holdings. The unexpected failure of any one of them will not cripple your plans. Using a group of mutual funds, exchange-traded funds (ETFs), or other investments that have been well thought out and researched can keep you from putting all of your eggs in one basket.

In fact, by using a three-part distribution system that I discuss in Chapter 14, you will actually always have three years' worth of your retirement needs invested in a diversified group of very safe instruments. Outside of insured bank deposits and Treasury instruments, nothing is guaranteed, but when your short-term needs are covered by a pool of money that is in ultraconservative investments, you can weather almost any financial crisis. (Think about this: if you had had three years' worth of your money stashed away like this in 2008, you would have sailed through the latest recession and ended up with more money to boot!)

Wake-Up Call: Not only can you lose money due to market volatility, but you can also lose it due to a wide range of fees and service charges when you are not careful about evaluating the true costs of investments—or the fees assessed by the firms helping you acquire them.

Things You Need to Know

Some of the biggest issues that affect your retirement planning come back to whom you choose to work with. It's natural to feel like you can't do it yourself—but I'll show you that you can. I'm also going to emphasize that taking an active role in the retirement planning process will help minimize the cost of retirement. After all, the business of retirement planning is a for-profit one!

The financial services industry makes money primarily by:

- Charging a fee for each transaction or service
- Collecting fees based upon the amount of assets that they manage for people

While that compensation structure gives them incentive to do well for their clients, it also gives them incentive to try to collect as much of your assets under their roof as possible.

> *Wake-Up Call: Many companies running your 401(k) are not necessarily acting in your best interests. Instead, they have an incentive to recommend their own products.*

Working with a professional does not necessarily mean that you are working with an expert. Remember the old joke: "You know why they call them brokers? You give them your money, and you become broker and broker!"

However, there are thousands of dedicated, qualified, and skillful advisers out there, and the chances are very good that you can find one with only a little bit of effort. Good advisers can (and should) be worth much more than their fees: they can guide you into the right investments, help you execute your plans, remind you of matters you may not have considered, and bring you an all-around improved peace of mind.

My Methodology and Your Plan

My approach is largely a commonsense approach that will require only occasional activity from you once it is in place. Ideally, this approach will:

- Reduce your worries
- Outpace inflation
- Support an enjoyable lifestyle

This is **not** a get-rich-quick plan, and it does not promise that you can do whatever you want whenever you want. Instead, this is about carefully tending to your assets. It is not completely immune to the movement of the stock market or the economy. My plan reduces the risk of loss due to market volatility, but no plan can eliminate that risk entirely.

I will give you the basic toolbox and instructions that you will need to manage your own retirement. But you will have to help me by doing some work along the way:

- There will be math, but it won't be too hard.
- You may need to learn a little more about investments and personal finance to get more comfortable with some of the concepts in this book, but luckily, learning about the markets and investments is easier than ever before.
- You will need to inventory your assets, evaluate your annual spending needs, review and manage your portfolio, and move assets around.
- More than anything else, what you will need most are the willpower and time to do it.
- There are resources listed throughout the book, and there are resources on the website http://www.940financialconsulting.com.

Retirement is **not** the time to be making bets on the "next big thing." You should plan to preserve your capital and grow it conservatively— instead of multiplying it quickly. With that in mind, there are a few single mistakes that can seriously harm you:

- Choosing the wrong adviser can certainly be a bad mistake if you give all of your money to that adviser.
- Making very large bets on risky assets can be damaging, like placing half of your retirement savings in a start-up company or a volatile asset like gold.
- Panic selling can put a big dent in the nest egg too. If you had sold stocks at a loss in 2008, it would have taken a lot of work to earn that money back. If you had held onto them, you would have actually been ahead of where you were when you bought them.

Here are some ways to avoid mistakes:

- Keep in mind that markets **can** drop 20 percent or more in a year, but these drops are relatively rare and they seldom occur in consecutive years.

- To limit market volatility damage even further, avoid putting the majority of your retirement wealth in risky stocks.
- Instead, keep your short-term retirement spending money in safer, fixed-income instruments and conservative stocks and funds so as to protect your immediate reserves. That type of investment will give you time to let the stocks recover without forcing you to sell into a weak stock market.

Each step in implementing my plan should not require more than a weekend afternoon. Once you become more comfortable with the system, your time commitment will actually get smaller. Beyond that, there are really no difficult steps that require advanced knowledge or any sort of confusing formulas. So, as long as you are patient and thorough, you can absolutely do this.

Quick Quiz

1. How much time do you spend on the following?
    Buying a car   _____
    Planning a vacation   _____
    Choosing an adviser   _____
    Choosing a restaurant for a big dinner on the town   _____
    Picking a stock or a mutual fund   _____
    Reviewing your portfolio   _____

    There's no "right answer," but if your retirement is going to run 20 years or more, I'd recommend spending more time on it than your dinner or your vacation planning!

2. Can you live on half your income?

3. How well do you know your broker or financial adviser?

4. List three goals for your life after retirement:
    Goal 1 _____
    Goal 2 _____
    Goal 3 _____

    We'll come back to your goals when the planning process begins in Chapter 3. And by the way, don't stop at three. List as many goals as you have!

5. What's the biggest asset in your portfolio?

2

You Can Do This

If you were lucky enough to inherit a sizable fortune, if you run a Fortune 500 corporation, or if you've won a lottery—congratulations, this book is probably not for you. If you fit into that other 99.9 percent of the population, chances are you have thought quite a bit about what your financial future is going to look like, and one of the biggest parts of that future is retirement.

A great retirement is a very worthwhile goal, but it takes planning and preparation—and that is the reason I wrote this book. I would love to see everybody make the most of their retirement savings and live the best retirement they can.

I began my career as a pediatric dentist after a great education at some of the best schools in the nation. I now am a Certified Financial Planner (CFP) advising my fellow health professionals and others who run their own businesses. I've always had a knack for managing money, but as I will tell you elsewhere in the book, a mere knack isn't enough to ensure someone's wealth and retirement. I've put in the work and attained the proper certifications to focus on the importance of being a smart and sensible steward of others' hard-earned money.

But I also know that those of you who have built a successful practice or business don't have a lot of spare time—or extra brain capacity—to tackle the art and science of investing and asset management. But if you physicians out there will pardon the pun, retirement planning is not brain surgery. I've been honored to help friends and peers secure their financial futures—and I can help you too if you can invest a little of your valuable time.

Loving Your Money Is Not a Bad Thing

You know what slogan you never hear from the financial services industry? "We love your money like you do." Even the most rapacious publicist knows that that would be a step too far into the unbelievable.

Does it sound strange to talk about money in such intimate terms? Hopefully, your answer is no. Thinking about your financial future and valuing your own money is not greed, and it is not the sort of preoccupation that leads to Scrooge-like behavior or the evils of Wall Street's wrong-doers. Instead, it is about taking responsibility for your future and doing right by yourself and your family.

Money is an essential tool for your present and your future. It is important for you to maintain this tool and give money matters the attention they deserve. A healthy relationship with money and a healthy preoccupation with your financial future are vital if you are going to reach your retirement goals and maintain your independence in the face of a lot of confusing and conflicting information.

Retirement *Is* Coming

Every one of us who works shares at least one thing in common: there will come a day when we stop working. For most of us, that will come with a formal decision to retire and 10, 20, or 30 years more of living. If we are fortunate (and if we plan well), those decades are something to be looked forward to as a time of enjoying a slower pace of life and fewer worries. If we do not plan well, those consequences are not so pleasant.

As scary as this may be, it is definitely better than the alternatives of the past. Until recently, retirement was not a comfortable process, nor was it something that people looked forward to with any enthusiasm. Nowadays, though, retirement can be about cruises and hobbies—not just about running out the clock and hoping to avoid sickness.

Some of this can be credited to the Germans. German Chancellor Von Bismarck in 1881 suggested that "those who had been disabled from work by age and invalidity had a well-grounded claim to care from the state." The Germans used the age of 70 as a time to start retirement, but later they dropped it to 65. In 1935, the United States launched the Social Security system. The government chose 65 as a retirement age because existing private pension systems, some state-run old age pensions, and the Railroad Retirement System were using 65 as a retirement age.

For all of its faults, the Social Security concept is really quite a marvel. Older workers today do not have the same anxiety about how they will manage to get by when they stop working, and the addition of the Medicare system guarantees a reasonably good quality of life. So, despite the complaints and worries about Social Security (including the gradual migration toward a retirement age of 70), it really was a step forward. But as you will later read, Social Security is not enough.

There's Good News and Bad News: Retirement Is Evolving

Earlier, I alerted you to the fact that average Americans fall way short with what they need to have saved for retirement versus what they have actually socked away. Many well-off and well-educated folks haven't even saved enough money to see them through 10 years of retirement! Even allowing for people who are struggling to just get by, that is a shocking gap in a wealthy and well-educated country like ours.

Clearly, people are not thinking about their financial future as much as they should, and the long-term consequences are going to be a decline in the standard of living during retirement or more government subsidies for retirement (which will mean higher taxes, higher interest rates, and higher burdens on younger workers).

Some of this gap may be a product of the recent recession, but a lack of planning and poor financial literacy is certainly the larger part of it.

Why are people not better prepared for retirement and more knowledgeable about their long-term financial needs? Unfortunately, this is not really something like driving a car or baking a cake—a lesson whose basic principles have worked for generations and will probably continue to do so. The financial rules are constantly changing, and what might have been true a decade ago is not necessarily still true today. Consequently, I think parents are at a loss as to what to teach their kids about finance and financial planning—in fact, they are probably still trying to figure it out for themselves!

Retirement is still an evolving concept. Labor unions fought hard for pensions in the first half of the twentieth century, and the New Deal gave us Social Security. To a certain extent, this trained a few generations of Americans to regard retirement savings as something that other people were already taking care of for them. The stock market was not seen as a place for regular people, and there was not much discussion concerning finance beyond simple rules about the importance of savings and living within your means.

Unfortunately, there have been a lot of significant changes over the years. About 30 years ago, companies began to realize that defined benefit pension plans were beginning to be an exceptionally expensive obligation. This led companies to shift to the defined contribution plans like 401(k)s that are so prevalent today. Odds are, unless you work for the government (state or federal) or a company in an industry with a strong history of union activity, you do not have a retirement plan that was prevalent 30 years ago.

At the same time, Social Security has changed significantly in its scope and purpose. Social Security was originally supposed to be a safety net so that seniors would not live in destitution. Instead, it has morphed into a quasi-retirement plan that it was never meant to be.

The only thing that really seems certain is that individuals are going to continue to bear more and more of the responsibility for ensuring that they have enough money to have a comfortable retirement.

What this has meant, though, is that the burden for taking care of your retirement needs has shifted squarely from "somebody else" to *you*. But who better to decide how you want to retire than you? After all, no one loves your money like you do. You are going to have to take charge of your finances in retirement, like it or not.

Where Do You Begin?

The big problem is that there is a decided lack of quality advice out there about how to prepare for retirement. Sure, there's a copious amount of information available and plenty of people with opinions. But most of these folks are going to help themselves first and worry about you later. They probably are trying to sell you something, and what works for them might not work for you. You really have to spend some time "interviewing" people and companies to help you.

You should use someone who doesn't sell "products" but, instead, sells advice. I should know. This is my business too. My philosophy has always centered on the long-term benefits for my clients and not on the short-term gains for my firm or me. That means I focus on my clients' goals and on building a personalized investment plan. And you know what? Things work out really well for both parties that way!

As the marketplace has shifted to employee- and self-directed pro-grams, the overall trend has shifted to one-size-fits-all solutions. That might seem like a relief when you are wading through tough choices on your plan—but do you want a generic retirement?

Because more and more companies have abandoned defined benefit plans and turned to 401(k)s and other employee-directed programs, employees are often given a limited set of investment choices (a fixed list of mutual funds or annuities, for instance), and there are few options for tailoring a plan to meet individual needs and goals. On top of this, the vast majority of companies offer only minimal (if any) tutoring or counseling for employees, leaving those employees to their own devices.

As an employer, you are probably facing few real choices as well. You may have a handful of different programs from a handful of companies to choose from, but there are very limited choices within these programs. You do get the benefit of having a point of contact with these firms, but these contacts are usually salespeople trying to work to their advantage while helping you.

After all, the funds offered in a plan may be a function of how lucrative they are for the sponsor to offer, as opposed to their quality or suitability for you. And when it comes to long-term planning, . . . well, those companies would be quite happy if you would just keep your money with them when you retire and move it into "appropriate" options like annuities (which are very lucrative for the providers.)

If you do not elect to use the choices the company running your retirement plan wants you to use post-retirement, then the company will often leave you to your own ideas. That is where this book comes in. My hope is that I can help shape how you think about your retirement and how you can begin setting up the plans that you will need to have in place to make the most of your money and the best of your retirement.

Whom Do You Trust?

Financial services is a big business. With over $52.6 trillion in assets under management, the financial services industry earns billions of dollars a year in revenue and employs millions of people. Think about all of those financial services ads you see on TV—the companies paying for them certainly expect to get a return on that money.

How much can you expect to pay for financial services? Let's look at annuities—one of the assets most often recommended for retired people:

- A financial services firm might charge you as much as 5 to 7 percent in commissions right off the top.
- In addition, there are annual fees that can easily exceed 2 percent a year.

- Likewise, a financial adviser might charge you between 1 and 2 percent a year (or more) to manage your money—on top of any fees charged by the funds. (None of that is rebated to you if the adviser's guidance is not up to snuff!)
- You may also pay additional fees and commissions depending on the size of your account and/or the types of investments sold to you.
- If you invested $100,000 in an annuity with total fees adding up to 6 percent, you would begin with only $94,000, and you would have yearly fees on top of that. You have given up a lot of your money just to invest in this product.

The financial services industry needs either ever-growing numbers of transactions or ever-growing amounts of money under management to continue its own growth. You might end up giving up a lot of your hard-earned money in fees if you follow a salesperson's advice to buy an unnecessary annuity instead of a no-load mutual fund that matches your goals. The salesperson wants to manage your money pre- and post-retirement so he or she can keep making a profit on you. Make sure that the industry works for you and not the other way around:

- Many firms are going to sell you only what they have "on the shelf."
- Those products and services may not be the ones you want or need, but it is rare for a broker to tell you this and suggest that you take your business elsewhere.
- Remember, they need to keep as much of your money in their hands as possible, so a partial match to your needs might be "close enough."
- Many brokers and advisers have relationships with mutual fund companies that incentivize them to promote those funds to investors.
- You can still buy almost any mutual fund you like through any broker you choose, but you may have to pay more for it than you would pay if you bought it directly from the mutual fund company or from a discount brokerage firm.

Whether you work with a financial adviser or manage your money yourself through a brokerage account, a failure to shop around can get expensive. Although there are numerous discount brokerage firms that offer extremely competitive commission rates, there are plenty more that are happy to charge you full rates. While it is not hard to keep your trading costs well below 1 percent of your principal, if you don't ask the right questions, it could cost you a small fortune.

I do not want to leave you with the impression that all (or even most) financial advisers are bad or inept people who only want to collect fees from you. There are many excellent advisers and managers who treat their clients with respect and work hard to develop and execute sound plans. However, no financial adviser will overlook his or her needs in favor of yours indefinitely. (Chapter 12 will help you evaluate and select the right adviser—and keep fees in line.)

You are fully capable of making the decisions that it will take to have a successful retirement. For some, a skilled and conscientious adviser is an invaluable asset in reaching your goals. However, remember that you do not need any particular "expert" to successfully manage your money into—and through—retirement.

There's No Time for Excuses

Just as there are for every other big project, there are plenty of common excuses available for delaying financial planning. But this is your life and livelihood we are talking about (as well as that of your spouse, family, and possibly even your employees). Few things are more important. It is complicated—but it can be done. You may be busy, but I'm asking for only a few days of your time, not weeks or months. And I'm here to show you where to start. But first, let's look at some of these excuses.

Excuse 1. "But I Won't Live That Long"

Some people convince themselves that they do not need to save or plan for retirement because they will not be around for it. Whatever the case may be, they tell themselves that there is no need to save for later days that are never going to come.

In most cases, though, it is just an excuse . . . and not a very good one. While the wonders of modern medicine are often overplayed, the fact remains that as science moves forward, people are living longer and better.

Most of you will live more than 20 years past retirement age, which is quite a long time. So what happens if you expect to die young but instead find yourself in reasonably good health? Maybe you can work a few more years than you expected, but it is pretty dangerous (not to mention depressing) to just assume that you will not be around for your retirement. You are also assuming that everyone else in your life is going to check out early too. If you can't make financial plans for yourself, do it for the people you care about.

Excuse 2. "I Don't Plan to Ever Retire"

Other people avoid planning for retirement by simply stating that they do not need to because they will never stop working. That is well and good to a point; loving a job so much that you never want to leave it is all but a dream to a majority of workers. However, just because you love your job, that is no guarantee that it will love you back.

Even if you cannot imagine a better end than being carried out of your office feet first, you may still be in for a surprise. Just because you *want* to work until the very end, that is no guarantee that you will be *able* to do so. Mandatory retirement ages are almost a thing of the past now, but more subtle means of showing older workers the door still abound in many companies and industries. They may even occur in your own business or practice if you bring on a younger partner or an outside investor.

Besides employers not wanting to keep older workers, health may be an issue as well. If you have an intensely physical job, it may be the case that you simply cannot do the work anymore. Even if your chosen line of work is not especially physical, age takes a toll on us all, and there may come a day when you simply cannot perform at a level that satisfies you, your employer, your partners, or your clients. That means that even if you do not want to ever retire, you may not have the privilege of making that choice and sticking with it. Just as in the prior example, you might find yourself facing many years of financial needs without the means to meet them.

As you'll discover in later chapters, there are ways to stay active in your business or practice while beginning your retirement. Yes, you can have your cake and eat it too!

Excuse 3. "I Can't Afford to Retire"

Some people may feel they are so far behind in saving for their later years that they might as well simply abandon any hope of retiring. Again, this is not a plan but something of a wish. After all, events outside of your control may intervene and force the issue such as illness or other life-changing events that are basically out of your control. These can force you to leave the workforce before you want to, creating a situation where you will not have an active income to support yourself.

Again, you can do this. There are ways to catch up on contributions to self-directed plans. You can cut living expenses to boost retirement savings, and you can work on taking a little more out of each paycheck.

What if you lack the extra cash at the end of the month to maximize these deductions? You could certainly consider the possibility of a second job. I realize working a second job late in life does not sound like a lot of fun, and I will not pretend that it is. But I feel confident in saying that it is better to do a little extra work when you can (and save those earnings) than to be caught short later in life when you cannot do much about it.

It is also worth mentioning that retiring at 65 is an *option*, and in the majority of cases, not a requirement. I believe as long as you can work and enjoy it with ample vacations, then you should work as long as you feel you are making a significant contribution. I am still working in my seventies, and I'm having a great time helping others. The most important point of all is to not give up.

Excuse 4. "I Have Social Security, and That's My Plan"

I've devoted an entire chapter (Chapter 11) to Social Security, but since it is such an important part of retirement—and such a common excuse for retirement avoiders—I need to mention it here. Social Security will almost certainly be around for the retirement of anyone reading this book today. What nobody knows, though, is how inflation, means testing, and taxation may affect what you receive down the road. Building a retirement plan around the idea that Social Security will fulfill all of your needs is tantamount to making the bet that the federal government will suddenly become honest, thrifty, and farsighted.

Moreover, people often overestimate just what Social Security will be worth to them when they retire. Average earners—people who earn approximately the average income for their age group throughout their lives—can expect Social Security benefits roughly equivalent to half of their income. That is all well and good if you plan to reduce your spending by half, but most people do not. Think about that—if I told you that you had to cut your total living expenses by half next month, could you do it? In other words, Social Security is not going to be enough for most people to live much beyond a subsistence kind of life in many places in the United States.

There is nothing wrong with incorporating your expected Social Security benefits into your retirement planning, but Social Security should not actually *be* the plan.

Finding Time to Deal with Retirement Planning

When I talk with professionals about planning for their retirement, one of the first things I hear is, "I don't have time to deal with it right now. Work is too busy." I can only reply, "It took you years of school and hard work to get to where you are now. Are you telling me you can't devote a handful of days to invest in the rest of your life?"

Your retirement may easily last more than 20 years, but to get started, you really just need to devote a couple of weekends to it. So take the time to make time on your busy calendar. On your first weekend, set your personal goals and your business goals for retirement, inventory your existing assets, and consider who (if anyone) you will use to advise you. This is going to take more time than jotting something down over a cup of coffee. You and your spouse may be discussing this all weekend! On your second weekend, it's time to carefully consider the pros and cons of each prospective investment.

It's perfectly fine to take some time between your two planning weekends, but don't drop the ball by waiting too long. Once your plans and investments are in place, you should actually walk away from everything for a while to let long-term market growth work its wonders. From there, I recommend reevaluating your goals, your situation, and your investments every four years. (Imagine that, you already have more time for work!)

Let's Get Started

You've no doubt heard that old saying, "If you fail to plan, you plan to fail." Planning is important because if you suddenly realize close to the time you had planned to retire that you do not have enough money, you may not have too many options. Going back to work is likely not going to be a realistic option, and many people will be loathe to depend on others taking care of them. A good plan will also bring you peace of mind, and it will go a long way toward helping you maximize all of the options available to you.

Independence is absolutely an important part of a happy retirement, but independence does not mean only the capacity to live alone and take care of yourself. Independence also means that you are *financially* independent and able to enjoy a retirement that fits your goals and interests. This comes at a cost though. You must not only have the financial resources to remain independent but also the discipline and willpower to plan ahead, build those resources, and manage them carefully.

Retirement is inevitable for almost all of us, and it could very well last for quite some time. Since the average person has a greater than 50 percent chance of living to 85, you could spend as much time in retirement as you did from infancy to college graduation. That is why planning is so important.

I know that some people find thinking about their finances to be a painful experience, but I promise I will make it as comfortable as I can.

In the following chapters, I hope to show you how to evaluate your assets, determine your financial needs in retirement, build and rebalance an appropriate portfolio, and draw down your assets in a disciplined and careful manner.

Honestly, that is really all I need from you to make this plan work. Instead of dreading retirement, I hope to leave you looking forward to it and prepared to build a plan that will give you peace of mind and an optimism for your life after retirement.

PART TWO

GOALS AND
SELF-ASSESSMENT

3

Establishing Your Goals

I want to give you a road map to a happy and fulfilling retirement, but there is one very important thing you have to decide for yourself: what road you want to take. Lewis Carroll, the author of *Alice in Wonderland*, once said: "If you don't know where you're going, any road will get you there."

The right financial advice for you is based on your goals, expectations, and needs for your own life. We'll start by building a list of goals, prioritizing them, and figuring out how to pay for them. This will take us through methods to match your current financials with your future plans—and budgeting methods to fund everything. As I warned earlier, there will be math, but first, you get to use your imagination and picture your dream retirement.

Your List of Goals

Setting your goals is no easy feat. It requires balancing your bucket list of dreams and ambitions with a sensible, logical approach to ensure that you have money for (almost) every possible scenario. It also requires that you take into consideration your spouse, your family, and others who are a part of your life.

Often, your goals may seem a little hard to pin down. "Freedom from worry" is a great goal, but it's hard to put into a budget, just as "being happy" or "helping my family" might be. Be prepared to dig deeper. What makes you worry? Debt? Uncertainty? Health issues? Planning is easier if you can express your goals in terms of something concrete like "freedom from worry over medical expenses and rising insurance premiums."

The best place to start is by listing your biggest dreams and ambitions. After all, you want a retirement that is fun, happy, and meaningful, right? (Don't worry, I won't let you get too wild. We'll focus on making sure the money doesn't run out too.) It's perfectly fine to be a little self-centered here. You've worked hard to get to this point in your life. You should dream big and list everything that you can think of.

Next, get a little more practical with your goals. Make sure you've got items like "Cover all housing expenses, including mortgage payments, property taxes, and upkeep" or "Establish a fund for assisted living expenses." This is far less fun, but now that you've addressed wants, you've got to address needs too.

Let's look at that goal of "Freedom from worry over rising insurance premiums" more closely as an example of how to translate a goal into a plan. Start with your current premium costs, and mark them up at least 10 percent a year to ensure that your plan will have money to spare for those expenses. Over the decade of 2001 to 2010, healthcare costs rose 100 percent for many people, and that pace is expected to continue. The rising cost of healthcare represents perhaps the most significant threat to the long-term economic security of workers and retirees. It's impossible to know how much prices of anything will go up, but they **will** go up. Allow for increases in your goals and plans.

Finally, think about what things you might wish to do for the important people in your life, if you haven't addressed this already. This may feel like you're writing your will—and there could be some overlap—but if you want to help put your grandchildren through college, for example, you'll need to have enough money available when **they** are ready.

Now, one little caution. Stay true to yourself. If your ambitions sound out of character, give them a second look. Often, when retirement is bandied about a dinner party, you hear things like "I'm going to take a trip around the world." That's a fine goal—don't get me wrong. But if you are prone to seasickness and prefer to put your feet up to read a book instead, you aren't giving your retirement plan an honest approach. If, after some thought, you still want to go for a big out-of-character step, go for it. Make sure you've got enough socked away for a new iPad or Kindle or TV every few years, too, if you'd rather stay home.

In Table 3.1, there's a sample worksheet that you can use to build your list. List your goals, and then circle back and rank them—and assign a

Table 3.1   Retirement Goals Worksheet

Retirement Goal	Ranking	Cost

cost. Your rankings should be broken into three categories so you can shake out the things you may find that you can't afford later:

- **Essential.** Things that you need for basic survival such as housing, food, and healthcare
- **Important.** Things that will keep you happy without breaking the bank such as an annual vacation, club memberships, or regular dinners out
- **Ultimate.** Everything else from your bucket list that you've dreamed up

Try to give your best estimates for costs, whether it's a one-off expense or an ongoing expenditure. When in doubt, err on the side of overestimating the cost. You can tally up the expenses for each category, and when we look at the financial means testing, you'll know what you can easily achieve and where you might need to work a little harder. We'll come back to the goals in this worksheet throughout the book.

Funding Your Dreams: Figuring Out What You Need

Here are two different ways to think about your retirement needs and goals: the Bottom-Up Method and the Top-Down Method.

Bottom-Up Method

The Bottom-Up Method begins with an assessment of what you will need to live on a year-by-year basis and then calculates what level of savings you need to have to support that lifestyle. It takes factors such as inflation, market appreciation, and other income sources into consideration. You can refer back to those rankings on your plan worksheet and create assessments for your different levels of retirement. Folks who are still a distance from retirement might find this to be the most useful because they have more time to adjust their savings rate and so on. Here's an example:

- **Background.** A couple are both 55 years old. They are in good health. Currently, their investments total $573,000 (not including their home). Some of their portfolio is from inheritance, but most is from savings and investing from the start of their marriage. Additionally, they are projected to get annual pension payments totaling $74,000 at 65.
- **Target goals.** They have determined that they will need $80,000 a year in today's dollars plus their Social Security to *continue* their lifestyle. (They have no big post-retirement plans that would require extra money.) Since they are 10 years from retirement, they must factor in inflation. (Always factor in a higher inflation rate than the current year so you have some breathing room. Since January 2000, the average annual inflation rate has been roughly 3 percent.) For our couple, let's budget a 4 percent annual inflation adjustment, so they will need **$118,500** a year when they retire at 65. After subtracting their pension payouts, they still need to have enough money to receive $44,500 a year from their personal investments. To preserve their capital, they plan to draw down no more than 3.5 percent of their investment for the first few years.
- **Needs.** To be able to draw $44,500 each year, they will need a total of $1,272,000 invested by the time they reach 65 to begin their retirement. Happily, by having a large sum of money invested already, their portfolio will likely grow to supplement their needs over this period. By forecasting a modest 7.5 percent growth rate for their investments, their portfolio should grow from $573,000 today to $1,180,000 in 10 years' time. (This is not a guarantee. The market can and will lose value in the short term, but in the long term, it will recover and grow.)

To get their portfolio to their target goal of $1,272,000, they need to add $92,000 to their investments—or at least $6,500 a year. Now, wait a minute, you might be saying. The amount of $6,500 a year times 10 years does not equal $92,000. But remember that any money they invest should also appreciate at an average rate of 7.5 percent per year. For example, if they invest $6,500 in Year 1, it will grow to be worth almost $13,500 by Year 10. The moral of this story is "Invest early!"

They can afford to save more—up to $10,000 a year—and that is what they plan to do. Choosing to save a lesser amount and hope for growth would not be prudent. Not only would they be "gambling" that the market would always go up but they would also be ignoring inflation. Even with their minimum contribution of $6,500, they would still need to make an average of 7.5 percent or more over the next 10 years to preserve their capital and protect against inflation. (That's 3.5 percent growth to replace the money they plan to draw down plus 4 percent to offset inflation.) Yes, inflation will not always reach 4 percent, and the markets may hit a big winning streak. If that happens, they end up with more money—and an extra cushion if the worst happens.

Table 3.2 shows you how the first year's investment of $6,500 would grow under the same conditions. And, yes, you are seeing that correctly: under normal market conditions, they would double their investment by investing it in a *conservative* mutual fund.

Now, keep adding the same amount yearly, and you'll see in Table 3.3 how investing $65,000 over 10 years can turn into almost $100,000 under even very conservative models.

I've provided you with all of the spreadsheet formulas shown here (plus a few more) on our website http://www.940financialconsulting.com.

Table 3.2   Investment Growth Over a 10-Year Period

Year	Percent Return	Initial Investment: $6,500.00
1	7.50%	$6,987.50
2	7.50%	$7,511.56
3	7.50%	$8,074.93
4	7.50%	$8,680.55
5	7.50%	$9,331.59
6	7.50%	$10,031.46
7	7.50%	$10,783.82
8	7.50%	$11,592.61
9	7.50%	$12,462.05
10	7.50%	$13,396.71

Table 3.3   Growth of Annual Investment Over a 10-Year Period

Year	Annual Investment	Previous Balance	Total Before Return	Percent Return	Estimated Year-End Total
1	$6,500.00	—	$6,500.00	7.50%	$6,987.50
2	$6,500.00	$6,987.50	$13,487.50	7.50%	$14,499.06
3	$6,500.00	$14,449.06	$20,999.06	7.50%	$22,573.99
4	$6,500.00	$22,573.99	$29,073.99	7.50%	$31,254.54
5	$6,500.00	$31,254.54	$37,754.54	7.50%	$40,586.13
6	$6,500.00	$40,586.13	$47,086.13	7.50%	$50,617.59
7	$6,500.00	$50,617.59	$57,117.59	7.50%	$61,401.41
8	$6,500.00	$61,401.41	$67,901.41	7.50%	$72,994.02
9	$6,500.00	$72,994.02	$79,494.02	7.50%	$85,456.07
10	$6,500.00	$85,465.07	$91,965.07	7.50%	$98,862.45

Whether you use my example on the website or use your own spreadsheet, you can build your own quick Bottom-Up analysis by entering the following:

- In Cell A1, enter your annual expense estimate. (To begin, plug in this couple's needs from their personal savings: $44,500.)
- In Cell B2, type 1.04 in the second row. (This is your 4 percent estimate of inflation.)
- In Cell A2, right below your expense estimate, enter this formula =(A1*B2) to multiply your expense number by the inflation estimate.
- Copy these formulas down the column for as many years as you expect to be in retirement.

If you used our examples of $44,500 and 4 percent inflation, after 20 years, you will see that your annual needs from personal savings would be $93,754.79 and that inflation has caused prices to more than double over that time (Table 3.4). If you don't have your money invested in a way to keep up with inflation, you'll have less and less to spend every year.

Let's take a quick look at how this couple's initial investment would grow from today to their retirement date 10 years from now. (There are no tax consequences factored into this "what if?" scenario. Taxes on capital gains and interest income would need to be paid out of pocket on money invested in non-retirement accounts—and would affect the true

Table 3.4   How Inflation Affects Your Annual Expenses

Year	Annual Expenses	Inflation Rate
1	$44,500.00	—
2	$46,280.00	4%
3	$48,131.20	4%
4	$50,056.45	4%
5	$52,058.71	4%
6	$54,141.05	4%
7	$56,306.70	4%
8	$58,558.96	4%
9	$60,901.32	4%
10	$63,337.38	4%
11	$65,870.87	4%
12	$68,505.71	4%
13	$71,245.93	4%
14	$74,095.77	4%
15	$77,059.60	4%
16	$80,141.99	4%
17	$83,347.67	4%
18	$86,681.57	4%
19	$90,148.83	4%
20	$93,754.79	4%

return on investment. Money invested in retirement accounts would not be taxed.)

In Table 3.5, we'll see how their current investments will grow at 7.5 percent per year. This is a conservative rate based on average market performance, but it's better to use an achievable rate than a market-beating rate, and it's enough to beat inflation *and* offset the expected drawdown of capital.

Finally, just for fun, let's pretend the couple invested that $573,000 in a real fund—one that lost money in the Great Recession of 2008 but that has posted gains every other year in the last 10 years. I've selected the Berwyn Income Fund (ticker symbol: BERIX). While I strongly urge you to forecast conservatively (using that 7.5 percent rate, for example), you may end up pleasantly surprised with the real results (Table 3.6).

Table 3.5   Example: Growth of One Couple's Initial Investment

Year	Percent Return	Initial Investment: $573,000.00
1	7.50%	$615,975.00
2	7.50%	$662,173.13
3	7.50%	$711,836.11
4	7.50%	$765,223.82
5	7.50%	$822,615.60
6	7.50%	$884,311.77
7	7.50%	$950,635.15
8	7.50%	$1,021,932.79
9	7.50%	$1,098,577.75
10	7.50%	$1,180,971.09

Table 3.6   Example: Growth of One Couple's Initial Investment in the Berwyn Income Fund

Year	Percent Return for BERIX	Initial Investment: $573,000.00
2001	14.12%	$653,907.60
2002	9.38%	$715,244.13
2003	16.23%	$831,328.26
2004	7.96%	$897,501.98
2005	1.96%	$915,093.02
2006	8.65%	$994,248.57
2007	6.84%	$1,062,255.17
2008	−10.19%	$954,011.37
2009	30.22%	$1,242,313.61
2010	10.06%	$1,367,290.36

Top-Down Method

Instead of calculating how much money you need to have saved for retirement to meet your expected annual spending needs, you can flip the process around. The Top-Down Method starts with the amount of money you have today and uses that to give you an idea of how much spending it could support on a year-to-year basis.

It is not hard to make a very rough estimate. Take your current savings, divide it by the number of years you plan to be in retirement, and add your annual expected Social Security payments. This approach completely ignores inflation or any increase (or decrease) in the value of your savings, so it is a very rough estimate, but it puts you in the ballpark all the same.

Let's walk through an example:

- You have $500,000 in savings.
- You will receive $15,000 a year from Social Security.
- You expect to spend 25 years in retirement.

You would be able to spend $35,000 a year by drawing $20,000 from savings and $15,000 from Social Security. This is essentially your "make-do" retirement income. Chances are that you'll find the amount somewhere between "a little low" to "disheartening." It can still get worse though. Remember, inflation will eat away at the value of that number; $35,000 today will be worth only about $17,000 after 19 years of 4 percent inflation.

Typically, a quick look at the Top-Down numbers tells me that we've got some work to do. If you aren't happy with the results of this quick analysis, circle back to the Bottom-Up Method and figure out what you need to do—and what you need to start saving—to get to the retirement of your dreams.

The Ups and Downs of Retirement Calculations

To have that wonderful retirement, you do need goals, hard work, and discipline to save the money required. However, you also need to be ready to deal with external forces. I've already touched on the biggest ones—market volatility and inflation—but let's look closer at how the market can help you—and hinder you.

We'll begin by looking at the performance of some key mutual funds, and we'll see how those funds can help your retirement savings grow. (As you'll see in Chapter 7, I believe mutual funds are one of the best instruments to grow your money while managing risk.)

Even quality mutual funds are not a guaranteed moneymaker, but they have a strong historical track record. It might be more exciting to talk about funds with double-digit returns, but when it comes to retirement, *safe* and *sound* are the keywords. As we build the financial models like the ones we've just looked at, I believe in presenting reasonable, achieveable returns.

What is a reasonable return? To me, it's a yield that history has shown long-term investors can achieve by sticking with their investment. Because I believe in playing it very safe with my retirement funds (and yours), I use a projected average yield of 7.5 percent even though all of the conservatively managed funds here have historically beaten that number.

Average Annual Yields, by Decade, of Conservatively Allocated Funds

In Table 3.7, we are looking at **all** of the funds that fit into these categories, and some are obviously not anything you or I would choose for an investment. These are **averages**!

It pays to understand the makeup of a mutual fund before choosing to use it. There are two categories that I prefer for retirement planning—*Conservative Allocation* and *Moderate Allocation* (see examples in Table 3.8)—because these

Table 3.7   Average Annual Yields, by Decade, of Conservatively Allocated Funds

Decade	Conservative Allocation	Moderate Allocation	S&P 500
1971–1980	12.64%	8.55%	8.48%
1981–1990	11.47%	13.82%	13.93%
1991–2000	10.15%	12.98%	17.46%
2001–2010	4.56%	4.02%	1.41%
40 Years	**9.66%**	**9.77%**	**10.15%**

Table 3.8   Mutual Funds: Objectives and Categories

Name	Symbol	Objective	Category
FPA Crescent	FPACX	Balanced	Moderate Allocation
Permanent Portfolio	PRPFX	Multi-Asset Global	Conservative Allocation
Berwyn Income	BERIX	Income	Conservative Allocation
T. Rowe Price Capital Appreciation	PRWCX	Growth and Income	Moderate Allocation
James Balanced: Golden Rainbow	GLRBX	Balanced	Conservative Allocation
Franklin Income A	FKINX	Balanced	Conservative Allocation
Vanguard Wellesley Income	VWINX	Income	Conservative Allocation
Vanguard Wellington	VWELX	Growth and Income	Moderate Allocation
Dodge & Cox Balanced	DODBX	Balanced	Moderate Allocation
Mairs & Power Balanced	MAPOX	Balanced	Moderate Allocation
Vanguard 500 Index	VFINX	Growth and Income	Large Blend

funds are not aggressive speculators in the market. They try to preserve capital and grow it without undue risk:

- **Conservative Allocation.** These portfolios invest in both stocks and bonds and maintain a relatively smaller position in stocks. These funds typically have 20 to 50 percent of their assets invested in equities and 50 to 80 percent of their assets invested in fixed income and cash.
- **Moderate Allocation.** These portfolios invest in both stocks and bonds and maintain a relatively higher position in stocks. These funds typically have 50 to 70 percent of their assets invested in equities and the remainder in fixed income and cash.

Average Performance of 10 Mutual Funds and the S&P 500

Table 3.9 shows 11 mutual funds with their objective and category, and it shows their returns for each year from 2001 through 2010. This was a very bad decade for all investments, and yet all of these funds grew over the long run.

The first 10 are funds that I track regularly. The eleventh is Vanguard's S&P 500 Index Fund, which I included as a market benchmark. These funds tend to perform well without taking undue risk. (Performance is easy to monitor. Risk is a lot more subjective. After all, none of these funds are guaranteed, which is important to remember as you press on.) I have ordered the mutual funds in this chart from the highest 10-year return on down to the lowest, which happens to be Vanguard's Index 500 fund (ticker symbol: VFINX) that mirrors the S&P 500. The Vanguard fund is shown *only* because so many people like to compare that fund as "the market" against how other investments do.

At the top of the table, you'll see the average annual return for each fund. For example, the FPA Crescent Fund (ticker symbol: FPACX) averaged a return of 11.56 percent each year over the last decade. But you'll also see that none of these funds were immune from short-term losses. Fortunately, the market tends to go up over the long term, and those short-term losses are regained and money is ultimately added to your coffers. That's cold comfort to the folks who turned 65 when the market dipped exactly when they were going to start drawing down their retirement savings. (If they had money safely stored in a Holding Pot, as I'll show you in Chapter 14, those people could have weathered those dips.)

Table 3.9   Average Performance of 10 Mutual Funds and the S&P 500

Average Annual Performance Over Time

Symbol	FPACX	PRPFX	BERIX	PRWCX	GLRBX	FKINX	VWINX	VWELX	DODBX	MAPOX	VFINX
3-year	4.54%	9.20%	8.78%	3.39%	4.90%	1.94%	4.99%	1.75%	–1.45%	3.21%	–2.90%
5-year	6.54%	10.75%	8.36%	5.77%	6.23%	5.85%	6.35%	5.58%	2.08%	5.15%	2.21%
10-year	11.56%	11.13%	9.09%	8.54%	7.13%	7.07%	6.44%	6.20%	5.93%	5.39%	1.31%
15-year	10.49%	8.54%	7.94%	10.14%	7.77%	7.81%	7.73%	8.45%	8.52%	8.82%	6.69%
20-year	N/A	8.28%	9.93%	11.19%	N/A	10.16%	9.09%	10.03%	10.13%	9.97%	9.04%

Year-By-Year Performance

Symbol	FPACX	PRPFX	BERIX	PRWCX	GLRBX	FKINX	VWINX	VWELX	DODBX	MAPOX	VFINX
2001	36.14%	3.81%	14.12%	10.26%	2.57%	0.65%	7.39%	4.19%	10.05%	–1.27%	–12.02%
2002	3.71%	14.36%	9.38%	0.54%	–0.81%	–1.06%	4.64%	–6.90%	–2.94%	–6.42%	–22.15%
2003	26.15%	20.45%	16.23%	25.47%	18.20%	30.96%	9.66%	20.75%	24.44%	21.65%	28.50%
2004	10.21%	12.04%	7.96%	15.29%	12.99%	12.17%	7.57%	11.17%	13.30%	12.02%	10.74%
2005	10.83%	7.62%	1.96%	6.85%	8.36%	1.85%	3.48%	6.82%	6.59%	4.47%	4.77%
2006	12.43%	13.82%	8.65%	14.54%	7.90%	19.12%	11.28%	14.97%	13.86%	12.10%	15.64%
2007	6.84%	12.43%	6.84%	4.56%	8.61%	5.31%	5.61%	8.34%	1.73%	4.28%	5.39%
2008	–20.55%	–8.36%	–10.19%	–27.17%	–5.52%	–30.51%	–9.84%	–22.30%	–33.57%	–21.12%	–37.02%
2009	28.37%	19.08%	30.22%	33.05%	7.12%	35.01%	16.02%	22.20%	28.37%	21.35%	26.49%
2010	12.04%	19.31%	10.06%	14.07%	14.06%	12.91%	10.65%	10.94%	12.22%	14.87%	14.91%

We'll explore ways to manage market volatility later in the book, including finding the safest havens for some of your nest egg. For the purposes of goals and planning though, I want to strongly emphasize that you cannot be sure that the market alone will grow your savings. You need to be an active contributor.

Budgeting 101

A good starting place for calculating what you will need in retirement is to figure out what you currently spend on a monthly basis. If you already keep a detailed budget, this will be pretty simple, but even if you don't already track your spending, it won't take much work to create a monthly budget. (There are plenty of sample budget sheets freely available on the Internet.)

Figure Out What You Are Currently Spending

Get out your checkbook and your credit card statements, and start looking at what you spend in each major category. Don't forget any cash items if they are significant—weekly shopping trips to the coffee shop or the local farmers' market can add up pretty quickly.

Hopefully, you will find that what you bring home as income every month is comfortably more than what you spend. After all, you need that surplus to help build your retirement savings.

Figure Out What Will Stay the Same and What Will Change

Now that you know what you have been spending, think a bit about what will stay the same—and what is likely to change. While you are doing this, make sure to factor in some less common expenses that don't occur every month (or even every year) but that may happen once or twice during your retirement:

- **Housing.** Your mortgage payments won't change if you have a fixed-rate mortgage until you pay off the house. However, your property taxes probably will increase, as will home repairs and upkeep. Expenses, like a new water heater or roof for your house, should also be a part of your planning. If you don't want to bother trying to guess about these expenses, you could simply decide to set aside 2 to 3 percent of your home's value every year for these eventual replacements and repairs that you will need.

- **Healthcare.** If you currently get healthcare insurance from your employer, that will not continue after you retire. Medicare may take the place of your primary insurance, but you may also need a Medigap plan plus prescription coverage.
- **Transportation.** If you drive a car, you will likely buy at least one or two more during retirement. Don't forget about insurance and repairs (and gas!).
- **Fun.** You may want to travel more often once you stop working. If you plan on taking a grand European tour or more modest vacations, be sure to include those costs. If you are staying closer to home, you might spend more time (and money) on a particular hobby, so those costs will be a factor as well.

Whatever the case may be, try to come up with a reasonable estimate or budget for those activities and include them in your future spending plans.

If you are planning on leaving any bequest or gifts *outside of your family*, those commitments should be laid out during this planning process. While you are not giving the money at this point, it is usually helpful that you make notes of your intentions now as you go through the financial aspects of what you would like to do someday. I personally would recommend that you have your estate make these bequests so that your generosity does not come back to haunt you during your retirement. You could, for instance, make a bequest of your home once you have passed on and no longer need it—that way you can still enjoy it while you are in retirement, but the eventual recipients still benefit from your generosity. Alternatively, you could set aside a certain amount of money and invest it with the idea that those proceeds will eventually be donated, but they will remain accessible to you if you should happen to need them. Once your retirement plan is formalized, it's a good idea to update your wills and trusts to reflect these plans.

Create Your Number

Once you know how much you are likely to spend each month, you can determine how much you are likely to spend on a yearly basis and over the course of your expected retirement. As I said before, this is an especially valuable approach to use if you still have a fair amount of time between today and retirement, which is time you can use to modify your spending, save more, or adjust your investment strategies.

It can also be an invaluable reality check that informs you that you may be living a bit too high on the hog or saving more than you really need for a secure retirement. We'll use this number in Part Four, when we look at living the good life while living off what you have.

The Hidden Cost of Retirement: Inflation

We've already seen how inflation can eat away at your retirement savings, but let's dig a little deeper. Inflation is the increase in the overall price level of not one particular item but rather, most prices generally.

Perpetually rising prices are a basic fact of life in the modern world, and you need to make sure to "bake" this in to your expectations. Recently, inflation has been historically low, but there are signs and worries all around that it may pick up in the future. Predicting inflation baffles even the most educated and experienced economists. If you assume a flat rate like 4 percent and you are off by a little bit, that's fine.

Inflation and the *Consumer Price Index* (CPI—or more correctly, the CPI-U) are used interchangeably but they are not the same. The CPI-U covers roughly 88 percent of the population, and it is compiled on a monthly basis for a particular "basket of goods." This allows us to compare prices from different periods.

The Consumer Price Index for the Elderly (CPI-E) is generally higher than the CPI-U, and it represents about 21 percent of the U.S. population over 62 years of age. Why is it higher? Primarily because of the sharp increases in prices for medical care and housing.

If you are curious about all the different CPIs and inflation data used by the government, visit the Bureau of Labor Statistics' website at http://www.bls.gov/data/. Also, http://www.inflationdata.com has a wealth of knowledge, and it is easier to maneuver for the average person.

What makes inflation even worse is that the statistics used by the U.S. government may not tell the whole story. The official inflation statistics do not just measure the simple increases in prices from one year to the next. Instead, the statisticians adjust the numbers in a variety of ways, including the fact that customers will simply substitute expensive products with cheaper ones. The bottom line is this: inflation is real and probably higher than the official numbers would suggest.

Table 3.10 is a chart showing the inflation rates from 1971 until 2012. The average annual inflation rate over this period was 3.77 percent. Although the inflation rate has averaged 4 percent or less for a long time, you cannot count on the inflation rate during your retirement to be under 4 percent every year. Remember those "WIN" buttons—"Whip Inflation Now"—in President Gerald Ford's presidency? They were everywhere. Inflation was 11.03 percent in 1974! Inflationary periods over 4 percent are in bold in Table 3.10. Your portfolio's return on investment over time should at least match (and ideally beat) inflation—but not necessarily year by year. As long as you are close, you still "get the cigar"—and you get to keep the extra money you budgeted.

**Table 3.10   Chart of Inflation Based on the
Consumer Price Index, 1971 to 2012**

Year	Percent
1971	**4.30%**
1972	3.27%
1973	**6.16%**
1974	**11.03%**
1975	**9.20%**
1976	**5.75%**
1977	**6.50%**
1978	**7.62%**
1979	**11.22%**
1980	**13.58%**
1981	**10.35%**
1982	**6.16%**
1983	3.22%
1984	**4.30%**
1985	3.55%
1986	1.91%
1987	3.66%
1988	**4.08%**
1989	**4.83%**
1990	**5.39%**
1991	**4.25%**
1992	3.03%
1993	2.96%
1994	2.61%
1995	2.81%
1996	2.93%
1997	2.34%
1998	1.55%
1999	2.19%
2000	3.38%
2001	2.83%
2002	1.59%

Table 3.10   (*Continued*)

Year	Percent
2003	2.27%
2004	2.68%
2005	3.39%
2006	3.24%
2007	2.85%
2008	3.85%
2009	−0.34%
2010	1.64%
2011	3.16%
2012	2.07%

Let's compare the annual inflation rate to the performance of the Berwyn Income Fund (BERIX), a conservatively allocated mutual fund that we looked at earlier. Most years, it comfortably outperformed the inflation rate, meaning that your overall savings and your purchasing power both increased. (In our Bottom-Up example, this fund would have grown every year except for 2005 and 2008 even after that 3.5 percent drawdown.)

But, as you can see in Table 3.11, no matter how hard you try, your portfolio will probably have years that do not beat inflation each and every year. (In Chapter 14, you are going to see how we get around that problem by

Table 3.11   Inflation Versus Berwyn Income Fund

Year	Inflation	BERIX
2001	2.83%	**14.12%**
2002	1.59%	**9.38%**
2003	2.27%	**16.23%**
2004	2.68%	**7.96%**
2005	**3.39%**	1.96%
2006	3.24%	**8.65%**
2007	2.85%	**6.84%**
2008	**3.85%**	−10.19%
2009	−0.34%	**30.22%**
2010	1.64%	**10.06%**

using Holding Pots for three years of "salary" from your investments.) The good thing is that for the decade 2001 to 2010, inflation was 2.39 percent and the return on the Berwyn Income Fund was 9.09 percent—a difference of 6.70 percent. (The higher rate for each year is featured in bold.) You could take out your 3.5 to 4 percent and still have money growing.

You can see by this example alone that your portfolio will not earn the same amount each year, nor will inflation be as consistent and predictable. Still, I hope I have made an important point: you need to beat inflation, but every little extra bit of savings and investment performance makes a big difference.

Tying It All Together

We've talked about the need to set goals, ways to assess what you will need to retire, and some of the biggest challenges facing you and your money. I invite you to return to your list of goals to refine and prioritize them. I'd like to conclude this chapter with a few thoughts, recommendations, and reality checks as you firm up your goals.

Remember, You Will Spend More Than You Think

Now, I need to remind you of an important point: you are going to spend more money in retirement than you probably think you will. You may not be filling up the car with gas every week to get to and from work, but you are still going to be eating three meals a day, using utilities, and so on.

Likewise, as things get older (be they cars, houses, or people), it takes more money to keep them going and in good repair. Whether or not you decide to include a "fudge factor" in your expense estimates is up to you, but be very careful about building a plan that requires everything to go your way.

Beware of "I Deserve"

If you have worked hard and planned carefully, you absolutely **do** deserve a comfortable retirement. But there is a big difference between a comfortable retirement and telling yourself that you can now buy all of the toys and luxuries that you denied yourself when you were working. If you are entering retirement with $400,000 in savings and you want to buy a $100,000 recreational vehicle (RV), that massive expenditure could create some potentially serious problems down the road. Unless, of course, you—and maybe more important, your spouse—are willing to live in that RV. A home lasts longer than an RV even though you have maintenance on both. But the home usually appreciates, and an RV will not.

Be especially careful if you find yourself "bargaining" with your future self. You might argue that you can afford a luxury car or vacation home because you will cut back on other expenses at some point in the future. Or maybe you'll tell yourself that you'll just work a few extra years or squeeze a few extra percentage points of performance out of your portfolio. This can be very dangerous because there really isn't any recourse if you buy something today and your future plans to earn back the money don't work out as you had planned.

As I said before, retirement should not be a period or process of denial, so I'll make you a deal: if you think that there is some big-ticket item that you really deserve, and you have a plan to pay for it, then execute your plan and buy the item *after* your plan works. In the meantime, build your plan from the basics on up.

Pick Smart, Sensible, and Achievable Goals

When thinking about your goals, it is important to make sure that they are not only **your** goals but also the right goals. What do I mean by this? Well, consider the goal of "beating the market." That is an enormous obsession in the investment world, but very few people stop to ask if that is really the right target. If you shoot for high market returns, you have to accept high market risks, and those risks can be pretty scary on a year-to-year basis when you're dealing with a fixed amount of money.

If you need a compound annual return of 5 percent to meet all of your goals, why worry if the market racked up a 10 percent gain? By all means, if you find that you can boost your returns by an extra percent or two *without* additional risk, you should do so immediately (and kindly drop me a note on the great underpriced investments you have found). But if a string of returns at 5 percent per year is all that you need, why risk losses (and missing your goals) just to reach for a little extra?

One of the easiest ways that managers can beat the market is to increase the riskiness and volatility of the portfolio. How much does it benefit you, though, if you are earning strong returns but you cannot sleep at night because you are worried about the monthly ups and downs in the value of your portfolio? As you transition into retirement, the major market averages matter less and less as appropriate benchmarks for performance. The world may fixate on the S&P 500 or Dow Jones Industrial Average, but it shouldn't be *your* benchmark!

Keep in mind that your goals and targets will change as you move through retirement. Someone who is just starting retirement at the relatively young age of 66 arguably needs to have a pretty healthy allocation to equities to generate enough portfolio growth. Someone in his or her nineties, though, probably does not have the same 20- or 30-year investment horizon anymore, nor the need for the same kind of allocation to stocks.

Your Top Priority for Retirement: "My Assets Will Outlive Me"

The two most important goals for any retirement plan are to ensure that (a) your assets outlive you (ideally without compromising your lifestyle) and (b) you keep up with inflation. I think the reasons that you want your money to outlive you are pretty straightforward and don't require a lot of explanation—nobody wants to run out of money and have to depend upon the kindness and charity of others to get by (or to drastically trim back their spending to mere survival levels).

Let me say one other thing about this though. While you absolutely do not want to run out of money, you also do not necessarily want to have a huge amount of money left over when you reach the end of the road either. Life is a funny thing; there are no guarantees, and it sometimes feels like a person's health can change in the blink of an eye. It would be a shame, then, *not* to take the once-in-a-lifetime trip to Spain or what have you and then have that opportunity stolen by the onset of Alzheimer's or some other terrible disease. I am not trying to contradict what I said earlier about not going overboard with spending. Rather, I am just trying to say that you should always remember that there is at least some element of "use it or lose it" to your retirement.

Not outliving your assets can be achieved largely by saving enough and being circumspect with your lifestyle choices, but outdoing inflation requires a different approach. In response to market demand, there are plenty of "inflation-protected" securities, including special bonds issued by the U.S. Treasury, collectively called Treasury Inflation-Protected Securities (TIPS). These securities tend to be expensive, and the real return (that is, the return you get after inflation) is usually very low—and occasionally in negative territory.

While a selection of inflation-protected securities may make sense for a certain part of your portfolio, they should not by any means be the bulk of your assets. Luckily, there are other ways to stay ahead of inflation. Historically, mutual funds and stocks have offered excellent protection against inflation because well-run companies are typically able to consistently grow their earnings in excess of inflation (and earnings are what ultimately power stock prices). However, no matter what investment you choose to put your money into, you are never guaranteed a positive return. Life just doesn't work that way!

Finalize Your Goals

Now that you've had a chance to think through your perfect retirement (or at least your very good retirement), wrap up your list of goals, prioritize them, and figure out the costs. Give one of the number-crunching exercises a shot as well. (Ideally, you should try the Bottom-Up Method, but the Top-Down Method will work too.)

I'd like you to have a sense of what your retirement will cost you before we proceed into a review of what you've already invested—and what you might need to put into your portfolio to get you there.

4

Assessing What You Have

Before you can really start to plan your retirement, you need to get a handle on what you have. You can put together a dream list of retirement goals, but you will need to fund everything on that list. You will need to know what you own—and what you owe. There's not much use in socking away money if you still have sizable debts. So, let's inventory your assets and your liabilities.

Just as it is hard to have Thanksgiving dinner with relatives spread across the country, it is difficult to manage your retirement with assets spread across numerous accounts. That task is even harder when you may not even know exactly how much you have.

A personal financial inventory should start with cash assets and move along in accordance with how easy it is to convert your other assets to cash. Stocks and bonds can be exchanged for cash with little more effort and delay than it takes to execute a transaction online or call a broker. Properties, trust funds, and insurance policies all take a little more time and effort to convert into cash. Keep in mind, this assessment is supposed to be about adding up what you have available for retirement—heirloom jewelry or a coin collection may be valuable, but if you do not plan on liquidating it as you retire, do not include it here.

As you build this inventory, consider doing it in an easily accessible and easily updatable format like a spreadsheet. This information is very useful at tax time and for estate planning, If your list becomes frustratingly long and far-flung, you might be ready to consolidate some of your accounts. I'll give you some hints on how to streamline your assets while keeping them diversified.

Cash and Cash Equivalent Holdings: Bank Accounts, CDs, and Money Market Funds

The odds are good that you already have a very clear idea of how much cash you have. People do not tend to forget about, or abandon, checking and savings accounts. Even still, there may be a primary checking account at one bank, a high-yield savings account at another bank, and a couple of CDs at a third bank.

There is nothing fundamentally wrong with doing business with multiple banks if you are getting great rates from them, but there is an inherent hassle when tax time arrives and you have to juggle a stack of statements. Having multiple accounts might mean that you do not immediately know how much you have in each, or in total, so now is the time to look at those statements and tally up what you have among your checking, savings, high-yield savings, and CD accounts. While you are doing this, make a few notes along the way. Why did you open this account with this bank? Are you sure you are getting the best rate? Does this bank offer you the same quality of services (at the same price) that it did when you first opened the account? Plenty of banks offer appealing teaser rates or promotions to get you through the door, but you may not realize a year or two later that your bank is no longer competitive. Along those same lines, make sure that you take advantage of what your banks do offer. If you have an account that gives you a discount on a safety deposit box, use that to keep important papers secure.

Considering that the United States has more banks than it needs, there is often a lot of competition among the banks for depositors. Use that competition to your advantage, and find the best deal you can. Some banks, for instance, will offer a slightly higher rate on CDs if you have a direct deposit account with them or a bundle of accounts. While earning 0.05 percent more won't mean the difference between retiring to Arizona or retiring to the south of France, it's still a few extra dollars just by walking across the street.

While you are at it, consider joining a credit union. Credit unions often offer slightly better interest rates on deposit accounts, and they can often give you a substantial bargain if you should want to borrow money. Since many of you have been in the Armed Services, you should look at the Pentagon Federal Credit Union (http://www.penfed.com), which is one of the best. Another good option is USAA. It is not a credit union, but many people think it is because its rates are usually better than the rates at other banks. It has a world of services available, and some of these are much better than those offered elsewhere (while some are not as competitive). Look them up at http://www.usaa.com. I think you will be very pleased.

Investments and Assets

While most investors take at least a cursory look at their brokerage statements, there are certainly people who inadvertently migrate from "buy and hold" to "buy and forget" with some of their stocks and bonds. Even if you do not always keep careful tabs on your holdings, inventorying your stock, bond, and mutual fund investments will not present too much of a challenge.

I will talk about investment selection and portfolio construction later, but you can certainly begin the process here. As you review your holdings, ask yourself why you bought each of them and whether that reason still holds true. Your review of the mutual funds you hold should include what you are paying, what sort of performance the funds are delivering, and how much overlap there is among your holdings.

Retirement Accounts: Pensions, Profit Sharing Accounts, 401(k)s, and More

Many health professionals and small business owners have to stay on top of the best retirement contribution plans available for their business or practice. But for many workers, retirement accounts may be the most far-flung and easily forgotten assets they own. People change jobs often, and when they do, they do not always remember to roll over retirement plans such as their 401(k)s. Over a 20-year period or longer, that oversight can lead to a large number of accounts spread out over many different brokers and money managers. Making matters worse, many plan administrators will send account statements infrequently if there is no activity, so it is even easier to forget where the money is.

You may have a wide array of IRAs, 401(k)s, profit sharing accounts, and other work-related retirement accounts. Round them up, and see what you have salted away already. You might be pleasantly surprised. And if you are intimidated by the sheer number of accounts and companies managing those funds, you might consider consolidating some of those holdings.

While we are exploring retirement accounts, let's talk about a pension you may have with a current employer. A pension is not a financial asset per se, but it absolutely belongs in an accounting of your financial assets and retirement plans. Every pension plan is different, but most plans will pay a regular amount based on a formula that factors in your service time and salary. Some plans also provide the option (and sometimes the requirement) of paying out a lump sum in lieu of regular payments. If you are going to get a lump sum payment, then perhaps the best solution is to roll it over into an IRA at a brokerage firm such as Schwab, Fidelity, Vanguard, or Ameritrade. If you are not comfortable with doing this right now, the lump sum payment can sit in money market accounts or very safe short-term investments until you decide what you are going to do.

Even though defined benefit pension plans are going the way of the horse and buggy, there are still many of them out there, and you may have one among your assets. Generally, defined benefit pension plans are required to provide you with an estimate of your expected benefit upon retirement, so it should not be too difficult to assess the contribution you can expect from one. Whether you expect to receive a lump sum payment or periodic payments over years, make sure to include your defined benefit pension plans on your list of assets.

What if you have forgotten a retirement account somewhere? Luckily, it is all but impossible to lose that money. If your account was worth less than $5,000 and you did not transfer it when you left the company, your employer could have moved it into a default IRA that would invest the funds in safe instruments like CDs and money market funds. If your account was worth less than $1,000, there is a chance that it was transferred to the state's unclaimed property division. If you have moved from one state to another, you may have to inquire at your old state's Treasury office to find out if you have money coming to you. It is amazing how many people have "lost" money!

The National Registry of Unclaimed Retirement Benefits website (http://www.unclaimedretirementbenefits.com) is a good starting place, and it may be able to reunite you with your lost retirement funds. Alternatively, contact your old employers for assistance in locating the assets, or the Department of Labor's database of abandoned 401(k) plans at http://www.askbsa.dol.gov/abandonedplansearch. (There are similar listings for dormant bank accounts as well.)

Once you have all of your retirement account records, the evaluation process is similar to what you did for your cash and stock accounts. Ask yourself whether you are holding these assets because you still really believe in them or whether they were simply the best options available at the time and you forgot to change them—after all, many retirement account providers allow only a limited choice of funds or assets. Ultimately, you will want to transfer these accounts into one or two rollover accounts at a low-cost brokerage firm. That will reduce your paperwork, simplify your financial life, and give you a broader range of options for your money.

Company Options and Stocks

From the 1980s forward, it has been increasingly common to compensate employees (particularly at the executive level) with equity in the company—either in the form of shares or options. As a result, company shares might make up a significant part of your financial assets.

If the firm is publicly traded, estimating the value of any shares you hold is straightforward. Assuming that the shares are registered and not otherwise restricted, they are worth the same as any other shares of that company. Even if these shares are held in an account administered by the company, it should not be difficult to eventually transfer them to another account if you decide to consolidate your holdings.

Owning shares in a private business is more complicated. Most larger private businesses that issue equity or options to employees also have some sort of auction mechanism at least once a year during which time employees can buy shares from or sell shares to other employees. Failing that, you can compare the company to similar companies that are public and use information like the price-to-earnings ratio (P/E ratio) or price-to-sales ratio to make a rough estimation of what your shares are worth. (I'll explain these ratios in Chapter 9.)

As far as *selling* those shares, things can be a little more complicated. Because these shares are not registered with the Securities and Exchange Commission (SEC), they cannot easily be sold to others, and you certainly cannot call up a broker and have him or her sell the shares for you. On top of those rules, many private companies have their own guidelines about how those shares can be transferred. Some companies allow for privately negotiated sales between those periodic auctions, while other companies will offer to buy shares at any time (at a price usually related to those auctions). In other cases, you may find it possible to borrow money using those shares as collateral, but that can be risky if the stock price falls.

Property

Property is another area where you are not likely to forget that you own something. States and municipalities are always looking to raise revenue, and there are not too many types of property that have real worth and manage to escape taxation. For purposes of assessing your financial health, focus on real estate, and do not include depreciating assets like automobiles and RVs.

Properly valuing property is a complicated topic that deserves its own book. For purposes of an initial inventory, it is reasonable to use whatever the assessed tax value may be. That will likely understate the true worth of the asset, but any sale of that property is likely to involve commissions and taxes so it is not as though you are ever going to get 100 percent of what your property is really worth.

Insurance Policies

Insurance policies are not really financial assets that should be part of a retirement plan, but they still have a role in your planning. For starters, taking a careful look at your policies might show you where you are over- or underinsured, and adjusting your insurance coverage may need to go on your to-do list.

A life insurance policy, if there is cash value in it, is also a potential source of funds if you encounter a sudden financial problem and need to raise money. Also, while it may be morbid or unpleasant to contemplate, the reality is that if you are married, it is almost certain that one of you will die before the other and that potential payout needs to be considered as part of your long-term retirement plan.

Annuities

If you've taken some tentative steps toward retirement savings beyond 401(k)s and Roth IRAs, you may have already been exposed to annuities. Millions of Americans have purchased this popular investment. In all honesty, they are not one of my favorite investments because the costs are not designed to be in your favor. In the simplest terms, an annuity is a contract that provides for a regular stream of payments over a fixed or indefinite period of time. The buyer of an annuity invests his or her money with a provider, either as a series of regular payments or a one-time payment. Over a defined period of time, the funds are "locked up," and they gain value. After that, the annuity provider makes payments back to the buyer.

Annuities come in many forms, with differing payment structures and tax implications. There are many advantages to annuities, the primary one being that they are "easy" to invest in. You pay a set price, and you get money back. Seems simple enough. But as always, when you pay for convenience, you aren't always getting your money's worth. Make sure you are considering the advantages of all the potential investment instruments available before leaping into annuities. But for now, simply list any investments you've made into annuities. I'll go into detail on annuities in Chapter 10.

Your House: It's Not the Asset You Think It Is

You may have noticed that I have not talked about the value of your house. While people often talked about housing as an investment before the recent bursting of the real estate market bubble, it seems likely that the dramatic declines in housing prices will have a long-term effect on how people regard housing as a part of their savings.

In the run-up to the bubble, some people began to regard their house as something more like a perpetual piggy bank than a physical asset. Unfortunately, real estate agents managed to pull the same trick that salespeople try all the time—convincing us that an expense is actually an "investment." Generally speaking, if something requires ongoing maintenance and provides a service to you, it is not really an investment.

So it is with a house. Certainly, houses are not like electronics or cars where no matter how well you care for them, they are almost certain to be worth less with every passing year. Housing prices *do* appreciate over time in healthy markets. Unfortunately, that appreciation has to be weighed against the cost of the interest (even with the tax deductibility of mortgage interest payments) and the ongoing maintenance needs. All in all, the net value of your house is unlikely to go up by more than a few percentage points per year—not exactly a scintillating return.

Realistically, the value of your house is all but irrelevant to your retirement unless you plan on selling it. There used to be an old system in which a couple would buy a small "starter home" and then progressively trade up to larger homes as both their family and financial resources grew. Upon retirement, the large family home would go up for sale, and the newly retired couple would buy a smaller house, taking advantage of the one-time tax exemption, and they would use the profits to help round out their retirement savings.

There is nothing wrong with that plan, but there is an important detail to remember: the only part of the home's value that impacts retirement is the difference between what your current home is worth and what the next one will cost. If you do not plan on selling your house, you should not include its value when you inventory your financial situation.

Today, more and more people want to downsize, so the value of the smaller homes in retirement areas may be *more* than you can sell your home for elsewhere. Do not sell your current house before looking for the next. Instead, look for houses where you may want to go, and then decide if selling your old home makes sense. You may have to compromise on the size or the location if you want to move during retirement, but it is better to know that well ahead of time.

Your Business or Practice: A Valuable . . . and Complicated Asset

Many of you own a business or a practice—or at least a share of one. It is likely to be a major asset for those who do, but it's a complicated one. When evaluating the assets you will have available for retirement, you will need to make some assumptions about whether you will continue to operate your business, whether you will transition to a nonoperating role (but still draw a salary or income to support yourself), or whether you will sell.

The important thing to remember here is that your business or practice might be the most illiquid asset you own, one that might take years to turn into the cash you need for retirement. Start your planning now to save a lot of trouble later. (We'll dig deeper into these complexities in the next chapter.)

Liabilities

Of course, assets are only one-half of a balance sheet. As important as it is to know what you have, it is just as important to know what you owe. After all, if you have $1 million in cash but $2 million in debt, you are not exactly a millionaire in the same sense as if you had that $1 million free and clear.

It may be easy for some of us to forget about the assets we hold, but our creditors do not tend to let us forget about the debts that we owe. As a result, "finding" your liabilities should not be all that difficult.

Mortgage

For most people, a home mortgage is the single largest debt they will ever owe. While many will have paid off their home mortgage by the time they enter retirement, that is not true for everybody. There is no reason to be in a rush to pay off a home mortgage, particularly if you have a favorable rate on the loan and/or no plans to relocate or downsize. However, a home mortgage payment is certainly going to be a significant factor in your month-to-month cash flow needs. Of course, some of you fortunate folks may have more than one mortgage if you've built your vacation home. Make sure you list all mortgage debt, including home equity debt.

Reverse mortgages have come into vogue lately. In a nutshell, a reverse mortgage works like this: in exchange for the deed to your house when you die, the buyer agrees to make monthly payments to you for however long you are in the house. In some respects, a reverse mortgage is a lot like an annuity—you agree to sign over your house in exchange for regular payments from now until death. However, it is still a loan with many obligations and contingencies attached. Because I see it mainly as an emergency option for raising funds, I will save the full discussion of this loan instrument until Chapter 16.

Credit Card Debt

Because of the abnormally high interest rates being assessed on credit card balances, this type of debt is arguably the most pernicious debt that you can have going into retirement. If your investment portfolio is earning 8 percent a year (an historically solid rate) but you are paying 19 percent interest on your credit card debt, you are on a conveyor belt to a very bad place. Unlike mortgage debt, credit card debt should be gotten rid of as quickly as possible.

Always use a credit card that pays you something back each month. Do not use one that does it once a year or one that offers you a lot of "junk" for your points. (One tip: credit unions frequently offer better deals on credit cards.)

Forget the TV advertisements you see about debt relief services— some of them are very nearly frauds, and even those that are legitimate enterprises offer little beyond what you can do for yourself. Your best bet is simply to pay as much as you can every month and reduce your spending. At a minimum, you need to cut your spending to match your level of income and look for any opportunities to squeeze some extra money out of your budget—money you can use to accelerate the payoff of those credit card bills.

Other Installment Debt

"Other" can be a pretty broad term, but it seems like the best way to categorize all of the other kinds of debt that people may have when they think about retirement planning.

Odds are that student loan debt will be something long in your past by now, but you may still have car payments or other kinds of installment debt (such as a loan for home renovations). Likewise, more and more people may find that they have to go into debt for healthcare expenses. Although these debts will not be as expensive as credit cards, they should be settled sooner than later.

Business Debt

For many small business owners, there is really no separation between personal debt and business debt—banks often will not lend to small businesses without having recourse to the owner's assets. Consequently, you should not separate the debt of your business or practice from your personal debt if you are personally liable.

However, as your business or practice matures or becomes more successful, you might consider getting out of personal liability, which you can do by incorporating your business. (We'll cover that further in the next chapter.) At a bare minimum, make sure that any value you assign to your business or practice is *net* of the debt that it carries.

Future Liabilities

Do not forget future liabilities when you draw up your financial inventory. Perhaps you promised to help with a grandchild's education or to make a substantial donation to a charitable organization. Even if these pledges do not rise to the level of legal obligations, you should still include them as liabilities if you intend to pay.

Conclusion

At this point, you should have a clear sense of what financial assets you have, as well as the liabilities you have yet to pay—two very important steps in building the plan for your retirement.

5

Your Business and
Your Retirement

Up until now, you've probably felt like this book is a retirement planning book for everyone. You're right. After all, money is money—and the need for a good plan is essential for everyone. But if you are running a business or practice, you are facing all of the same retirement issues as everyone else—plus a number of more complex ones.

Besides your full-time work and home life, you may have partners to deal with, financial decisions to make for your business, and income that isn't always as simple as a regular paycheck. Furthermore, a good deal of your wealth may be tied up in an asset that might be hard to value or sell. However, you are still going to retire at some point—and I expect that you'd like your retirement to be as good (if not better) as your life is right now.

Luckily, it can be done. I work with scores of health professionals and small business owners like you all the time. By working together, we make retirement planning simple and straightforward—and get everyone's retirements off to a winning start.

If you own your own business or if you are in solo practice, you know the "buck stops here." You are on the hook for all decisions. But read the following even if you don't have a partner. You may find that you have something like one, even if it is only for a short time of transitioning out of your solo practice or business.

Company Retirement Plans

Consider bringing in an expert who can advise you and your partners on retirement planning and tax issues. I would recommend engaging a third-party administrator (TPA) to talk with you about what type of plan would work best for you or your group. Third-party administrators design retirement plans, and they can show you what would work best in your particular case. You might find a plan with tax benefits that could help you today while also helping you get a better footing for retirement in the future.

TPAs are independent—that is, they are unaffiliated with a particular brokerage firm or insurance company. However, you have to be careful that they do not steer you to someone who sells high-fee, loaded funds and other expensive investments. Just as your attorney likes to work with a certain certified public accountant (CPA), a TPA who gets a lot of leads from someone in the financial community may return the favor and recommend that person. Have the TPA suggest several low-cost brokerage firms (for example, Schwab or Ameritrade) for you—or you can go independently to an online brokerage firm.

Be careful! Most of us know that money will have to sit in a retirement plan for a long time, so we don't pay as much attention to it as we should. Doing your homework up front makes a difference.

Most health professionals and small business owners are inundated by brokerage people and financial planners selling loaded funds to them from the day they hang out their shingle. You'll find that so many people are after your money that it is mind-boggling. Talking to your "friends" or golf buddies who work for a large brokerage house is a **no-no**! First, they will tell you that their existing plan is free and that you don't need to spend money on an individually tailored plan. The first thing you think is "Great!" The second thing you realize, many years later, is that you have been "sucker punched." Because you did not have enough experience, you chose a "freebie," but now, you are locked into buying their products.

In almost every case like this that I have seen, the client has been forced to buy exclusively the products of the brokerage firm or company that provides the retirement plan—such as expensive loaded funds in A, B, or C classes instead of more affordable versions of the same funds with better overall returns. (In Part Three, I'll give you an example of how some mutual funds and their "alphabet soup" of classes have significant differences in their costs and returns.)

Safeguarding Your Retirement Savings from Business-Related Loss and Liability

You've invested a lot in your business or practice. How safe is that investment? It's hard to protect your practice or business completely against everything that could happen, but there's a lot you can do to buffer your business (and your own wealth) from most bad things that could happen. This type of business planning provides protection for today, and it is also valuable when it comes time to sell or transfer your share of the practice.

You almost certainly know about these legal tools as commonsense safeguards for your practice or business, and they are far too complex to address in depth in a book on retirement planning. However, I encourage you to think about how these actions will also protect the assets that may constitute a big part of your retirement wealth.

I've combined the discussion of business structure and malpractice insurance in one section because I don't want you to have the rest of your life ruined by the actions of another person, especially one of your partners. You might have an impeccable record as a business owner or health professional with ample coverage against malpractice suits, but you can still make bad business or financial decisions. Is your business or practice set up properly to deal with both kinds of issues?

Structuring Your Business or Practice

The most common models for business structures today are these:

- C Corporations
- S Corporations
- Limited Liability Partnerships (LLPs)
- Limited Liability Companies (LLCs)

There are different advantages and disadvantages with any of these structures, but they all do one very important thing: they protect you (the individual) from legal and financial liabilities that your company faces. I cannot stress the importance of this. If a legal claim is made or if a bank note is called on your business and your business is structured correctly, no one can come and dip into your personal savings or retirement funds.

Of course, there are always ways that someone can come after you, but these structures afford you the best possible protection from personal risk.

In addition to the legal protection that S Corporations, LLPs, and LLCs provide, your business earnings are passed directly to your personal income tax returns, so that the business entity is exempt from federal taxes. You still have to pay taxes, but at least this income isn't being taxed twice. I view this as more money to put toward your retirement.

Malpractice Insurance

If you are in one of the health professions, I don't have to tell you that malpractice insurance is one of those things you hate to deal with, but you'll hate it even more if you don't. Again, I'm focusing on your retirement (not on how to run your practice), but if you don't have your ducks in a row today, it could really bite you down the road.

Take some time to reacquaint yourself with your policy. Ask your insurer if it covers you fully both now and through the rest of your life, even post-retirement. Find out how your policy covers you, your practice, and your partners.

Make sure that the way you structure your practice and set up your insurance protects you from any problems that another partner might incur. In many cases, an incorporated practice with proper malpractice insurance will buffer you from personal loss. But if you have the slightest doubt, double-check it with the experts. Now! As with most facets of retirement planning, a little legwork now pays off in spades down the road.

Liability Insurance for Non-Health-Related Businesses

Businesses outside of the health professions don't have as much to worry about, but a lot of these things (like professional liability insurance and partnership and corporate status) should be considered carefully. As with any legal matter, you should consult with your attorney, especially when things like insurance and business laws can vary significantly by state.

Business Ownership and Retirement

If you own a business or practice, you know just how big a part of your life it is, but you may not be clear on how big a part of *your wealth* it is. In fact, your business or practice is a critical part of your retirement planning process, and it is complicated. Throughout this section, I'll talk you through the valuation and the key decisions you need to make as part of your long-term retirement goals.

If you own a business or practice and you are heading into retirement, there is no rule that says you must sell it. Even if you decide that the day-to-day rigors of running the business are no longer fun or interesting, your business can still pay you. Decisions on whether to remain on the payroll or whether to pay yourself dividends involve a lot of complicated tax and legal issues, but for now, know that you can certainly continue to draw income from a business or practice even if you step down.

Dealing with Partners Today for a Happier Retirement Tomorrow

Running **any** business or practice by yourself is hard work. But running one with partners might be even harder! I had been in practice for a few years and I was thinking of bringing in a partner when I got a little advice from an older friend who had been in business on his own and with others. He told me, "It is best to know how you are going to get out of a partnership, or any other business arrangement with people, **before** you get in."

The practice or business should be valued before anyone new enters. It is just as important to be sure of what the senior partners are going to be paid to take someone in as it is for them to know what the senior partners are going to be paid should they decide to leave and cash out.

Too many people anxious to join a successful business or practice don't ask the "retirement" questions, and the senior members sometimes don't think to put it in writing. Don't assume anything!

When you are dealing with the complex tangle of assets, ownership shares, and personalities in a partnership on a day-to-day basis, it's already a challenge. You make an awful lot of life's decisions with your partners, so you should add retirement issues such as these to the discussions:

- At what age do you retire?
- Can you practice or be an owner for as long as you wish?
- How much notice do you have to give partners when you would like to exit?
- Who is going to retire first?

That last question really throws a monkey wrench into many partnerships. In fact, there can be a great deal of ill will created when a younger partner decides to retire before an older, more senior partner retires. The younger partner may elect to exit first, thinking that the business would implode if the senior partner weren't there to continue to bring in referrals or to promote the business in the community.

If you've got a few years before you are planning your exit from your business or practice, you might want to collaborate with your partners on proactive retirement planning. It is important to understand how to make it seamless for the practice or business.

Valuing the Business or Practice

Valuing a business or practice is complicated and time-consuming, and frankly, it would take up the rest of the book just to get started. So I'm going to focus on *why* you should do it—and leave the "how" to the specialists.

Because you've spent blood, sweat, tears, years, and heaps of cash on building your operation, it's a significant (and perhaps the biggest) part of your net worth. So how much is it worth?

If you don't know the answer to that question, you don't know how much you've got for retirement. If you are planning on selling or handing over your business or practice when you retire, you've got a huge question mark looming on the horizon. Of course, this ties into your personal exit plan. Are you planning to sell the business or practice outright? Are you looking to have your partners buy out your share?

There are numerous groups around the country who value practices or businesses for sale. Most professional organizations have a list of those who value your particular type of practice or business. My advice: talk with more than one valuator, and talk with a few people you may know who have used them recently.

You cannot use the same rule of thumb for all businesses. Different industries have different valuation strategies. Not all businesses and practices are equally valuable in the absence of the owner. If you are a dentist or physician or accountant or lawyer running a small practice, the odds are basically 100 percent that your clients are interested specifically in the services *you* provide. In cases like these, it is necessary to stay awhile with the new owner to ensure a smooth transition. If you don't want to help with a transition, it may be difficult to get much value out of the business or practice beyond selling equipment, customer contact lists, and/or personal referrals to the buyer. My recommendation is that you plan a few years in advance; then you'll have the option of bringing in a partner or protégé and gradually transferring or selling the business or practice to this person.

If you own a business or practice for which you do not personally provide the service, its value may have little to do with your continued involvement— and your sales and income figures are much more important.

To come up with a simple valuation estimate, you can look at the value of publicly traded companies in similar businesses and use that to make comparisons based on gross income and other factors. You should remember to assign a discount to this estimate, because private businesses often sell for 10 to 30 percent less than their large, public peers.

Alternatively, you can create a quick valuation based on income. Let's say you have a general health profession practice. Add up the last five years of gross income, and then divide that by 5 to get an average annual income for the five-year period. If the income of this general practice has been going down slowly each year, the practice might be worth 50 percent or less of that average. If the practice has been growing and the practitioners have kept up with the latest techniques, it might be worth closer to 70 percent or more of the average five-year gross income. Do not use these numbers in any way except to get a ballpark estimate. There are large variances by region and business type.

When it comes time for the real thing, work with a professional. Start the conversation with your accountants or financial advisers. They might be able to conduct a simple valuation, or they can point you in the direction of an expert. Your professional or trade associations can refer you to specialists in your field as well.

How often should you conduct a valuation? It certainly doesn't need to happen often, but when things change dramatically in your industry or your community, it's probably a good time to dust off the numbers.

Once you get a fix on the worth of your practice or business, you'll have a much better sense of the cash proceeds that will stock up your retirement nest egg—and the tax liability you might be facing when you do sell. You (and your partners) will also have fair warning on how much cash you'll need to shell out when buying out a departing partner.

It's a good idea to discuss an exit plan with partners as early as possible. You might be able to maximize the value of your business or practice by mapping a transition—and you don't want *your* retirement to be delayed because someone else took his or hers before you did!

One thing to consider: if the valuation takes longer than you thought it would, selling may take even longer. Although my focus in the book is on your money, your time is obviously a retirement asset too. Give yourself plenty of time to deal with the valuation process. It often takes longer than you think.

Selling the Business or Practice

Selling your business or practice might be the most symbolic act of your shift from working life to retirement. It's also going to be one of the most complicated.

As with business valuations, there's not nearly enough room here to tackle such a big subject. But it is important to think about how this move will affect your retirement. (If you are planning to stay active in your profession, there's more for you in Chapter 17.)

You know how they say you shouldn't go to the grocery store when you are hungry, because you'll make bad decisions? Don't wait until you are fed up with the business to sell it. You risk getting a bad deal if you are too anxious to move on.

Similarly, don't let the calendar force your hand. That's not just a "hurry up and settle for a lower price" thing because you're ready to retire. There are other considerations as well. For example, you should also be careful not to start a sale too close to the end of your fiscal year. Things invariably run long, and you don't want to begin your retirement with two tax returns' worth of complicated tax events.

As with the rest of your retirement goals, plan ahead. It's not too early to identify potential buyers. (Whether you **tell** them now or not is a whole different story.) Proceeding with a formal legal restructuring of the business or practice into a corporate entity and formulating a transition strategy for the sale today may make the transfer of the business far easier when it actually happens. You've probably seen what other professionals in your area have gone through. How long did the average deal take? What "surprises" did they run into? How could things have gone better?

Start assembling your dream team of people who might be involved: lawyers, accountants, real estate brokers, and so on. One tip: pick some experts who are younger than you. Your retirement plans shouldn't be held up because your key person retired before you!

Speaking of accountants, assume you'll have a tax whammy. Your accountant might be able to identify some immediate tactics to minimize your tax burden—and at the very least, he or she can tell you just how much of the sale proceeds you can keep.

Transferring Ownership

When it comes time to exit your business or practice, you may find that you'd like to turn it over to someone else instead of selling it outright. The valuation may be relatively low or the local market may be too illiquid to make it worth selling. For example, if you run the older of two businesses in a small town, you might find that there is no true gauge of a fair market value. There might even be a tax advantage to "giving away" the business or practice.

As with valuing and selling your business or practice, I'm not here to tell you how to go about doing this. But I want you to think about how transferring one of your biggest financial assets might affect your retirement. For greater details on the how-to side, talk with your attorney and accountant before you do anything else.

The obvious outcome from not selling your business or practice outright is that there is no windfall from a sale. In addition, in terms of your post-retirement budget goals, remember that there's also no more salary, profit sharing, or quarterly dividends, nor are there any other current income sources on which you might rely.

It's also important to make sure that you are free and clear of any liabilities related to the business or practice. This isn't just good business sense. This is about insulating your retirement savings from unnecessary claims. Such liabilities could include financial ones (such as bank debt with personal guarantees) or legal ones (such as malpractice claims) that could come back to haunt you. Make sure your legal documentation addresses liabilities, and follow up with outside parties directly whenever possible.

On the tax side, by not selling your business or practice outright, you may be sparing yourself from a big tax bill from a sale-related windfall, but you might also be setting yourself up for taxes related to the transfer of valuable assets. There's nothing like the feeling of getting a big tax bill for money owed when no money has been received. The laws vary greatly by state, but be on the lookout for business and/or real estate transfer taxes.

Things will also vary depending on the structure of the business (whether it is an LLC, a C Corporation, or an S Corporation, for example). If you believe that a transfer (rather than a sale) is in your long-range plans, you can start preparing in advance by installing the transferees as minority partners or officers. (Laws sometimes favor "insiders" in a transfer, as opposed to "outsiders" who suddenly assume ownership of a sizable asset.) You may also find that the enterprise (or your ownership) share can be put into a trust to help ease the transaction—and minimize the tax impact.

Speaking of taxes, you should also take the federal income tax gift exemption into consideration when you are working on the transfer. This is most relevant when you are transferring your personal share of the asset. You may be able to get a full or partial tax exemption if you haven't used up your annual or permanent gift exemption. The exemption levels vary greatly so there's no point in putting the current amount in print in this book. Suffice to say, the exemption ceiling changes every year.

Ultimately, if you decide to hand over your business or practice rather than sell it, the important thing is to make sure that your generosity (and your retirement nest egg) isn't punished.

Retaining a Share of Your Business or Practice

You may elect to keep a part of your business or practice into your retirement. You might do this as a way to help your partners out financially, to keep an active interest in the business or practice you built, or to stave off boredom.

Those are all good reasons, but be aware that things will change. As you move into a less active role, you won't have the same influence you used to have. You might find that liberating or frustrating . . . your mileage will vary.

From a retirement standpoint, you've got two things to consider: the liability and the long-term impact. It's great to have an active revenue source throughout your retirement, but you do not want the liabilities of a business or practice to have a negative impact on your future. Make sure you are insulated from the debt that the business or practice may hold or incur—and from the worst-case scenarios that could occur (lawsuits, malpractice cases, and so on).

As for the long term, you may or may not ever fully retire, but you will fully expire. Have a clear exit mapped out contractually for yourself (if you ever decide you want out of the business) and for your survivors (who will almost certainly want out).

Conclusion

As a busy professional, you've got a lot to think about when it comes to your retirement. Planning makes setting up your retirement a whole lot easier. Investing the time to consider your personal wishes and your business needs is critical.

Take the time to set your goals, to assess what you have and what you will need, and to make sure that the large asset that is your business or practice is aligned to support your retirement—not slow it down.

In Part Three, I'll take you through the critical tools and resources you need to implement the plan—and to begin investing your hard-earned money for retirement.

RETIREMENT TOOLS AND RESOURCES

6

Understanding the Market and Your Investments

Just because you love your money, there's no reason why you can't put it to work. In order to build a sizable nest egg that covers all of your wants and needs with a little extra left over, your money needs to work hard starting today.

Investing is the key to a truly healthy retirement portfolio. Saving the money you invest is important, but making that money work hard makes your nest egg bigger (and it makes it easier to fund your retirement overall). I'll show you my strategies for creating a healthy and secure investment portfolio for retirement.

Investment Fundamentals That Fuel Your Retirement Plan

There are two forces in the market that can erode your savings quickly: inflation and market volatility. They will derail your retirement permanently if you aren't planning to deal with them constantly. But also, over time you can grow your money wisely to offset volatility and beat inflation. That's why some of these fundamentals—the time value of money, compounding interest, and Dollar Cost Averaging—are so important to embrace.

The Time Value of Money

Time is money—you've heard that over and over. The *time value of money* refers to the principle that the purchasing power of money varies over time. If you were given the choice of receiving $5,000 today or in three years, what would you do? It seems obvious that you'd take it now, but why? There's a lot more than immediate gratification at play here.

If you took the money today, you could spend it or invest it. But if you waited three years to get the $5,000, after inflation (at an average rate of 3 percent) did its dirty work, its real-world value would be approximately $4,564. That would be a drop in value of almost $436 in just three years. Yes, you would still receive $5,000, but it would not go as far. Gas would be more expensive, food would be more expensive, and frankly, everything would be more expensive. That would be money that you couldn't get back. If you had spent it when you got it, you could at least have gotten some use out of your purchases. However, if you had invested it, you'd have likely increased or at least retained most of the value. So yes, take the money now.

Ever heard the expression "leaving money on the table"? That's one way to define *opportunity cost*—losing the opportunity of being able to use money by not taking it now. You have the opportunity to save it, invest it, or spend it now. There is also an opportunity cost in paying a bill early if there is no fee charged for waiting until the end of the month. Perhaps you should leave the money in the bank and let it earn a little interest and still pay the bill on time.

We all know that a dollar is not worth what it once was. If you want to grasp inflation's toll, sometimes you need to turn the clock back to truly understand the "sticker shock." In 1990, a new Ford Mustang Convertible cost $14,289. In 2014, that same car has a starting price of $27,200, *not* including the extras. Wow, it has almost doubled in price over 24 years. The salespeople get around the inflation issue by focusing your attention on all the newest features and improvements so you forget about the steep price hike.

If you have to have that car, you can dip into your pocket right now, or you can save for it. If you passed on the car in 1990 and invested the $14,000 instead, there's some good news. By investing in mutual funds or stocks that yielded a modest return of 6 percent per year, you would have over $57,000 saved by now. You can buy the Mustang and all the bells and whistles and still have money left over. That $14,000 has been working hard, even during some very rough economic times. It has beaten inflation and created wealth.

If you socked that $14,000 away in a simple savings account that earned just 1 percent, you would have $18,000 in the bank. Oops, that's not enough! You ended up ahead technically, but inflation beat you. That's why investing in the market is a critical factor with the time value of money.

(If you decided to spend that money on the car in 1990, you would not have earned anything on your money. That's an important part of the time value of money too. If you don't save money, you probably won't have money. And if you don't have money, it's awfully hard to buy the next car after the old one stops running.)

In retirement, you probably aren't going to have the deep pockets to make big purchases as easily as you do now. So, start saving that money now. Every dollar you invest today is going to be worth more than the dollar you invest tomorrow.

Compounding Your Money

Money saved grows—and over time, it grows faster and bigger. That's *compounding*—that is, generating earnings on assets you have placed in investments *and* reinvesting those earnings. Think about the savings account you had when you were a child. You put $10 in the bank for five years at 5 percent annual interest. The first year you ended up with $10.50. The chart below shows how your initial investment grew to $12.76 as each year's interest compounded on the next year (Table 6.1). Compound interest starts with the first amount of money you put in, and then the accumulated interest is added. The faster money compounds, the larger amount of money you will have over time.

Without doing a lick of work and without investing another penny, you earned a greater amount of money each year. (If you'd left that childhood money alone from the age of 10 until you retired at 65, you'd have $146.36!) That's the power of compounding!

Putting Your Numbers to the Test

Using a financial calculator is a great way to become proficient at working through your financial plan. It might bring some clarity to your goals if you

Table 6.1 Simple Compounding Interest

Year	Interest	Amount on Jan. 1	Interest Earned	Amount on Dec. 31
1	5%	$10.00	$0.50	$10.50
2	5%	$10.50	$0.53	$11.03
3	5%	$11.03	$0.55	$11.58
4	5%	$11.58	$0.58	$12.16
5	5%	$12.16	$0.60	$12.76

see how much value your own savings could have if invested wisely. There is a wealth of online resources such as the specialized investment and savings calculators at http://www.bankrate.com/calculators.aspx, and there is a wealth of apps for your smartphone or tablet that also work through these time-value-of-money and compounding exercises. You can also buy a Texas Instruments or Hewlett-Packard financial calculator at any office supply store or online for $30 to $40.

Here is how to solve the problem above—if you put $10 in the bank for five years at 5 percent annual interest, how much would you end up with—with a simple financial calculator. Each calculator is slightly different, so be sure and read the instructions first:

Present value (PV) = $10.00 (principal amount, or *P*)
Period (*N*) = 5 years (number of years)
Percent return (*I*) = 5 percent
Future value (FV) = $12.76

There are a number of scenarios, like savings and spending goals and assessing the real value of your money, that you can work through. With the flexibility to put your own data through a number of what-if scenarios, a financial calculator might just be your best friend during your retirement planning process. I've posted several exercises at http://www.940financialconsulting.com.

The Power of Dollar Cost Averaging and Regular Deposits

The *Dollar Cost Averaging* (DCA) model is another investment fundamental that you should understand. While making the most of compounding and the time value of money helps you do battle with inflation, using DCA helps you deal with the unpredictable volatility in the financial market. It also helps you become a more disciplined and dedicated investor.

It's a very simple concept: *Dollar Cost Averaging* means investing a fixed amount of money in your chosen investments regularly. Seriously, that's it. Most people who follow this model have money automatically transferred monthly from their bank account to a mutual fund or other investment account.

By making regular transfers, you take yourself out of the "market-timing" mindset. Investors who believe in *market timing* try to buy only when the market is at its lowest, and they try to sell only when the market is peaking. However, no one knows exactly when the market hits those points, so people who practice market timing spend a lot of energy to create a best guess. In contrast, those who practice DCA and make regular purchases might be paying relatively high prices every once in a while, but it's offset by the fact that they are also buying at relatively low prices quite often. The average cost of your investment is always well under the highest price you paid. Given that the market always trends upward over time, your average cost will yield a healthy return if you stay invested for the long haul of 10 years or more.

Mathematically, it's simple enough, but there are some benefits to Dollar Cost Averaging that are very important.

First of all, you are making a regular contribution to your retirement every month. If you are serious about having a happy retirement, you need to show that kind of commitment. Luckily, it's quite easy. When the money is automatically deducted, you typically don't miss it. It's off to work, so to speak. Even if you are deducting $100 monthly, look at how the time value of money is fueling your retirement. (Your first year's investment alone of $1,200 will be worth almost $4,000 after 20 years, assuming a conservative average rate of 6 percent. Nice work!)

The other advantage of Dollar Cost Averaging is more psychological. When you invest regularly, you aren't "overthinking" it. Getting too caught up in the market might cause you to panic when the usual commentators cry about a market crash. Some of the investors who got hurt the most in the Great Recession were those who panicked and sold at the market's lowest point. If they had stayed the course, they'd be pretty happy today since their investments would be surging ahead healthily.

While there is a real financial benefit to Dollar Cost Averaging, the greatest value might be in the long-term commitment of your retirement strategy.

Critical Investment Strategies

With the fundamentals introduced, it's time to look at two very important strategies that will keep your money working and protected from risk. The philosophies of *asset allocation* and *diversification* allow you to embrace risk while maintaining safe and sane practices to safeguard your money.

Asset Allocation: The First Step

The simplest way to define *asset allocation* is balancing the risks and rewards of your portfolio by dividing your money between cash, stocks, bonds, and other investments such as gold, property, and business holdings. It may be a new term to you, but it is a time-tested philosophy. The Talmud has this quote: "Let every man divide his money into three parts, and invest a third in land, a third in business, and a third let him keep in reserve."

Distributing the money is simple. Choosing the right categories will take up the rest of this section of the book. However, Figure 6.1 gives you a quick look at a very simple allocation model. We'll get into specifics and the right allocation targets for you later on.

There are two main asset allocation strategies: strategic allocation and tactical allocation. I recommend strategic allocation. Why? Because *strategic allocation* is based on designing a portfolio that takes into account your investment objectives, time horizon, and ability to withstand volatility through all market conditions. It is a relatively hands-off strategy. It just requires that you rebalance the portfolio regularly (but infrequently) by reallocating funds back to their original target percentages that you established in your plans. (I'll show you how—and when—to rebalance in Chapter 8.)

Tactical allocation requires active management of your portfolio. You are going to be constantly moving money around trying to beat the market. As I noted earlier, this is a full-time job, the success of which still rests on your best guesses most of the time. If you have enough education and experience in the market, tactical allocation may be the one for you, but it is not for me. I pay management fees to individual managers and mutual fund managers to make those decisions for me because they are better equipped than I am to do that.

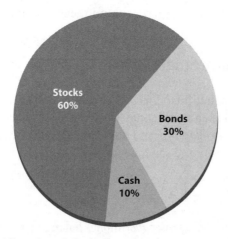

Figure 6.1   Asset Allocation: A Basic Overview

My Personal Allocation Model

Almost every investor has his or her own specific allocation models. There is no one right formula. I believe you can be healthily diversified with just six different funds, as long as you have researched the categories carefully and matched them to your goals. Here's my basic allocation model, using mutual funds exclusively. For this example, I will use the fund categories set up by Morningstar.com, a great information resource for investors.

As shown in Figure 6.2, in the Six Fund Portfolio, there are the following:

- **Three World Allocation Funds.** *Fund objectives: two are Multi-Asset Global Funds and one is an Asset Allocation Fund.* Multi-Asset Global Funds invest in various combinations of stocks, fixed-income investments like bonds, and other asset classes. A significant portion of these global funds are composed of securities of foreign companies. The two such funds in my portfolio have very different holdings and different investment philosophies, but they both share a goal of owning investments from the best regions and market sectors around the world. Asset Allocation Funds also own stocks, bonds, and other instruments but are managed with greater flexibility to move money to the optimal sectors for income and capital appreciation.
- **Two Moderate Allocation Funds.** *Fund objectives: one is a Balanced Fund, and the other is a Growth and Income Fund.* Growth and Income Funds aggressively seek growth and current income through stocks, whereas Balanced Funds also seek growth and current income, but generally invest in a greater proportion of stable fixed-income investments. Typically, a Balanced Fund portfolio is composed of at least 25 percent bonds and other fixed-income investments.
- **One Aggressive Allocation Fund.** *Fund objective: this is a Balanced Fund with similar parameters as defined above, but with a smaller proportion of fixed-income investments—and therefore, a more aggressive weight placed on growth stocks—than the Moderate Allocation Balanced Fund.*

When you decide on your personal allocation goals, you'll be able to research investments that will support those goals. The allocation shown in Figure 6.2 matches my personal goal of having a portfolio that is diversified across multiple fund categories and funds. It also reflects my tolerance for risk. Your model may be different from mine.

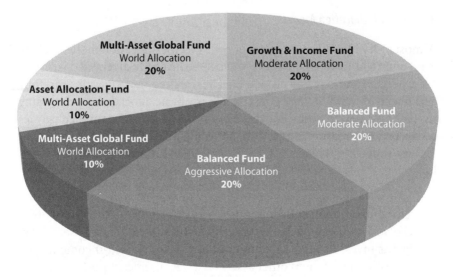

Figure 6.2   Asset Allocation of the Six Fund Portfolio

Strategic allocation and a mutual fund portfolio make this strategy easy for me to implement. I choose funds with objectives that match my goals regarding the allocation of money put into the funds. (Fund objectives can be found in a fund's prospectus or on the fund company's website.) Because the funds' goals are aligned with my goals, I do not get bent out of shape if my return is not the highest in any given year. I know I will end up with an excellent return over the long run.

The biggest amount of time you should spend with your portfolio is in the initial phase of investing. Set up your allocation based on your goals, and then select the investments that fit your goals and your planned allocation. That allows you to make the best choices for the long run. By beginning with a strategic allocation strategy, you'll have a well-thought-out balanced portfolio representing many asset classes. This type of portfolio has a better chance over time than one that is constantly being adjusted.

Diversification

Diversification is an important way to reduce risk in a portfolio by using different types of investments. If you put your money into diversified types of investments, you will be able to keep a reasonably steady return over time even when some are going down in value. Failing to do that could cause you a lot of sleepless nights.

Diversification is the central concept of asset allocation, but it goes beyond allocation. It's about distributing your money in a way that lets you capitalize on a wide range of opportunities while reducing your exposure to risk. You should diversify your portfolio at a high level (choosing a greater concentration of growth and income funds versus conservative investments, for example) and at a more tactical level (choosing an array of mutual funds and stocks within the growth and income category of your core asset allocation.)

Why diversify? Often, there are one or two parts of the market that are not in sync with the others. In any given year, one fund will outrun another fund, so it behooves you to check the performance of individual funds to be sure that they are consistent performers and have reasonable returns over a long period of time. When we watch the market, it seems like we are always comparing investments in the here and now, but that often does not give us a clear picture of what is going on. I rarely buy a fund that does not have at least a five- to eight-year track record. You want to see how well a fund performed when the market was up—and when the market tanked.

How you diversify between stocks, bonds, cash, and other investments is going to be based primarily on your (1) *risk tolerance* and your (2) *time horizon*.

Risk tolerance is basically a decision you make as to how much money you are willing to lose at any point in time. Are you willing to put more money at risk in hopes of a higher return? If the market goes down 25 percent, are you willing to "ride it out," or are you an uneasy investor who should have more of your money in less risky securities?

There are some risks that you will be able to manage and some you will not. The latter are known as *nondiversifiable* (or *systematic*) *risks*. Let's think about these risks first. You cannot control changes in interest rates, stock market crashes, wars, major earthquakes, or other events that will have a major impact on the entire market. (In other words, if the market tanks, pretty much everyone takes a hit. There are exceptions, but they are not relevant to an individual investor planning for retirement.) Therefore, you cannot escape these—and you'll have to expect the ups and downs that these broad changes have on the markets.

Diversifiable (or *nonsystematic*) *risks* are specific to certain investments. Suppose you want to invest in a fast-growing market like Latin America or a hot sector like technology or gold. There might be big potential returns, but there's much more risk because the waters are largely untested. (I knew an acquaintance who kept investing all of his money in gold during the go-go 1970s, only to watch his undiversified portfolio's value plummit to one-sixth of its value as he prepared to retire in the mid-1980s.) How do we control this? By creating a diversified portfolio with investments in multiple instruments, market sectors, and regions. Simplistically put, don't put all of your eggs in one basket!

Over time, you are going to see the market go up and down, but often you don't really "get the picture" until you see a graph like the one shown in Figure 6.3. Those little blips are more than they seem on a long-term chart. For example, during the dip in 2008, the market lost **37 percent** of its value as shown in Figure 6.4!

Your *time horizon* addresses the time that you will need the money you have invested: a down payment on a house, sending a child to college, or eventually your retirement. When you are younger, your time horizon for retirement may be 30-plus years, so you can afford to invest in slightly more risky investments with hopes of a higher return. Younger people are more capable of riding the market's ups and downs. They can chase big gains and still have time to replenish their savings with earnings if those risks don't pan out. But older people may not have the same degree of flexibility. When you know that the money you have been investing is for your child's college tuition, you need that money to be there when you need it.

Remember the saying, "No pain, no gain"? You have to decide how much pain you are willing to take as the market goes up and down. An old English proverb suggests, "A bird in the hand is worth two in the bush." For investors, there is something to be said for having a smaller, but certain gain, rather than *hoping* that they will have a larger, riskier gain that may not materialize.

Many beginners move into the market as it reaches its highest points because they think it will keep growing constantly upward. When the market takes one of its inevitable drops, they take their money out, vowing, "Never again!" That's buying high and selling low. What you want to do is to buy low and sell high, but that is hard to accomplish. Putting in a little money at a time (using Dollar Cost Averaging) is always the best way to invest.

Understanding the behavior of a stock or mutual fund during downturns is very important to mapping out your time horizon. In 2002, as the stock market recovered from the technology stocks' downturn, novice investors thought all was fine and that the market was heading up. Of course, in 2008, the market tanked again.

Those who put their money exclusively into an S&P 500 Index Fund (a mutual fund that mirrors the makeup of common market indicators) between 2002 and 2007 got a real surprise when the S&P 500 plunged in

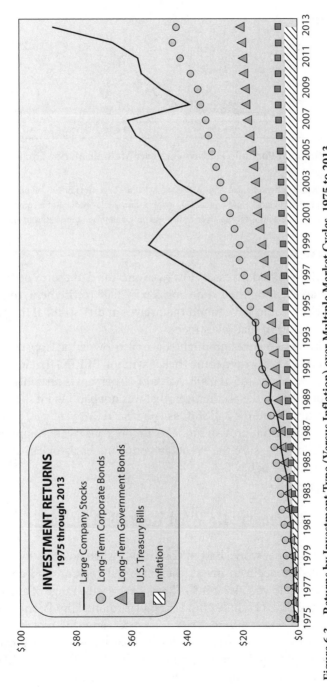

Figure 6.3   Returns by Investment Type (Versus Inflation) over Multiple Market Cycles, 1975 to 2013

Note: The graph represents a hypothetical value of $1 invested in stocks, bonds, and Treasury Bills at the beginning of 1975. This graph assumes reinvestment of income and no transaction costs or taxes. This is for illustrative purposes only, and it is not indicative of any investment.

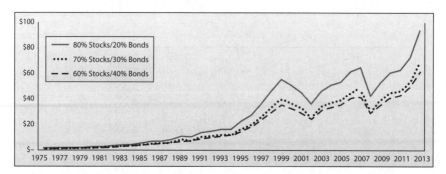

Figure 6.4   Retirement Portfolio Performance over Multiple Market Cycles, 1975 to 2013

Note: The graph represents a hypothetical value of $1 invested at the beginning of 1975 in portfolios of differing proportions of stocks and bonds. This graph assumes reinvestment of income and no transaction costs or taxes. This is for illustrative purposes only, and it is not indicative of any investment.

2008. Those undiversified investors lost over one-third of their portfolios. Investors with an event on their time horizon in 2008 (retirement, tuition, or something else) would have found themselves in dire straits if they had put all of their money in that investment.

A more diversified investor might have also owned a Conservative Allocation Fund like Berwyn Income (ticker symbol: BERIX) that lost only 10.19 percent of its total value in 2008. A loss of 10 percent is certainly scary enough, but considering the alternatives, that was not bad! As I'll show you in Part Four, your allocations will shift as you near retirement age, moving some of your money from growth mode to a more conservative approach. That's designed to make sure the events in your time horizon can stay on schedule and risk stays at bay.

Investing and Retirement: Do What Works Best for You

You have to decide what works best in your hands when it comes to investments. When people begin to invest, they naturally look around and ask their friends, "What do you invest in?" They'll hear a wide range of answers: specific stocks, bonds, ETFs, index funds, "regular" mutual funds, and so on. They have different goals, different risk tolerances, and different incomes and spending habits—so their friends' solutions may not fit their own needs.

There is a lot of bragging in investing. That's true of friends and family who are in the market, and it is even more true of many brokers and financial planning professionals. Someone at a party who "made a killing" may sound great as he spins a tale, but remember, no one is going to advertise that he "lost his shirt" last year. No one has a perfect record playing the market. Don't blindly follow someone's advice on a hot stock until you know more about his investment philosophy and his overall track record.

Creating a Diversified Portfolio Model That Supports Your Retirement Goals

Now that the core concepts of asset allocation and diversification have been put forward, let's put them into action. In my opinion, diversifying your portfolio is one of the most important decisions you can make. It's the key to making your investments support your retirement plan and goals—while keeping your money as safe as possible.

Before we address specific investments in subsequent chapters, we'll create a portfolio model that supports your goals. Although you can build a portfolio containing many types of investments, I'm a believer in mutual funds making up the majority of your portfolio. Let's start this discussion with the investments that make up a large part of most mutual funds: stocks. What we say about them can be translated into any other sector of the market.

Stocks are usually divided into groups depending upon their capitalization, or how much money they are worth. Two examples of giant-capitalization companies are Microsoft and Google (both have market capitalizations over $250 billion). There are also tiers of large-, medium- (or midsize), small-, and micro-cap stocks. Micro-cap stocks usually have between $50 million and $300 million in capitalization. If you choose to invest in a common stock mutual fund, that fund will more than likely own stocks from each of these categories—and reach a far greater degree of diversity than you could achieve if you invested directly.

Looking at the size of companies is just one element of a mutual fund's composition. Table 6.2 is just a sample of the many domestic and international stock categories. You'll see many different types of categories that include stocks at all levels of capitalization and some with a blend of sizes.

Let's move beyond size and start to consider a fund's objectives. You are going to build a portfolio that matches your retirement plan's goals and philosophies. With Table 6.3, you can start to zero in on fund categories that mirror your goals. (Table 6.3, "Fund Objective Categories," covers stock-based funds as well as different bond classes such as general, government, municipal, and speciality bonds, and it includes funds that carry a blend of stocks, bonds, and other instruments.)

Table 6.2   Domestic and International Stock Categories by Size

Domestic Stock	International Stock
Large Value	Foreign Large Value
Large Blend	Foreign Large Blend
Large Growth	Foreign Large Growth
Mid-Cap Value	Foreign Small- to Mid-Cap Value
Mid-Cap Blend	Foreign Small- to Mid-Cap Blend
Mid-Cap Growth	Foreign Small- to Mid-Cap Growth
Small Value	Individual Country Stock
Small Blend	World Stock
Small Value	

Table 6.3   Fund Objective Categories

1	Aggressive Growth	21	Money Market: Government
2	Asset Allocation	22	Money Market: Single State
3	Balanced	23	Money Market: Taxable
4	Convertible Bond	24	Money Market: Treasury
5	Corporate Bond: General	25	Multi-Asset Global
6	Corporate Bond: High Quality	26	Multi-Sector Bond
7	Corporate Bond: High Yield	27	Municipal Bond: National
8	Diversified Emerging Markets	28	Municipal Bond: Single State
9	Equity: Income	29	Pacific Stock
10	Europe Stock	30	Small Company
11	Foreign Stock	31	Specialty: Communications
12	Government Bond: ARM	32	Specialty: Financial
13	Government Bond: General	33	Specialty: Health
14	Government Bond: Mortgage	34	Specialty: Natural Resources
15	Government: Treasury	35	Specialty: Precious Metals
16	Growth	36	Specialty: Real Estate
17	Growth and Income	37	Specialty: Technology
18	Income	38	Specialty: Utility
19	Money Market: Federal Tax Exempt	39	World Stock
20	Money Market: General	40	Worldwide Bond

In Chapter 7, we'll return to the Six Fund Portfolio for an example of diversification in action.

A Quick Look at Common Retirement Investments

Now that we've explored asset allocation and diversification, let's go beyond the fundamentals of investing and talk about the kinds of investments that you might be considering, before we move into the more detailed chapters on those instruments.

First, I want you to understand that there is a big difference between investing **for** retirement and investing **in** retirement. When you invest **for** retirement, your goal should be conservative to moderate growth of your money. **In** retirement, you continue to stay invested but in more conservative instruments than before while you begin to spend the income (dividends and gains) from the money you have saved. At times you may find that you have to "borrow" a little principal itself. Accordingly, it's important to remember that your portfolio needs to evolve over time, and it's up to you to manage that.

I do not believe that all of your money should be in any one type of investment (mutual funds, individual stocks and bonds, ETFs, or others). However, it is both possible and easy for you to construct a balanced and diversified portfolio for yourself.

No matter what you plan to invest in, you need to ask the right questions—something that investors often forget to do. In 1940, Fred Schwed, Jr., wrote *Where Are the Customers' Yachts? or A Good Hard Look at Wall Street*, and it still is worth reading! Schwed tells us that it is up to us to keep our goals at the forefront. You may not be interested in buying a big yacht, but I'm guessing you *are* interested in maintaining your pre-retirement lifestyle.

When it comes to retirement, don't try to beat the market. You should be interested in buying quality investments that are going to provide for you and your family in the future without trying to make a "killing."

Focus on *why* this mutual fund (or stock or ETF or other investment) is the right one for you to purchase—not *when* you should purchase it. Morningstar checks investor returns, and it has found that, in most cases, many funds are bought when the market is high and sold when it goes down. So even though the fund may have returned 10 percent a year for 10 years, most investors' returns are always below that (and sometimes, no more than half the return of the fund). That has to do both with investor anxiety and with the class of funds (A, B, or C, for example) they own. A regular monthly investment gives you a better chance of achieving your goal. If you insist that you know more than Mr. Market, you will likely do far worse.

You should not research the fund or stock you want to purchase while you are watching the very convincing people on television. They "hype" investments so that their programs will get great ratings, which will get them a contract renewal and a higher salary. Sorry, folks, but that is just the way it works!

Read everything you can find about stocks and funds you are interested in. Note the source of the material you read. Ask yourself, "What's in it for them? Are they going to profit from my investment?" A brokerage firm profits directly from fees and commissions so take their recommendations with a grain of salt. The talking heads on TV and online bloggers profit indirectly, but they get paid nonetheless. Finding a resource that is relatively unbiased is very valuable. That's why I turn to Morningstar, Value Line, and other unbiased sources for information on stocks, ETFs, and mutual funds.

Before You Get Started

No matter what you are investing your money in, you must match your retirement goals with an investment's objectives. When you begin researching mutual funds, you can do that by tapping into research sources and even the funds' websites, and you'll be able to quickly find the management philosophy and objectives for each fund. With individual stocks and bonds, you aren't going to have an easy time finding the information you need to match these investments to your goals.

There are a few paths to follow. If income and cash flow are important to your goals, you can track dividend stocks, for example, and you'll look at the concrete facts of past and current dividend payouts. But if principal growth and beating inflation are key goals, you will be overwhelmed with copious and *incomplete* information. After all, every stock is intended to be an instrument of growth. It's just that some of them actually aren't. If you build your own retirement portfolio, it's up to you to do the research to find the best stocks and bonds with strong upside potential and stability. (Aren't those professionally managed mutual funds sounding good right now?)

Finally, **don't panic!** Most people do, but take a deep breath and remember that you can do this. Even though people in the investment field like to believe they are "rocket scientists," those who are worth your time and money are really few and far between.

Why Mutual Funds Are Better Than You Think

I believe that mutual funds can, and should, be the largest component of your retirement portfolio. Even though there has been a lot written about the drawbacks and flaws of mutual funds, the benefits outweigh the problems for a large percentage of investors. Mutual funds are cost-effective, relatively simple to analyze, liquid, and pretty transparent—all of which are major arguments in their favor as cornerstones to a retirement portfolio.

Although it is true that the average mutual fund manager *does not* beat the market on any regular basis, I would never suggest that you invest with *average* managers. That's why I stay away from index funds and stick with well-managed funds that meet the objectives that match my goals. The fact is, talented managers, the real cream of the crop, **do** beat the market on a fairly consistent basis. They don't win every year, but over the longer term their performance really rises to the top, consistently producing returns that are a few percentage points above the market over any 5- or 10-year period.

Mutual funds also give you healthy, cost-effective diversification. Bonds, for instance, have a valuable place in almost every retirement portfolio, but it is very difficult to build a diversified portfolio of individual bonds unless you are exceptionally wealthy. Because most mutual funds own hundreds (if not thousands!) of positions, a couple of bad decisions really will not hurt their performance. Moreover, virtually every fund available will reinvest any dividends or capital gains automatically if you so desire, and that can lead to powerful (and convenient) compound growth over time.

The advantages go beyond the investing process. When you need to draw down your investment, it is easy to remove money from no-load mutual funds when you need it, without having to worry about selling a few shares and paying the sales charges for doing so.

Why Stocks Aren't for Everyone

Some people will no doubt notice that I am encouraging readers to buy funds and not individual stocks. I have no problem with the idea of people investing in stocks as long as they *know the risks, have the time, and can achieve proper diversification*. Let me give you an example.

If you look at the prospectuses of mutual funds or you look at individual accounts run by investment management firms, you'll see that they put certain percentages of different categories of stocks, bonds, and other investments into the portfolios. Let's use oil and gas as an example. These investment firms allocate 6 percent of the money to that category, and they may have 2 percent in three separate stocks (or some variation), but they do not put all 6 percent in just one stock. That is where I see the biggest difference in how a mutual fund manager or investment management firm can control a portfolio better than an individual investor.

Too many individuals get carried away with a particular segment of the market that is doing well, and they put entirely too much money in one stock. Sure, I know the "one-stock" stories—that one hot stock that went through the roof and made someone very rich. Just like the stories of winning the lottery, there is always going to be a lucky duck, but that duck, in all probability, won't be you! Why take a chance with your retirement when you can make a good deal of money with much less effort?

After all, another problem with individual stocks is that it takes a lot of time and energy to manage a portfolio containing them. Since my primary goal is to make the process of planning and managing your retirement as painless as possible, it is difficult for me to recommend that you invest a lot in individual stocks. In other words, it's just plain easier to own a portfolio of funds.

Stocks have what is called *idiosyncratic risk*—bad things can happen to a specific company that have nothing to do with any of its competitors. Because of that, you have to own stocks from multiple companies at the same time, or you run the risk of a single piece of bad news wiping out a large chunk of your money. Not only is it harder to achieve diversification with a portfolio of individual stocks than it is with mutual funds, but rebalancing that portfolio can also be more problematic.

Rebalancing a stock-based portfolio doesn't just require more effort. It could involve more cost too. With stocks, there is no discount in commissions if you want to trade just 20 shares instead of 100—so selling a few shares here and buying a few more there to rebalance your stock positions can rack up sizable commission costs before you know it. Transfers between mutual funds (when they are held with the same fund company) typically do not have additional fees attached.

That said, it is a near certainty that many readers will already have some stocks in their portfolio—whether as deliberate investment decisions or as by-products of their employers' compensation systems via employee stock awards, stock options, stock purchase plans, or 401(k) matching. As a result, some readers will find that they are about to enter retirement with a large amount of a single company's stock.

There is nothing wrong with keeping some of that stock, but you don't want the stock to skew the balance of your portfolio. Bad things can happen to any and every company, and it would be tragic to see a happy retirement derailed because too much of your money was tied up in a single company. I don't think it really makes sense to have any more than 5 percent of your portfolio in any particular stock, so I would recommend selling at least down to that level.

In some cases, the company may have policies that will take care of this automatically since some private companies do not let employees keep shares after they leave the company. Even in cases in which such sales are not mandatory, the company almost certainly will have some sort of auction, buyback, or arranged sale mechanism to allow for retired (or retiring) workers to cash out their shares.

The Cost of Investing

Investing for retirement costs money. But don't get caught up worrying about fees. If your portfolio is performing well, you won't mind if a brokerage fee or a mutual fund's expenses are a little higher than normal. You wouldn't blink at paying more for the house or car of your dreams, so think of your investing costs that way too.

Naturally, I do not want you to pay any more than you have to, but I also want you to spend time learning about the quality and performance of the investment you are considering, regardless of what it is.

Fees on stocks are fairly straightforward. You pay the brokerage firm a flat fee when you buy or sell the stock. You'll typically pay a broker a percentage commission on those transactions, so if you want to save money, do it yourself online. Mutual funds fees are much more complex, so that's why many investors get hung up on fees and don't spend the needed time researching the fund as a whole. (We'll get into fees when we dig into specific investments in the next few chapters.)

Remember, when you are spending money, especially on something as important as your retirement, "Caveat emptor," or "Let the buyer beware."

Resources

When you are thinking about your retirement at a high level, including your goals, your plan, how to allocate and diversify wisely, and how to invest your money, this book will serve you well. When you start actively implementing your retirement plan and begin investing, you need the freshest data, information, and analyses to evaluate specific funds, fund companies, and the ongoing performance of your portfolio.

Throughout this part of the book, you may find yourself craving more information. I'll list key resources throughout these chapters, and I'll post the links at http://www.940financialconsulting.com.

I suggest starting at your local library to find all of its resources first. Library online resources are some of the most thorough I've found, and if you subscribe to my "Look before you leap" philosophy, you'll be glad you stopped by and had a reference librarian talk with you for 10 minutes.

My personal recommendations for resources are these:

- Morningstar (http://www.morningstar.com)
- Value Line for Mutual Funds (http://www.valueline.com)
- Steele Mutual Fund Expert (http://www.steelesystems.com)
- Yahoo! Finance (http://finance.yahoo.com)

I highly recommend tapping into all the resources that Morningstar, Value Line for Mutual Funds, and Steele Mutual Fund Expert have to offer. While there are many other information sources, these are the ones I use most. You can research their fund categories, discover the top-rated funds in each category, and learn more about individual funds, including each fund's philosophy, performance record, and even the specific stocks it invests in. There is a wealth of information for free on these websites, although there is much more available for subscribers. (Many libraries have access to the full Morningstar website, so you may want to plan a research outing if you can't find what you are looking for on the free site.)

There are many great online resources for data, prices, and performance like Yahoo! Finance, Bloomberg, and most other financial media companies' websites. Be careful about taking recommendations for specific stocks and funds online. There are a million sales pitches on the Internet. Stick with the data from a reputable site, and don't buy into a "hot tip" until you are certain of the reputation and track record of the person or company making the recommendation.

If you want to learn more about the fundamentals of investing like the time value of money, you might want to check out the Khan Academy's Finance and Capital Markets online videos and tutorials. This is a *free* service. It's a great way to learn and better understand a concept in just a short time frame: http://www.khanacademy.org/economics-finance-domain/core-finance.

The major brokerage firms (Schwab, Fidelity, Vanguard, and so on) have very clear models to help you understand how to work well with asset allocation. Online, I would suggest that you go to the SEC's website (http://www.sec.gov/investor/pubs/assetallocation.htm) and read their "Beginners' Guide to Asset Allocation, Diversification, and Rebalancing."

If you'd like to learn more, get a copy of *Asset Allocation: Balancing Financial Risk* by Roger Gibson. It is an excellent commonsense, in-depth book. You will be well rewarded for having read it.

Conclusion

More often than not, investors tend to get caught up in stock picking and trading their accounts, when in almost all cases, they would be better off spending their time on developing a diversified portfolio with appropriate asset classes and funds with objectives that mirror their goals.

Yes, playing the market can be exciting, but your retirement plan shouldn't be focused on thrills. You want stability and reliability—and freedom from worry about risk and inflation. Smart asset allocation, diversification, and goal-driven fund selection will get you there, and they will provide you with plenty of wealth to spend on all of the exciting things you want to do in your retirement.

7

Understanding Mutual Funds, Exchange-Traded Funds (ETFs), and Index Funds

Mutual funds are the ideal instrument for investors who are planning, implementing, and managing their own investments in their retirement plans. They are easier to evaluate and select than individual stocks, and they are much easier to manage than a large portfolio of stocks and bonds. Furthermore, you have a team of mutual fund professionals managing your money wisely. In addition to traditional mutual funds, you may run across mutual fund–like investments such as exchange-traded funds (ETFs) and index funds, which have different criteria to consider. When it comes to investing and retirement, mutual funds offer many advantages *when properly chosen*. (I emphasized "when properly chosen." I don't want you to buy from the almost three-fourths of the fund choices that are dogs!) Good funds offer diversification, professional guidance, and protection against risk and volatility, just to name a few benefits.

In this chapter, we'll look at linking your overall retirement goals with a mutual fund portfolio strategy.

Mutual Fund Basics

A mutual fund is simply a professionally managed collection of investments that support the investment objectives of the fund as well as *your* objectives. It can contain a wide variety of investments (dozens of individual stocks and bonds, if not more—as well as other instruments) that are carefully selected and traded to increase the value of the fund. If you already own a portfolio of stocks and/or bonds, you essentially have your own mutual fund. However, unless you have a very large portfolio of individual stocks and bonds, chances are you are not sufficiently diversified, and a lack of diversification invites more risk into your retirement portfolio. Of course, a diversified portfolio means that you have more work to do to manage your money. In that case, you will find it easier to own mutual funds and let someone else handle the work for you.

That is why I left individual stocks and bonds years ago and started using mutual funds. I *do* use individual investment managers as well, but for my investment portfolio, those managers function like a mutual fund to a certain extent in that they make the everyday decisions. If I don't like what's going on with either a mutual fund or an individually managed account, I have the freedom to change direction by moving my money to other funds or individual managers. However, when you carefully plan your own portfolio and thoroughly research your mutual fund choices, you probably won't even have to consider moving your money around. Personally, I have used one carefully selected individual manager for over 20 years with excellent results.

Wading into the world of mutual fund investing unprepared can be just as risky as making any other investment—and risk is something we want to reduce when it comes to your retirement.

For one thing, there are too many choices—and that is intimidating to new investors. At the end of 2012, there were over 7,500 funds, managing more than $13 trillion. In fact, there are now more mutual funds than there are publicly traded stocks on the New York Stock Exchange and Nasdaq combined. Many are good, but many more aren't right for you and your retirement needs.

The data for Table 7.1 is from the *2013 Investment Company Fact Book* (http://www.icifactbook.org)—a great resource for information and data on the mutual fund market. There's no way you will be able to analyze each and every fund—and the wrong choice could add unnecessary risk to your portfolio. You need to narrow your search, but luckily, your goals that you established back in Part Two will help you do that.

Table 7.1   Total Net Assets Held by Mutual Funds

	Total Net Assets (in trillions of dollars)	Number of Funds	Number of Share Classes	Number of Shareholder Accounts (in thousands)
2012	$13,045	7,596	22,634	264,131

Source: Data from the *2013 Investment Company Fact Book* (http://www.icifactbook.org).

No investment arena gets to be this large without serving some sort of need. For mutual funds, the needs being served have arisen from the proliferation of 401(k) plans—both large and small. In the case of mutual funds, it is the need for the long-term growth that only equities can provide, combined with needs for cost-effective diversification, professional management, and exposure to a variety of industries and asset classes.

The vast number of available mutual funds means you have more choices of where to invest than ever before—but it also means you have more decisions to make. And when it comes to your retirement, you need to make the best decisions possible. So, where do you begin?

Planning and Designing Your Fund Portfolio

Before you start choosing funds, you should map out an overall strategy that supports the retirement goals you put together in Chapter 3. After all, this is the point where you are going to be putting your hard-earned money on the line.

Make sure you know that the funds and fund companies you select are in alignment with *your* plans. This includes dealing with some of the issues previewed in the previous chapter like asset allocation, diversification, and cost—as well as investing philosophies with regard to the basic mix of fund investments, growth investing versus value investing, fund categories, and international versus domestic investing.

The Right Number of Funds to Include in Your Portfolio

One of the best things about mutual funds is that you need only a relatively small number of them to achieve your investment goals. In the previous chapter, I introduced the Six Fund Portfolio model—and I believe that number is all you need to be sufficiently diversified. It has adequate exposure since six funds are enough to give you the asset allocation and diversification that you need.

This is the portfolio that I have run for myself for a long time—enough time to know that I can "trust" it even when the market is down significantly:

Moderate Allocation Funds (by Objective)
- Fund 1. Growth and Income Fund
- Fund 2. Balanced Fund

Aggressive Allocation Funds (by Objective)
• Fund 3. Balanced Fund

World Allocation Funds (by Objective)
• Fund 4. Multi-Asset Global Fund
• Fund 5. Multi-Asset Global Fund
• Fund 6. Asset Allocation Fund

In Table 7.2, you can see the average returns of my portfolio versus the commonly used market benchmark, the S&P 500, since 2001.

For the 13 years ending in December 2013, the S&P 500 returned an average of **4.86 percent** per year, and the Six Fund Portfolio returned **10.46 percent**. Starting with $500,000, and even after making yearly withdrawals of 4 to 5 percent (totaling $380,000) and adjusting for inflation, this portfolio grew to a total value of over $1.1 million. This is what diversification will do for you.

Table 7.2   Six Fund Portfolio Versus S&P 500
Returns by Year

Year	Six Fund Portfolio	S&P 500
2001	**14.02%**	−12.02%
2002	**1.99%**	−22.15%
2003	27.24%	**28.50%**
2004	**13.58%**	10.74%
2005	**11.50%**	4.77%
2006	15.24%	**15.64%**
2007	**12.45%**	5.39%
2008	**−21.64%**	−37.02%
2009	25.38%	**26.49%**
2010	12.60%	**14.91%**
2011	0.19%	**1.97%**
2012	12.24%	**15.82%**
2013	20.70%	**32.18%**
Avg.	**10.46%**	4.86%

Remember, the S&P 500 is composed of the 500 largest stocks traded publicly in the United States—and nothing more. The Six Fund Portfolio is a mixture of U.S. and global stocks, bonds, and other instruments. When one segment of the market or an economic region goes down in value, the other investments in the portfolio protect you from the drop. Nothing can totally protect you from a global crash like the one in 2008, but you can see that diversification helped to stop the bleeding. In 2012 and 2013, this portfolio didn't go up as quickly as the overall market. However, it is much safer—and over the long run, more successful.

The Six Fund Portfolio can be held in an IRA. There are no capital gains and dividends to pay taxes on each year until you withdraw from it. You can just let it grow.

I started my Six Fund Portfolio with a lump sum—mainly due to my age when I set it up. However, this type of portfolio also works very well if you are adding money regularly. My own portfolio has grown sufficiently to allow me to take out 4 to 5 percent each year. (I'll detail how much you should plan to withdraw annually in Part Four.)

Let's take a look at how the money within the Six Fund Portfolio is distributed across different investment categories. This really illustrates the beauty of mutual funds when it comes to diversification. With the simple creation of six different fund accounts, the funds invested are spread across a number of categories and a larger number of specific stocks and bonds within each category.

Within those six funds, diversification continues further. For example, let's look at Fund 1 (see Table 7.3), which makes up 20 percent of my total portfolio. Fund 1 includes U.S. and foreign stocks, U.S. and foreign bonds, cash, and other investments. The fund owns a range of stocks with capitalization sizes from giant to smaller-sized companies. What is "other"? It could be gold or foreign investments that don't fit the common category niches.

Figures 7.1 and 7.2 show the Table 7.3 data reproduced as pie charts. This makes it easier to understand for a lot of investors. A picture is still worth a thousand words!

To achieve a diversified portfolio, it is much easier to use quality funds that can serve several purposes, such as allocation funds that distribute money through a wide variety of global regions, market sectors, and individual company stocks and bonds. Because the funds in this portfolio are well diversified among Aggressive, Moderate, and World Allocation Funds, just six funds achieve a healthy balance of positive returns and protection from risk.

Table 7.3   Six Fund Portfolio: Fund Allocations by Asset Category and Company
Capitalization Size

Asset Allocation by Investment Type						
Percent of Portfolio	Fund Name	Domestic Equities	Foreign Equities	Bonds	Cash	Other
20%	Fund 1	64.56%	8.69%	11.27%	10.55%	4.93%
20%	Fund 2	42.19%	10.07%	14.30%	29.49%	3.95%
20%	Fund 3	56.20%	4.60%	24.41%	10.81%	3.97%
20%	Fund 4	33.39%	40.26%	0.18%	21.65%	4.52%
10%	Fund 5	31.60%	25.20%	13.99%	17.92%	11.28%
10%	Fund 6	33.07%	35.53%	5.32%	14.01%	12.07%
100%	Avg. allocation across entire portfolio	45.68%	18.79%	11.92%	17.99%	5.62%

Asset Allocation by Investment Market Capitalization						
Percent of Portfolio	Fund Name	Giant	Large	Mid	Small	Micro
20%	Fund 1	27.77%	43.25%	27.25%	1.54%	0.19%
20%	Fund 2	44.85%	36.80%	15.12%	3.23%	0.00%
20%	Fund 3	29.85%	54.13%	14.00%	0.76%	0.00%
20%	Fund 4	34.16%	45.07%	18.37%	1.65%	0.53%
10%	Fund 5	50.28%	34.86%	13.06%	1.79%	0.01%
10%	Fund 6	69.94%	18.78%	11.28%	0.00%	0.00%
100%	Avg. allocation across entire portfolio	40.06%	40.66%	17.38%	1.62%	0.15%

Here's an example of how diversification protects you from risk. When the market was down 37 percent in 2008, the Six Fund Portfolio was also down but only by 21.64 percent. When the market reversed itself and moved up the next year, the portfolio bounced back, gaining 25.38 percent in 2009. There was only slightly over 1 percent difference in the return of the S&P 500 and the Six Fund Portfolio account.

However, working with a small number of funds also means that you must look at the funds going into your portfolio carefully to be sure that they have a good long-term track record with good management. In the case of my Six Fund Portfolio, one manager has been with his fund for

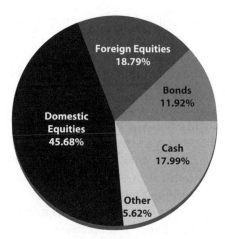

Figure 7.1 The Six Fund Portfolio: Asset Allocation by Investment Type

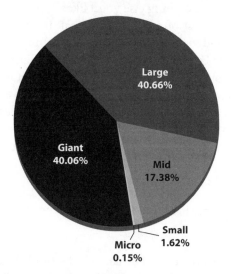

Figure 7.2 The Six Fund Portfolio: Asset Allocation by Company Capitalization Size

almost 25 years, and the shortest tenure is about 6 years. Even in the case of the newer ones, these managers came up through the ranks of the funds, and they are not totally new to the job. The funds are also from firms that run a number of other mutual funds and have a depth of qualified managers in case something untoward should happen.

Funds are defined by both what they own and how the assets are managed in the fund. You will find the investment objective in the prospectus of a fund. (A list of fund objectives can be found in Table 6.3 in Chapter 6.)

The objective tells you what the investment approach is, and what the managers would like to accomplish in the fund. The category that a fund is placed in depends on its individual investment style, which shows up in the stocks, bonds, and any other holdings in the portfolio.

Having too many funds can make your portfolio hard to manage. I would never own more than 10 funds. You could certainly add an additional fund to your main 6 funds, and you could consider a very specialized fund that meets your personal goals (for example, funds specializing in real estate, precious metals, or small-cap stocks). However, the advantages of diversification start to shrink pretty quickly, and the extra hassle, paperwork, and time requirements start to go up.

You'd probably like to know the exact funds in my Six Fund Portfolio. Because the portfolio may change and because your goals may be different from mine, I prefer you get them in real time. Just go to my website (http://www.940financialconsulting.com) and e-mail or call me, and we can talk about those funds and anything else you'd like.

Table 7.4 shows a list of mutual funds that, in most cases, can do the things you need a fund to do. These are among a number of funds that I track regularly, but I don't necessarily own them. The Years Since Inception column is important. Each of these funds has been around for at least 18 years—and the Vanguard Wellington fund has been around over 84 years as of this writing. As the chapter progresses, let's apply the ideas and theories discussed to this group of funds to show the many different areas you should be considering as you develop an investment philosophy and begin to select funds.

Asset Allocation Funds: Categories and Objectives

When I constructed my Six Fund Portfolio, I focused on the following *categories* of funds:

- **Conservative Allocation Funds.** These funds generally own 50 to 80 percent in fixed income (such as bonds) and cash—and 20 to 50 percent in stocks.
- **Moderate Allocation Funds.** These funds own 50 to 70 percent of these assets in stock—and the rest is held in fixed income and cash.
- **Aggressive Allocation Funds.** These funds typically own 70 to 90 percent of these assets in stock—and the rest is invested in fixed income and cash.
- **World Allocation Funds.** These funds hold at least 10 percent in bonds, less than 70 percent in stock, and usually 40 percent in non-U.S. stocks or bonds.

Table 7.4   Tracked Funds: Category and Years Since Inception

Name	Ticker Symbol	Objective	Category	Years Since Inception
Oakmark Equity and Income	OAKBX	Balanced	Aggressive Allocation	18+
FPA Crescent	FPACX	Balanced	Moderate Allocation	20+
T. Rowe Price Capital Appreciation	PRWCX	Growth and Income	Moderate Allocation	27+
Vanguard Wellington	VWELX	Growth and Income	Moderate Allocation	84+
Dodge & Cox Balanced	DODBX	Balanced	Moderate Allocation	82+
Mairs & Power Balanced	MAPOX	Balanced	Moderate Allocation	53+
First Eagle Global A	SGENX	Multi-Asset Global	World Allocation	43+
BlackRock Global Allocation A	MDLOX	Multi-Asset Global	World Allocation	19+
Ivy Asset Strategy A	WASAX	Asset Allocation	World Allocation	18+
Permanent Portfolio	PRPFX	Multi-Asset Global	Conservative Allocation	31+
Berwyn Income	BERIX	Income	Conservative Allocation	26+
James Balanced: Golden Rainbow	GLRBX	Balanced	Conservative Allocation	22+
Franklin Income A	FKINX	Balanced	Conservative Allocation	65+
Vanguard Wellesley Income	VWINX	Income	Conservative Allocation	43+

Within those categories, there are differing *objectives* that support different investing goals. Here are the ones I look at:

- **Objective: Asset Allocation.** Funds that use a combination of stocks, bonds, and cash. The management team's interpretation of the business cycle determines the investment strategy.
- **Objective: Balanced.** Funds that seek both income and capital appreciation. These funds usually hold at least 25 percent in fixed income.

- **Objective: Growth and Income.** Funds that seek current income and capital appreciation. Consequently, the managers look for dividend paying stocks with growth potential.
- **Objective: Multi-Asset Global.** Funds that invest in stocks, fixed income, and other asset classes and often have a large amount of securities issued by countries other than the United States.

In Chapter 6, I discussed the importance of asset allocation—splitting your money among multiple types of investments. To reiterate, the gist of asset allocation is this: you will increase your returns and lower your risk if you own a diversified portfolio. Stocks and bonds move up and down in response to different conditions—as do investments in different regions of the world—and what is bad for one can be good for the other. Consequently, over the long term, you can do better by owning a mix of funds than you can by owning only one fund.

Before you start matching specific investments to your retirement planning needs, you need to create your allocation plan. Luckily, the same basic allocation model works for both mutual funds and individual company stocks and bonds.

Remember, you are fighting two key factors here: unexpected expenses post-retirement and inflation. Both can deplete your principal investment, so your portfolio must have a healthy allocation of investments that will grow in value.

A portfolio of six mutual funds with a collective allocation of 60 to 70 percent in individual stocks, 30 to 40 percent in bonds, 5 to 10 percent in cash, and up to 5 percent in so-called other investments is a good place to start. With a stock-centric allocation, if your overall portfolio matches or beats the overall market, you'll be able to achieve an 8 percent (or better) annual return. That will beat inflation (in all but the worst-case scenarios), and it will allow your core investments to grow, even when you start dipping into them.

Remember, it's your job to keep your portfolio in the black—or in bad times, to stay ahead of the market's temporary decline. You are the manager of the funds in your portfolio. If they are growing at an average pace of 8 percent per year (over a 10-year period or longer), you are doing great. If the funds are outperforming their peers, you are ahead of the game. What you want is to have stability and income from this or any portfolio.

When it comes to retirement, safety is paramount. I first look at the Beta ratio of a stock or fund. The Beta number is easy to find in most mutual fund data you'll come across. It measures volatility—the primary measure of market risk. The risk of my Six Fund Portfolio was one-third less than the risk of the S&P 500 Index. (I present a complete set of complex analytical tools at http://www.940financialconsulting.com.) It's hard to beat lower risk *and* solid returns—and that's our goal.

If you want to have a diversified portfolio, it does not require a lot of work on your part, after the initial research and due diligence. Once you have chosen a particular fund, then the managers of the fund determine which is the best allocation for the money held in that particular fund.

For instance, a Moderate Allocation Fund is usually invested with 50 to 70 percent in equities (domestic or international or both), and the remaining amount is in fixed-income investments like bonds and/or cash. Depending on market trends, a fund may change its stripes temporarily by investing more in a particular area. However, most of the time, the fund will quickly revert to its original ratios in order to stay true to its mission.

Types of Funds

It's time to allocate your money into a portfolio and allocate your resources between different fund types. First, let's consider which fund types to use:

- Domestic and International Stock Funds
- Domestic and International Bond Funds
- Balanced and Asset Allocation Funds
- Growth versus Value Funds

As you design your retirement portfolio, you must consider how much weight you are giving to funds that primarily trade in stocks or bonds. In fact, deciding how you should allocate your money between all the choices you have is one of the most important decisions you can make. You have to look at the entire portfolio and its return, not just one particular part, because one part of the market may be up while another part may be down.

Domestic and International Stock Funds

The stock market can have big drops, and that risk pushes many people into portfolios that have too few stocks. It is true that stocks can be risky, but they are a major source of portfolio growth. Keep a significant portion of your portfolio in stock-concentrated mutual funds. Because stocks typically provide much higher annual returns than bonds, those returns can help you grow your portfolio and stay ahead of inflation, unexpected costs you may face during retirement, and the risk of living substantially longer

Table 7.5   Stocks Versus Bonds

What Is It?	Stocks: Equity (Ownership)	Bonds: Debt (Creditor)
Ownership	Yes. Owners share in future profits.	No. Bondholders only get principal repaid plus interest.
Bankruptcy	Owners get paid second.	Bondholders get paid first.
Value	Sold at market price.	Sold at par value (or at a premium or discount).
Maturity	No maturity.	Usually a set date (when principal gets repaid).

than you currently expect. If you put too little money in stock funds, you run a bigger risk of *running out of money*.

Table 7.5 is a simple chart giving you some idea of the differences between stocks and bonds. It does not list all of them, but it does provide enough information to ensure that you have a beginner's understanding of the differences.

In any portfolio allocation that includes U.S. and international stocks, you should have at least 15 to 20 percent of your money in International Funds. You might want to use a Global Fund along with U.S. and International Funds. Personally, I think that a Multi-Asset Global Fund works best. Why? If the international markets are not doing well, the fund can reinvest where the managers feel the best returns are possible. It is not bound to stay in one specific international arena. For example, a fund specializing in Asian stocks cannot pick up stakes and move into European markets if the Pacific Rim economy goes into the tank. A Multi-Asset Global Fund has that flexibility, and you have an experienced team of investment managers scouring the globe for the best investments.

Domestic and International Bond Funds

Bonds, when chosen carefully, are good sources of income, thanks to their periodic interest payments. Those payments can help fund a regular drawdown when you are planning your retirement income sources. Buying and managing a portfolio of bonds can be complex, however, so owning a bond fund simplifies things greatly. But you need to understand some bond basics before you proceed.

If you have the time and means to invest in individual bonds, they can be very useful to your retirement plan. One of the main reasons is that you can select bonds with maturity dates that match your pre-retirement plans *and* post-retirement cash flow needs. Maturity dates matter if you own bond funds as well, so let's walk through the maturity process. If you plan to own individual bonds, I strongly recommend that you *ladder* them—that is, that you buy a series of bonds with *staggered maturity dates*. For example, this could be a bundle of 10 bonds with maturity dates spread over each upcoming year for 10 years.

Duration becomes important for you to understand and take into consideration if you are buying a bond or a bond fund. Bond funds are constantly selling and replacing bonds, and this strategy is much more complex than simply buying a ladder of 10-year bonds and holding them until maturity. As an example, let's consider a Long-Term Bond Index Fund that has a duration of 14.03 years. What does that mean? The higher a bond's duration, the more sensitive it is to interest rate changes. If interest rates rise on a bond fund with a 10-year duration, the fund will lose 10 percent of its value if interest rates rise by 1 percent. But if interest rates fall by 1 percent, the fund will gain 10 percent in value. So a 1 percent rise in interest rates will mean that this particular bond fund will lose 14.03 percent of its value.

Interest rates have come down since 1981—not in a straight line, but they have come down. In 1981, a 10-year Treasury Bond was paying 15.8 percent interest. More recently, the rate was under 3 percent. With interest rates at historic lows, there's a high probability that they'll climb in the mid- to long term. Bond funds with a high duration factor face a high risk of drops in value if interest rates go back up, so use caution when looking at duration.

Quality matters. Because bond funds are continually buying and selling bonds, it is important to look for those funds with the lowest risk. It's always a good idea to look at bond ratings before you buy any bonds. Table 7.6 is a quick reference chart of risk grades.

The rating firms listed in the table (Moody's, S&P, and Fitch) are constantly tracking the quality of bonds, and the bond funds act swiftly if a rating changes. Therefore, when a bond fund has a listed objective of having only AAA bonds in its portfolio, the fund managers will stick very closely to that objective. Remember, when it comes to retirement, you are including bonds in your portfolio because you are minimizing risk and volatility. So stick with the highest grades on this chart.

Compared to stocks, annual returns from high-grade bonds are typically not that good—often just matching or being barely above the rate of inflation. But bond returns do not bounce up and down the way stocks

Table 7.6   Major Bond Rating Agencies, Grades, and Risks

Moody's	S&P	Fitch	Grade	Long-Term Ratings	Risk
Aaa	AAA	AAA	Investment	Minimal credit risk	High quality
Aa	AA	AA	Investment	Very low credit risk	High quality
A	A	A	Investment	Low credit risk	Upper medium grade
Baa	BBB	BBB	Investment	Can be speculative	Medium grade
Ba and B	BB, B	BB, B	Junk	Substantial credit risk	Speculative
Caa, Ca, C	CCC, CC, C	CCC, CC/C	Junk	High credit risk	Very speculative
C	D	D	Junk	Typically in default	Usually in default

do—and they do not sink into negative territory as stocks can unless interest rates go up. Bonds *can* lose value, but it is a much rarer occurrence. A portfolio of individual bonds laddered for 10 years can generally produce more income than a portfolio of stocks, and that income can be a critical part of your near-term retirement planning needs. While this has not been the case in the last few years, over time, a laddered bond portfolio does very well. Stocks that pay dividends also generate income, and that is why a combination of stocks and bonds is always a good choice.

Many people don't have a lot of money to invest in a fully diversified and laddered group of individual bonds—and many simply don't understand the rather arcane world of bonds. If you opt for a bond fund instead of individual bonds, be sure that you look at bond funds with reasonably short maturities for the next few years.

I recommend that you allocate 30 to 40 percent of your portfolio toward bonds or bond funds and cash (or in the case of the Six Fund Portfolio, that you use mutual funds containing the right proportions of stocks, bonds, and cash). The closer you are to retirement age, the closer you should be to the high end of that allocation. Bonds and bond funds protect your money; they don't grow it. As you get older, protection becomes more and more important. However, you do not necessarily need to own a bond fund to get the benefits you need. Balanced and Asset Allocation Funds hold stocks and bonds, and they may be an easier way to get the allocation mix you need.

Balanced and Asset Allocation Funds

Let's take a closer look at mutual funds that will help you match your retirement goals and plan to your allocation strategy. Balanced Funds and Asset Allocation Funds are great tools because they offer a broad portfolio of investments to you while working within very clear objectives and risk tolerances. All of these fund types carry a mix of stocks, bonds, and cash, which can be confusing to the untrained eye. However, the ratios of investments are tuned to meet different kinds of investors' objectives, so it's worth a closer look at the differences.

New investors often get Balanced Funds and Asset Allocation Funds mixed up, and rightfully so, because many information resources blur the distinctions between them. However, Table 7.7 should help you understand the differences.

Some Balanced Funds act like Asset Allocation Funds. What do I mean by that? A Balanced Fund is usually designed to have a certain and steady ratio of bonds and stocks, and it rarely alters the amount in each category by more than a few percentage points. Any small change the fund managers make is often because they are adding a new position in one of the categories with cash available before they sell off a currently owned stock or bond.

As an example, one Balanced Fund states it will contain 60 percent stocks and 40 percent bonds. That fund will hold its percentage allocation in each investment type as closely as possible to their stated allocation. Any deviations from that ratio are generally reset to their originally stated allocation when the market allows.

Table 7.7 **Balanced Funds Versus Asset Allocation Funds**

	Stocks	**Bonds**	**Cash**	**Other**
Balanced Funds	Usually have a *fixed* mixture of stocks and bonds. Bond holdings are rarely less than 25% of the portfolio.			
Conservative Allocation	20%–50%	50%–80%	Remainder	N/A
Moderate Allocation	50%–70%	30%–50%	Remainder	N/A
Aggressive Allocation	70%–90%	Remainder	Remainder	N/A

Asset Allocation Funds generally will tell you that their objectives are capital appreciation and income. To reach those loosely defined objectives, fund managers will go where they think they can get the best returns with the risk exposure parameters that investors are expecting. It is not unusual for an Asset Allocation Fund to move assets based on the fund managers' analysis of the current markets. Read the fine print on a fund's prospectus to see how much leeway funds have with their charter.

As you consider funds for your portfolio, take a good look at the Balanced and Asset Allocation Fund categories. They match with retirement goals nicely, and they offer simple, well-managed diversification.

Growth Versus Value Funds

When you are reading about mutual funds, you often encounter the terms *Growth Fund* and *Value Fund*. What's the difference?

Growth Funds (and the growth stocks they hold) are interested primarily in capital appreciation, and they are not given to paying dividends. If they do pay a dividend, it is a meager amount of money. These funds usually have above average growth, and their main focus is to have the companies they invest in grow. Growth Funds, at times, carry an above average risk, more so than Value Funds. Because of this volatility, a mutual fund that holds growth stocks should be a fund that you plan on holding for 10 years, roughly two market cycles, depending on when you choose to purchase the fund. Otherwise, you'll end up trying to time the market, which is counterproductive.

Value Funds buy their holdings at undervalued prices, and they hold them until those holdings rise in value. In the meantime, the funds pay reasonable dividends, which generates income for the investors. Many investors purchase only those individual stocks that pay a dividend (or mutual funds that specialize in dividend stocks). These stocks and funds are considered less volatile, and they combine income and some upside potential in price.

Index Funds and Exchange-Traded Funds

I've shared some recommendations for fund categories that are worth a closer look for your retirement portfolio. Now, I want to raise a caution on some fund types that you will encounter: *index funds* and *exchange-traded funds* (ETFs.) These are popular investments, and they are frequently offered to retirement-minded investors, but they may or may not be a good fit, depending on the retiree's ability to monitor them.

Index Funds

Some financial advice givers will tell you that actively managed mutual funds (or your own portfolio of stocks) are a bad idea. They will point to the fact that some funds fail to match the performance of the market, and so "if you can't beat 'em, join 'em" by buying an index fund (funds that mirror market benchmarks like the S&P 500 Index or the Dow Jones Industrial Average). Index funds do have a certain appeal to them. They generally have low fees (or at least lower than actively managed funds). Because they are designed to match particular indexes, they will never underperform their chosen "market" by very much—usually only if there is a management fee included.

Nevertheless, I don't like them. It is true that an index fund will not underperform its index by much, but it is equally true that it will *never* outperform it either. You are settling for guaranteed mediocrity, while many good mutual fund managers *do* manage to do so much better. What's more, not all indexes are created equal—some indexes give very large weightings to a relatively small number of stocks, and if those stocks underperform, the whole index (and index fund) can do poorly.

Exchange-Traded Funds (ETFs)

Exchange-traded funds (ETFs) are one of the most popular and successful Wall Street inventions of the past decade. An ETF is an investment that is constructed like a mutual fund, but it is actually based on an index of holdings like stocks and fixed-income investments. Typically, the ETF is run on autopilot and not actively managed by experts. ETFs of every stripe are available for purchase today, and the number is growing. They do not trade the way mutual funds do, but they often have a portfolio similar to that of a mutual fund. ETFs (the right ones) can be a cheap, tax-efficient way to invest in the markets. If chosen and used properly—and that's the key—they can be good investments.

Unlike mutual funds, which are purchased from the fund company directly (or a broker) and are priced once at the end of the day, ETFs are traded on the major exchanges, just the way stocks are traded. An ETF is traded at the *net asset value* (NAV) of its underlying stocks. ETFs may trade at a premium or a discount. In most cases, the variance is 1 percent or less, but there can be a big difference in a volatile market.

Fewer than 200 of the more than 1,500 ETFs are what I would call safe. Over half of the ETFs are underfunded and illiquid. ETFs are relatively new, and most don't have the track record that a high-quality mutual fund has. Be sure you understand a particular ETF's strategy and trading history during volatile times before you put your money in it.

Of the 150 or so that I think qualify for your money or mine, many are good investments if you monitor the results. If you are very careful, you can set up an ETF portfolio that works. But keep in mind that there is no seasoned and successful manager making active decisions and watching your ETF investment for you.

Despite claims that they have smaller expense ratios, many ETFs are often just as expensive as mutual funds. I don't mind paying a small percentage of my mutual funds' value annually to compensate a skilled management team, but I have a harder time paying almost as much to a company that simply programs a computer to match the weightings of someone else's index.

ETFs have a number of advantages that I like. My favorite is their continuous pricing, which allows you to get in and out over the course of a day—not just at the close of the market the way mutual funds do. The holdings of an ETF are priced every 15 seconds throughout the day. That allows you to know the price at which you are buying or selling the ETF.

Another advantage is the diversification of ETFs. They track a myriad of indexes and benchmarks, which allows a lot of flexibility when you buy an ETF. For example, if you are trying to decide which ETF to invest in for large-cap stocks, you can consider ETFs that follow the Dow Jones 30 Index, the Russell 1000 Index, or the S&P 500 Index. Because there is more than one benchmark to consider, an ETF can really be a good solution—if you do your homework.

ETFs have a number of disadvantages and unique risks. While they are supposed to replicate a particular index, there may be reasons the ETF cannot do that. Often, it is because the index is not large enough or it has been "invented" by one of the companies selling ETFs. That might not make much difference, but when the market is in turmoil, you may find a variance (often negative) in the returns. That's not the only problem with ETFs. These securities trade like stocks, and brokers will charge you commissions every time you want to buy or sell. Some brokerage firms are now rolling out lists of no-commission ETFs that you can buy through them, but these lists are small, and they tie you to that broker. In comparison, there are many high-quality mutual funds that charge no-loads, and you can buy and sell shares at no expense to you.

ETFs are also just as prone to bubbles and panics as any other type of investment. When money rushes into an ETF, it can push the shares to unsustainable levels. If a mutual fund sees more cash flowing into it than it can prudently invest, the administrator can close the fund to new investors. Alternatively, it can liquidate holdings as prices get too high and move money into areas of the market that are less expensive, which will shield fund holders from risk. Those really are not options for the passively managed ETFs.

Because ETFs trade like stocks, they can have considerable volatility over the course of a day. During the so-called Flash Crash of May 6, 2010, several stocks saw huge waves of selling and irrational plunges in price—plunges that dragged the ETFs along with them. Mutual funds basically just floated on past the chaos without any major problems.

If that were not enough, some ETFs are not even ETFs at all. They are actually exchange-traded *notes* that essentially mirror or mimic the performance of a real ETF. Furthermore, there is a credit risk element at work with all ETFs: if the sponsoring firm gets into trouble, any losses incurred are passed on to the ETF and the fund could plunge in value. Seeing how the last market crisis toppled Lehman Brothers and AIG, that is a risk that investors should not ignore.

Vanguard did some research on accounts that held ETFs for a five-year period, and it found that ETF holders were *more than twice as likely* to trade and not be buy-and-hold investors as they were with mutual funds. I believe that most ETFs are traded too often, and consequently active traders often end up with *poorer* results trying to play the market. Most retirement portfolio investors should follow the buy-and-hold model, and they should not engage in a lot of active trading, especially those investors with neither the time nor experience to trade regularly.

A *well-managed* collection of ETFs as part of your total overall portfolio is fine. Our firm manages 401(k) portfolios in ETFs for clients, and the ETF shares are bought at very low (or no) cost, which allows us to charge a small fee to manage these accounts. It always boils down to expert management. A quality mutual fund provides this as part of the purchase price. For an ETF, solid, ongoing management costs extra.

Other Investments

There is no rule that says you can invest only in mutual funds that own stocks and bonds. You may decide to take a smaller piece of your total allocation (say, 5 percent) and devote it to a mutual fund specializing in real estate or precious metals. These investments are not strictly necessary, but there are some high-quality individual investments that can add even more diversification (and protection) to your portfolio.

The Asset Allocation Mix

Before we get into the selection process for individual funds, let's recap and finalize your portfolio's overall allocation.

I believe that an allocation of 65 to 75 percent in stock-centric funds is a good place to start. As you get older and revisit your investments, you may decide to reduce this percentage, but equities should always be a part of your portfolio. Personally, I think anything more than 25 to 35 percent in fixed-income holdings (bonds, cash, and so on) creates the risk of running out of money in retirement. A portfolio balanced between 70 percent stocks and 30 percent bonds and cash could be expected to give you a solid retirement portfolio.

Let's take another look at the Six Fund Portfolio. In Chapter 6, Figure 6.2 shows the overall allocation of retirement savings across the six funds. Then in this chapter, Figure 7.1 shows the current allocation of the amounts of stocks, bonds, cash, and "other" held by the six mutual funds in the portfolio.

Because I wanted an overall balance of roughly 70 percent stock and 30 percent bonds and cash, I selected an array of allocation funds. I chose not to invest in specific stock or bond funds, choosing instead to let the expert fund managers handle the balance. Ultimately, the holdings of these six funds do achieve my desired 70/30 mix.

There is an *old* rule of thumb that your allocation to bonds should match your age. For example, if you are 50 years old, that formula suggests that 50 percent of your savings and investments should be in bonds. However, we are living much longer than when this rule was first stated. Although I can understand the intent to create a safe haven for an elderly person, adhering to that rule is flirting with danger. You can run out of money in many ways (too much risk or not enough risk), and being too conservatively invested is certainly one way that it often occurs. Prices keep going up, and the need for growth to offset inflation is extremely important. Following that old rule-of-thumb advice would leave you underexposed to stocks, and it would reduce the growth of your portfolio, leaving you short if you live longer than you expect.

Remember, you are fighting two key factors here: unexpected expenses post-retirement and inflation. Both can deplete your principal investment, so your portfolio must have a healthy mix of investments that will grow in value.

Today, there is a lot of talk about a "reverse glide path into retirement." Under this model, you would have more invested heavily in bonds than in stocks at 65 as you begin your retirement, and you would then slowly add stocks to the mix. Categorically, I am opposed to this idea. If you did this, you'd need a sizable nest egg invested overall to fund new stock purchases without compromising your money's safety.

Honestly, I think it depends on your goals, your desired budget, your initial capital, and how you set your portfolio up and how you manage it. Personally, I have been withdrawing my planned 4 to 5 percent yearly from my Six Fund Portfolio, and it has left me with enough money to reinvest and grow. It has worked extremely well for me.

Before You Buy: The Cost of Mutual Funds (Load Versus No-Load and Other Fees)

All investments have a price—and mutual funds are no different. You'll see mutual funds with and without loads. Some loads are *front-end* (charged to you when you buy the fund), and some are *back-end* (charged to you when you sell the fund). These loads can vary greatly—as can the expense ratios and the transaction fees of the funds. *Expenses* are the operating costs that the fund companies regularly deduct from the value of the portfolio. If you understand the costs, you can avoid many of the fees involved.

Ultimately, results matter most—not fees.

Here's the Lowdown on Loads

A *load* is basically a commission that the fund company charges for allowing you to invest in the fund. Most of the time, these commissions are given to the broker, financial planner, or investment adviser who is helping you. Due in large part to competition, front-end loads are not as common (nor as high) as they used to be. And yes, there are back-end-load funds, although most of back-end fees diminish over time if you own the fund for a certain number of years.

There is a wide variety of no-load funds—funds that do not charge a fee for purchasing or selling the fund. But, again, don't be lulled into thinking they are the best deal because some no-load funds have *very high* expense ratios. Just stopping a minute to appraise expense ratios, the highest I see is 8.33 percent, and the lowest is 0.010 percent.

Many fund companies offer a variety of funds with a broad range of load structures (which you will see shortly). You just have to be careful that you don't get carried away about any particular aspect of a fund's fee structure. Remember, you and I are paying for results!

As an example, First Eagle Global A (ticker symbol: SGENX) is a front-end-load fund. However, for a Multi-Asset Global Fund in the World Allocation category, this fund's return after fees *and* the load over 10 years was better than all of the funds in that category, regardless of whether it was a load or no-load fund.

We use Schwab Institutional for our clients, which allows us to avoid the loads on many loaded funds. As you check out all the low-cost broker-age firms, such as Ameritrade, Fidelity, and E*Trade, you may find there are others that will also waive the loads.

When you invest for the long term (10 years or longer), loads are less significant. As your fund gains value, you essentially pay off the load charge, and you begin to earn in earnest. You should expect to hold onto your shares at least through two market cycles (both boom times and recession-ary times)—and generally, you will hold them much longer.

When you evaluate funds, do not get caught up in short-term suc-cess. Funds posting a large return over a one-year (or less) period attract attention, and new investors jump on board in droves. That rapid influx of money often puts the fund managers in a quandary. They cannot invest in the way they used to, and the results go down significantly. Although it may be counterintuitive to what you may expect, a fund with a load or high fees may actually help you in this situation. High fees scare away specula-tors and traders who like to quickly move money in and out of funds—something that can be very disruptive to a manager's strategies.

Performance Is the Priority

Maybe it seems strange when I say that mutual fund expenses are not as important as a lot of people think. Contrary to what you might read else-where, I think there is *too much* attention paid to the question of mutual fund expenses. What you and I should focus on are the *results*—net of expenses.

Here's a hypothetical question for you. Would you rather (a) pay a 1.00 percent fee for a 12.04 percent return per year, for 10 years, net of fees, or (b) pay a 0.71 percent fee for a 9.50 percent return per year, for 10 years, net of fees? Since both are net of fees, I know you and I both would choose the fund with a 12.04 percent return. The difference would be an addi-tional $6,387 on an initial investment of $10,000. If you have researched the fund's performance over a number of years, then you would feel more comfortable paying more—*and getting more.* The song in the Broadway show *Seesaw* says it better than I can express it: "It's not where you start; it's where you finish. It's not how you go; it's how you land."

When you find a mutual fund with a 5.75 percent load (Table 7.8), those load fees will knock down the starting point of your investment from $10,000 by 5.75 percent. So your initial investment is really just $9,425. You

Table 7.8   Front-End-Load Funds Versus No-Load Funds

No-Load Fund			
Year	Investment on Jan. 1	Growth Rate	Investment on Dec. 31
1	$10,000.00	10%	$11,000.00
2	$11,000.00	10%	$12,100.00
3	$12,100.00	10%	$13,310.00
4	$13,310.00	10%	$14,641.00
5	$14,641.00	10%	$16,105.10
6	$16,105.10	10%	$17,715.61
7	$17,715.61	10%	$19,487.17
8	$19,487.17	10%	$21,435.89
9	$21,435.89	10%	$23,579.48
10	$23,579.48	10%	$25,937.42

Front-End-Load Fund with a Load of 5.75 Percent				
Year	Investment on Jan. 1	Investment Minus Load	Growth Rate	Investment on Dec. 31
1	$10,000.00	$9,425.00	10%	$10,367.50
2	$10,367.50	—	10%	$11,404.25
3	$11,404.25	—	10%	$12,544.68
4	$12,544.68	—	10%	$13,799.14
5	$13,799.14	—	10%	$15,179.06
6	$15,179.06	—	10%	$16,696.96
7	$16,696.96	—	10%	$18,366.66
8	$18,366.66	—	10%	$20,203.32
9	$20,203.32	—	10%	$22,223.66
10	$22,223.66	—	10%	$24,446.02

may be able to find a similar fund without a load. If the two funds have the same annual return, the no-load fund is the clear winner. If the fund with the load fees performs signficantly better than the "cheaper" fund, you may find it's worth it to pay the fees, but only rarely does that happen!

Note that in some instances, the fees are not charged when you have your account meet certain critieria—for example, you have an automatic monthly deposit or a minimum initial investment. So, if you are truly focused on getting the best deal, you might be able to beat the fees on most funds.

The problem is that investors often overfocus on relatively small differences in expenses between funds, and they lose sight of the bigger picture. Two-tenths of 1 percent of additional expense really does not amount to much, especially if the slightly more expensive fund delivers *significantly* better performance.

Not All Expenses Are Easy to See

Don't just worry about the load fees. Make sure you are considering all of the obvious and "hidden" fees. (All fees must be disclosed to investors. Some fees are just not as clearly disclosed as others.) These costs are typically not "billed" to the investor, but instead, they are deducted from the total value of the investment nonetheless.

People are often surprised at just how Wall Street accounting can work sometimes. Not all expenses get grouped under the label of "expense ratio," but that does not mean that they aren't real. If a fund manager trades often, that trading cost does not go into the expense ratio, but it does come out of your performance. The *expense ratio* consists of operating expenses, management fees, 12b-1 fees, administrative fees, and all other asset-based costs, but *not* brokerage costs. You don't really know whether a fund company is getting the best deal it can on services like commissions. It is still quite normal on Wall Street for investment managers to pay for research from brokerage firms in the form of higher commissions.

Along similar lines, the capital gains incurred by a fund can significantly impact your actual performance in a personal account. A successful fund that makes frequent trades will have more capital gains or losses in any given year, and capital gains taxes will be passed on to you, the investor. That is not really a problem if your funds are being held in a tax-advantaged account such as a retirement plan or an IRA, but it does make a difference in other types of accounts.

Again, the overall performance of the fund—especially over a long period of time—is the critical factor here. Remember, you have to spend money to make money—and if the fund is making money, so are you. When you realize that results are more important than fees, then you are on your way. Some fund companies brag about their low fees, but if the results are not good, it does you little good.

Just as an aside, the Six Fund Portfolio has an expense ratio of 0.994 percent, or just under 1 percent—a good price for very good results.

It's Possible to Beat the Fees

Not only do you have to make a decision on what funds to buy but you also need to choose the right brokerage firm (or firms) and the types of accounts you have with those firms. Often, it is cheaper to buy straight from the fund company, and by doing so, you may avoid most brokerage fees, depending on the firm you are using. When it comes to front-end loads, shop carefully. Some companies will waive the load if you buy from them directly (or through a brokerage firm that they have partnered with) or if you buy a certain dollar amount or if you agree to a monthly purchase plan.

If you are offered a "deal" from a brokerage firm to buy a mutual fund, before you buy, be sure to check all the options. You may not want to work through a brokerage firm that charges its own fees on top of all the fund charges we've just discussed.

Brokers may try to make you think that you are doing the very best you can by using their company. However, that may not be true. I do not think that financial planning or investment management firms that work with only one fund company can necessarily give you the best result in the end. No one mutual fund company, regardless of its strategy, has the best set of funds for you, so look for advisers and brokerage firms that offer a broad array of fund (and fund company) choices.

Do Your Homework

If you go to the Securities and Exchange Commission website (http://www.sec.gov) and look up "Mutual Funds Fees and Expenses" and "Mutual Fund Investing," you will get a good idea of what is really going on with mutual funds and the costs involved. As with all government papers, it would be great if this material, which contains a lot of good information, were more entertaining to read and not "just the facts" reporting. Don't let the sheer amount of the information inundate you. Keep your eye on the ball.

I believe in careful planning when it comes to retirement, and unfortunately, there are many traps awaiting those investors who aren't careful. I am highly critical of what many financial services firms charge for advice and the products they push, such as high-load mutual funds and annuities, especially when sometimes these firms are paid more money to push an inferior product. I guess you can convince a client of *anything* if you're getting paid well to do so, eh?

Matching Fund Types with Your Retirement Goals

As you link your allocation plan to your personal retirement goals, here are some potential fund types to consider.

Optimal Fund Types for People with 10 Years or Less Until Retirement

Type A. For the Risk Averse

- Conservative Allocation Funds.
- For a foreign or international fund, I would use a Foreign Large Blend or a Foreign Large Value Fund.
- For an intermediate bond fund, my choice would be a High-Quality Bond Fund.

Type B. For Someone Who Can Take a Temporary Loss in Stride

- Moderate Allocation Funds.

Optimal Fund Types for People with 15 to 20 Years or More Until Retirement

Type A and Type B

- With a longer time until you retire, you have more flexibility, so these fund types work for those who are risk averse *and* for those who can take a temporary loss in stride.
- Moderate Allocation Funds can be used at any time and for those with longer than 10 years to retirement.

Conclusion

For me—and for millions of investors—mutual funds are one of the best ways to fuel a retirement plan. With just 6 to 10 well-diversified mutual funds run by market experts, you spend less time and effort than buying and managing individual stocks and bonds—and you typically get much better results. On the whole, mutual funds are less expensive (especially if you consider the time to do a good job researching each investment you buy) than other investments like stocks, and they are easy to track, review, and manage.

ETFs *can* be just as good, if you are willing to put in the extra time it takes to manage them, but like exercising, it's easy to make excuses and let things slide. Finding a good management team to run your ETF portfolio for you can be an effective way to pursue the ETF investment route.

Because you *have* to beat inflation and find a way to grow your nest egg, mutual funds are the optimal route. With a strategy in hand, the next chapter will discuss how to begin investing in the mutual funds that support your goals—and how to manage and evaluate the funds in your portfolio.

8

Selecting and Managing Your Mutual Funds

Now that you've mapped out the fund types that match your goals and your desired allocation of those funds, it's time to pick the individual funds that will go into your portfolio.

What to Look For in a Mutual Fund

Having made the case for mutual funds, it is important to state that not all funds are alike. In fact, they're not even close. Picking the right group of funds is critical if you are to meet your investment goals. Your asset allocation plan is the important first step, but selecting specific funds to support your goals is an even bigger challenge. Here are some of the important things to consider and analyze when evaluating funds for your portfolio.

Arming Yourself with Information

Before you wade into the thousands of funds out there, you need reliable sources of data and other information about funds. What if you've never bought a mutual fund before? Where do you start? Information is key, so your first step is . . . go to the library!

As you would expect, you can find a wide variety of books and guides on mutual funds. Everything from *Mutual Funds for Dummies* to the most involved and complex books on investment strategies are in your library. What I like about the "Dummies" books is that they are a good *starting point* to get your feet wet in understanding mutual funds. You should not take that book or any other book as gospel, but rather you should use them to start your learning process. Your reference librarian can provide recommendations.

Libraries have access to my favorite mutual fund data sources like Morningstar and Value Line. Ask the reference librarian to help you get started online with Morningstar (http://www.morningstar.com), and take an hour or so to dig deeper into their ratings, performance data, and analysis. Although I don't necessarily believe that Morningstar's star rating system is the best way to pick a fund, it is a quick way to sift through the good ones and avoid the duds altogether.

In addition to Morningstar, I use Steele's Mutual Fund Expert (http://www.steelesystems.com), and it is often easier to use for new investors. Steele's MutualFundPro edition is a good place to start. You can try it out free for 30 days, and you will probably find that a quarterly subscription gives you enough insight and analysis to make good informed decisions.

Both Morningstar and Steele have reports that contain a lot of good information in an easy-to-read format. Value Line (http://www.valueline.com) is most often associated with individual stocks, but the company does have a mutual fund site.

These services for investors online offer a lot of free information—and even more for subscribers. Most offer a trial subscription, demos, and other useful support for the beginner investor. Take advantage of the free trials so you can decide which of the services are most helpful to you.

A free alternative that many use is Yahoo! Finance (http://finance.yahoo.com/funds/), which provides current and historical data and even offers Morningstar's ratings as part of its data.

Fund Goals and Management

When you start looking at funds, the best place to start is with a fund's philosophy and the person (or persons) managing that fund. You can find that information on the fund's own website as well as on the other online resources I've listed.

I happen to think that it makes quite a bit of difference who manages your money. After all, you have set out your personal goals for your money. The people managing the fund should mirror them.

When I look for mutual funds, I look for championship *teams* and not individual stars. Individuals might just be hot managers riding a good streak. Likewise, a successful mutual fund manager is eventually going to start fielding calls from hedge funds desiring that manager's services, and then the fund will no longer have that superstar manager. Additionally, individual managers may have a little too much discretion with their investment decisions. Without someone to challenge their ideas, they may inadvertently stray from their own systems and methodologies, and they may diverge from the sort of strategy they advertise in the prospectus—or worse, they may start underperforming as a result.

Investment teams help mitigate a lot of these risks. Although it is possible for an entire team to be poached away by a rival, it is less likely. Even if one or two members leave, there will be a fair bit of continuity in terms of investment philosophy and decision making. Teams also seem to create a degree of consistency and discipline in the investing process.

In addition to a team approach, I also look for long track records. After all, one of the best indicators of what people will do in the future is what they have already done. Underperforming managers are not likely to learn how to invest better overnight (and you certainly don't want them "practicing" with your money!), and likewise, great managers are not going to forget how to do their job.

Make sure that the management team that has delivered a strong past performance is still intact. Large companies, such as T. Rowe Price, have enough skilled fund managers in their organization to shift managers around, if need be. In small firms, if the lead manager leaves, he or she may be replaced by someone who has never led a fund of that type before. Past performance is no longer a reliable indictator when an all-new team takes over.

Many Happy Returns

The returns that a mutual fund will earn are extremely important. In fact, that's the whole reason we are doing this—so that you earn the best returns possible on your money. At the bottom line, you should want to own only the best funds that your money can buy. Limit your search to funds that are in the top 10 percent of all funds for long-term performance.

How long is "long term"? A 10-year track record is a good starting point because that is usually long enough to include two complete market cycles. A *cycle* includes a market peak, a period of decline, a bottom, and finally, a recovery and growth period. I would rather look at 15 to 20 years. Going further back, unless you are very familiar with the markets at that point, is interesting, but it will not help you make a better decision.

There are many young funds with great short-term performance records, but when it comes to your retirement, I strongly advise focusing on funds with a long, positive track record. New funds often include incentives to invest in them such as lower trading fees, so the true return is often lower after the initial launch period. (Newer funds are certainly fine—and fun—for your nonretirement savings.)

In addition to the long-term returns, look at the year-by-year results. It is not necessarily vital that a fund be the top performer in its category every year (in fact, this is almost impossible), but you want to get a sense of the year-to-year volatility that you should expect. Many information services will also provide you with information on the best and worst one-year returns, as well as the best (and worst) three-year periods. This last one is actually a very valuable piece of information because it gives you a good sense of what you can expect the worst-case scenario to look like.

I recommend that you evaluate funds on "apples to apples" performance. If a particular fund charges you more in expenses than other funds charge but it routinely outperforms its peers by more than the difference in costs, you still come out ahead. Now it will probably never be possible to compare funds on a truly equal footing (after all, capital gains taxes will not matter if the shares are held in a tax-shielded account), but there are many information sources out there that will at least show returns net of stated expenses.

Let's take a look at an example of why you should look at long-term results—and at the management approach of a fund. Comparing the Fidelity Magellan Fund (ticker symbol: FMAGX) to the Dodge & Cox Stock Fund (ticker symbol: DODGX) provides a good example of why I prefer to invest with teams (Table 8.1). Even though Fidelity Magellan is a Large Growth Fund and Dodge & Cox Stock is a Large Value Fund, both have been around for 50 years.

Under the leadership of fund manager Peter Lynch, Magellan was one of the best performing funds in the world. From 1977 to 1990, Lynch averaged a 29 percent return for fund holders. Some assume if it happened once, it can happen again. Subsequent managers have not done as well as Lynch, and the fund's performance has also been more uneven.

Table 8.1   Dodge & Cox Stock Versus Fidelity Magellan

Name	Symbol	3-Year Avg.	5-Year Avg.	10-Year Avg.	15-Year Avg.	20-Year Avg., Ending Dec. 2013
Dodge & Cox Stock Fund	DODGX	18.04%	19.63%	7.95%	9.48%	11.64%
Fidelity Magellan Fund	FMAGX	12.19%	17.50%	5.15%	3.03%	7.14%

I believe that it is important to see how well a fund has done over no more than 20 years because most investors, for one reason or another, do not hold a mutual fund for more than 20 years. The team-run Dodge & Cox Stock Fund has been a more consistent performer over the last 20 years (though some of those years have been bumpy), and the consistency of the investment approach has worked well. Table 8.1 shows the returns of the two funds over the last 20 years ending December 2013.

As you can see, Magellan looks good enough in the short term, especially if you are hunting for funds that achieve that 8 percent per year minimum goal to beat inflation and if you want to be able to withdraw 4 percent annually. But obviously, the Dodge & Cox Stock Fund wins the battle across the board. That's why doing a head-to-head comparison over 20 years is a good idea. Find a good fund, and then try to beat it with another fund with similar objectives, before you buy!

Risk and Volatility

I always look at the fund's risk and volatility factors. All of the research sources I mentioned earlier have these statistics listed prominently. Visit Morningstar .com, and enter a symbol of a fund you are considering purchasing. Let's put in the FPA Crescent Fund (ticker symbol: FPACX). Look just below the name, and you will see a line that starts with "Quote." Look a few spaces to the right, and you will see "Ratings & Risk." Click on that, and you will see "Risk and Ratings Statistics, MPT" (modern portfolio theory statistics), and below that you will see "Volatility Measures." You can review several funds to understand how much risk you are taking for the returns you are getting. (If you need help understanding the complex ratios you encounter, you can visit http://www.940financialconsulting.com for a detailed rundown.)

Exposures

It is also worth taking a little time to investigate the kinds of stocks and bonds that a mutual fund holds. You'll quickly see what market exposures are impacting the fund: industry sectors, locations, and capitalization, just to name a few of the big factors. There is no need to go down a list company by company, but every fund will give you a breakdown by industry category.

The reason this matters is that when you own multiple funds, you do not want too much overlap between them. Significant overlap of investment holdings reduces some of the benefits of diversification. For example, rather than owning two funds that both focus on Treasuries, it would probably be better to own one bond fund that focuses on Treasury securities and a second bond fund that focuses on corporate or foreign debt. In the Six Fund Portfolio, there are three different World Allocation Funds, but there is almost no overlap in the stocks those funds hold.

When you are reviewing funds at Morningstar, look for the tab marked Portfolio. There's a wealth of information related to exposure featured there: Asset Allocation, Style Details, Market Capitalization, Sector Weightings, and much more. While you're at it, check out how many stocks (or bonds) the fund holds in general. There isn't really a magic number here, but you want to be careful with a fund that invests in a small number of issues (say, less than 75). Some managers like to run concentrated portfolios and put their eggs in relatively fewer baskets, the idea being that they want to hold only their absolute best ideas. That's fine when they are right, but it can be dangerous when the market turns against them. For retirement investing, then, I would suggest you stick to well-diversified funds that own sizable portfolios.

Expenses

It is important to look at all types of fees, but don't be consumed with buying a fund just because its fee is smaller than another. I buy funds that are pure no-loads, or I buy funds through an account that allows the sales charges to be forgiven.

Pay close attention to the differences in mutual fund share types offered. Many funds are no-load. But some brokerage firms sell loaded shares of the same no-load funds, and the loads differ across the board. A significant number of the **27,000 listed mutual funds** are duplicates of other funds with slightly different packaging. Look at the fund in Table 8.2—yes, *fund*, not funds! It is the same core portfolio, packaged 10 different ways. First, look at the expense ratios—a range between 0.36 and 1.51 percent depending solely on which package you picked. Now, look at the performance. As the fees increase, the performance dips. With the varying fees being charged for the same fund, it is paramount that you understand what you are paying for. You want the best return with the most reasonable fee that you can get.

Buying the Fund You Want

When it comes time to actually buy the funds, you should buy directly from the fund company or from a reputable low-cost online brokerage firm like Schwab, Ameritrade, E*Trade, Vanguard, or Fidelity. You want

Table 8.2 Fund Fees

Fund Name	Expense Ratio	12b-1 Fees	Front-Load Maximum	Deferred Charge Maximum	3-Year Avg. Return	5-Year Avg. Return
Fund 1	0.36%	0.00%	0.00%	0.00%	10.92%	12.59%
Fund 2	0.50%	0.00%	0.00%	0.00%	10.78%	12.46%
Fund 3	0.63%	0.24%	5.75%	0.00%	10.63%	12.29%
Fund 4	0.66%	0.25%	0.00%	0.00%	10.60%	12.26%
Fund 5	0.66%	0.25%	0.00%	0.00%	10.59%	12.25%
Fund 6	0.72%	0.22%	5.75%	0.00%	10.54%	12.21%
Fund 7	0.96%	0.50%	0.00%	0.00%	10.26%	11.90%
Fund 8	0.98%	0.50%	0.00%	0.00%	10.25%	11.88%
Fund 9	1.38%	1.00%	0.00%	5.00%	9.80%	11.41%
Fund 10	1.51%	1.00%	0.00%	5.00%	9.67%	11.29%

to use a firm that offers many services and not just a firm that gives you good deals and discounts when purchasing investments. Over time, you will need those additional services (such as helpful advisers or diversified investment instruments).

There is no reason to pay any sort of commission or inflated load just for the dubious "convenience" of buying through a broker or a bank, especially when you are buying something that you've already carefully researched and weighed. It's cheaper and easier to buy direct—or through a discount brokerage firm. Don't waste your money!

Most companies will also allow you to set up a regular deduction from your checking account into your fund account. It's a great way to fund your retirement without having to think about it—and to take advantage of Dollar Cost Averaging. Signing up for these automatic withdrawals often entitles you to have many load fees (if there are any) waived.

You should be aware that many of these brokers I've mentioned may not carry the same shares of a particular fund. In other words, you may be able to buy a certain share type from one firm that is not sold at the other. Just be aware and careful.

If you have retirement accounts elsewhere already, it is usually no problem to transfer the funds you buy from a company to your regular retirement account. You can also easily roll over existing retirement savings into your new funds. That's something to consider if you didn't research your older choices carefully—or if a past employer's plan forced you into that company's limited options.

Although buying directly is very easy, if your current brokerage firm or financial adviser already offers the funds you want with no difference in costs or commissions to you, why not use him or her and save yourself some paperwork? There's no benefit to paying extra though.

Prospectuses

How many times have I heard a client or friend say, "I didn't know they were going to invest in that!" Many people decide to buy a particular fund purely on how well it has done.

There's a wealth of information that you can get from outside resources, but ultimately, you should plan to do a little more homework before you make your purchase. Investigate the factors we've been discussing—risk and volatility, exposures, fees, and so on—to select your finalists, and then read the funds' prospectuses. Both types of resources are available online at the fund company's website. Companies are required to send investors a prospectus after they purchase the fund, but you will want to read it before that.

The *statutory prospectus* is long, and for many it is a put-off, but read it anyway. Start with the shorter, reader-friendly *summary prospectus*. Both of these are important because they give the fund's investment objectives, how it intends to accomplish those goals, past performance, and the fees and expenses charged by the fund. The statutory prospectus gives information about the managers of the fund, the advisory firm the fund is a part of, and how to buy and sell (redeem) shares in the fund. The material in the prospectus is required of every fund by the Securities and Exchange Commission (SEC). If you are comparing two funds, the "apples-to-apples" data from the prospectuses is most helpful in your decision making.

The *statement of additional information* is often mailed along with the *annual report*, but if you want one earlier, all you need to do is request it. It usually contains rules about what investments can and cannot be made. The actual holdings are found in the annual report. Funds buy and sell investments every day, so by the time you get the annual report, holdings will have changed. But you'll get the general idea of what they are doing with your money.

Other Details That Matter

When evaluating funds, there are a lot of other details to monitor. Pay attention to the *minimum investment amount*—it does you no good to find the perfect fund, only to learn later that the minimum investment is $1 million. Likewise, it is worth making a note of the *minimum follow-up amounts*—the minimum amounts you can invest after your initial purchase.

Advanced Analytics

As you research mutual funds, you will encounter several other concepts and terms that describe important parts of the fund's performance. For the most part, these are statistical measures of volatility and risk that tell you something about how much of a fund's performance is due to manager skill and how much is due to the manager buying risky securities. I've created an *advanced analytics resource* at http://www.940financialconsulting.com for those of you who want to dig into statistics like Standard Deviation, Alpha and Beta risk ratios, and the Sharpe, Treynor, Information, and Sortino Ratios among others.

How to Manage the Funds You Own

By this point, you've set up an allocation plan for your retirement savings, and you've researched and purchased the funds. Trust me, it gets easier, but you've still got work to do. Most of your work is just a simple review of your accounts, but you should plan to actively rebalance your portfolio regularly. If you are using the Six Fund Portfolio model featured in the book, I recommend rebalancing every four years, shortly after each presidential election, but you may want to do it more often if your actual allocations are shifting away from your plan. (Remember, the fund managers of each mutual fund you own are actively rebalancing their holdings continually, so *you* don't have to do so very often.) Finally, you'll start making adjustments tied to calendar milestones (like turning 60) when you may want to shift your allocations toward a more slightly conservative mix.

Regular Reviews

How often should you review and evaluate your portfolio?

Once you have a mutual fund portfolio set up, you should look at it monthly. That doesn't mean you need to do anything such as buy and sell. You're just looking for anything untoward. If you understand how a particular fund "works," you won't be worried if one fund is down or another fund is up. You don't expect every member of a baseball team to hit a home run every day! You own a *diversified* portfolio, and you should think of it in that way.

If a particular fund is not doing as well as you had expected or if a fund is in negative territory, just stop and think what it owns that would cause that to happen. Funds with a specialized focus (gold or technology stocks or Asian equities, for example) do well when that overall sector is up. When that sector cools off, expect this fund to lag behind the other funds and maybe even to dip into negative territory for a while. I wouldn't take action at this monthly check-in (remember, don't panic!), but you should start watching laggards more closely. Before I buy a fund, I look at previous drops and recoveries from those drops, and I compare the fund to the S&P 500 or another more appropriate index. That gives me a better sense of what to expect, and then I basically know what to expect in a downturn.

Life is full of changes, and your funds are no exception. Keeping up with your fund manager or management team for each of your mutual funds is important. When management changes, the fund company does not usually broadcast it. Once a quarter, you should go online (either at the fund's website or a resource like Morningstar) and check in on your funds. This can be a simple quick effort, but make sure your funds' management and objectives are still in line with your expectations.

During your quarterly check-ins, you should take a look at the fund's short-term performance and compare it to its market category. This is best done with an objective source like Morningstar or Steele. Again, you aren't looking to make rash decisions and change ships too quickly, but a quarterly review of performance keeps you tuned in. When you review the fund's year-end performance, you might consider making those changes if one fund is drastically underperforming.

Shifting over Time

As you get older and closer to retirement, you may want to shift your allocation. (You'll see in Part Four that you will **definitely** need to make some changes about two years before your retirement.) As I mentioned before, there is a tendency for older people to move toward a higher concentration of bonds. This can be a mistake. If your portfolio is generating results, don't change for the sake of change. Nonetheless, if your goals are to start protecting assets more carefully after a certain age, you may want to schedule some self-reviews when you hit those ages.

One reason I have filled my Six Fund Portfolio with Moderate Allocation and World Allocation Funds is that the managers are responsible for any shifts in stocks, bonds, and other holdings as they see the market changing. As I have mentioned before, if something goes terribly wrong, I would "fire" the fund and put another one in its place. My investments may have lost money on paper in the 2008 recession, but I did not sell anything. Why? Though my portfolio was down, I felt that the managers had proven themselves, and I was not going to fire either the mutual fund managers or the individual investment management teams.

Keeping Everything in Balance

Regardless of the types of investments you own, rebalancing is an important part of investment management, but one that I think does not get enough attention. Rebalancing keeps the asset allocation of your portfolio in line with the risk you are willing to take. If you choose the right investments carefully, you can avoid the expense and the frustration of constantly worrying about rebalancing too often. Almost from the start, the portfolio will fluctuate and move away from the initial percentages you chose for each component of your portfolio. Therefore, when you set up your percentages, you should also establish an amount that you know is not going to upset the mix in your portfolio.

No matter what group of funds or other investments you buy, some of them are going to do better than the others. If you owned one fund that outperformed the others significantly one year, that fund will now make up a larger proportion of your total portfolio worth. (Likewise, one or two of your investments will now be smaller parts of your portfolio, even if they are performing well.) Your portfolio has now deviated from your original plan.

Sometimes, shifts come from poor performers with low or negative returns. It's easy to justify making those changes. But often, a portfolio goes out of balance when one investment delivers amazing results. Why mess with a good thing? Mainly because your risk exposure could be growing beyond your comfort level.

It may seem odd to walk away from a winner, but your retirement savings need to have balance. A high performing part of your portfolio likely carries more risk, and you don't want your total portfolio to be more susceptible to risk than you have planned. Let's say Fund X was originally 20 percent of your mix, and it has doubled in size over five years to become 40 percent of your portfolio. Chances are a fund with explosive growth carries a lot of risk and a lot of downside potential. It's fine to have some risk in your holdings but not in almost half of your savings.

You don't want to keep funding losers either, so a regular rebalancing is a good time to reassess and reallocate the different investments in your portfolio. Rebalancing allows you to keep your gains and restock your other funds to the level you planned.

So why rebalance? There is an idea in statistics called *reversion to the mean*. In plain English, this means that over a long period of time, there is a stable "average" performance. If an investment has a period of years during which the performance is above that average, it is increasingly likely that the performance will be below average (and vice versa). Rebalancing on a regular basis, then, can have a positive effect on your portfolio—it helps you sell more of what is expensive and buy more of what is cheap.

Assuming that you originally bought the same amount of each fund or stock, a simple way to rebalance would be to add up the total value of the portfolio, divide that by the number of positions you own, and then buy or sell whatever amount of each investment it takes to get to that *target allocation*. Even if you did not start off with an equal amount in each fund or stock, rebalancing is not too hard. In this case, you still calculate the total value of your portfolio, and then you multiply that amount by the target percentage for each investment (and then buy and sell accordingly).

A *strategic allocation portfolio* is ideal for those investors who want their portfolio to stay on track, with minimal hands-on involvement. If you use allocation funds, as I do, the mutual fund manager takes care of rebalancing if things are getting out of whack, so to speak.

Too many people fall for the idea of rebalancing their portfolio every six months or even more often, and all it does is cost them money—and a fee if their financial guru is doing it for them. I do not believe in rebalancing a portfolio more than once a year.

I rebalance the Six Fund Portfolio every four years, after each presidential election. For this type of portfolio, it is much easier. While this is a long time for many types of portfolios, I find that it has worked well. Four years is a good length of time in the market. There have probably been ups and downs during that time, and Wall Street tends to make adjustments before and after an election, so it's a convenient time to take a close look. You might consider rebalancing more often than that if you are not using the same fund strategies I am, but an annual rebalancing should be fine if you have chosen the parts of your portfolio carefully.

During rebalancing, you may simply want to redistribute your money to your planned proportions, but you may also find that it is a good time to revisit your basic allocation decisions. Perhaps you can afford a little more risk, or you may see it's time to invest a little more conservatively. A rebalancing is a good time to make those kinds of changes.

Conclusion

You've seen how to construct a mutual fund portfolio, fill it with invest-ments that match your goals, and manage it without a lot of effort. For many of you, you have done the work required to put your retirement sav-ings plan into action. That being said, there is room for stocks, bonds, and other investments in a retirement portfolio—if you are willing to do the work. Let's take a look at those instruments next.

9

Stocks and Bonds

By now, you know that your retirement plan's success hinges on your money working hard for you—and growing enough to outpace inflation *and* your planned withdrawals. Owning stocks—either directly or within a mutual fund or exchange-traded fund (ETF)—is the best way over time to do both.

As I showed you in Chapter 6, a successful retirement portfolio needs to be balanced and diversified, with an appropriate allocation of your assets. In other words, if you are going to own stocks, you need to own bonds too, although I will caution you about being too heavily invested in bonds. The ideal allocation with individual stocks and bonds is the same for mutual funds: your portfolio should be 60 to 70 percent stocks and 30 to 40 percent bonds and cash.

What to Look For in Stocks

I have never seen absolute rules carved in stone about what you have to do to successfully invest in stocks, but I can tell you that it takes time and research to end up with a good portfolio. You learn almost anything you need to know about a mutual fund within three or four hours of research. With individual stocks, it typically takes much more time to really understand a company, its prospects, and the appropriate price for its stock.

Owning a stock portfolio is a little like owning a pet goldfish: it probably does not need hourly attention from you, but you had better check on it reasonably often if you want it to do well. In addition to the quarterly earnings reports that every public company provides, you never know when important news might come out about the company or its competitors.

Because of this constant flow of information, you need to check the latest updates on your holdings and keep a careful eye on your portfolio.

By comparison, owning a mutual fund portfolio is more like owning a tree—it needs a little attention now and then, but things don't change much from month to month. It is easy to keep up with who is managing the fund, how it is performing versus others in that category, and all of the key metrics we discussed in Chapter 8. There really is no need to monitor the progress or fortunes of the companies owned by a fund (that's the manager's job, after all), and there really isn't going to be important news very often that is specific to your fund.

When you buy individual stocks, you take on specific risks. In a mutual fund that holds over a hundred stocks, all of these risks blend together and somewhat balance themselves out. The failure of any one investment idea is unlikely to have much of an impact on your fund's results. With individual stocks, though, it is much more difficult to diversify away those risks, and they become a more significant part of your overall returns.

One of the biggest risks with stocks is *company-specific risk*. Simply put, some companies just don't do as well as you think they should. For every Apple Computer, there are plenty of Tandy and Commodore corporations that do not make it. Even investing in "stable" companies can go sour, as new competitors take away business or the very market itself changes. While it's true that picking the right company (and the right stock) can result in big returns, the opposite is also true.

Company-specific risks are not the only thing you need to worry about if you own a portfolio of individual stocks. Stocks from the same general business sectors usually move up and down together. You may be able to find the best semiconductor stock out there, but if the market moves against semiconductors as a group, that knowledge may not do you any good.

A Portfolio of Stocks: More Work and Responsibility

Even though I definitely recommend a portfolio of *mutual funds* for most people in their retirement, I do not want to give the impression that a retirement stock portfolio is automatically a bad idea for everybody. If you want the work and responsibility, and particularly if you have a long personal track record of successfully investing in individual stocks, by all means continue. There is no shortage of people who manage to do quite well for themselves with a carefully watched portfolio of stocks, and if you are one of those people, you probably already know it!

One other word of caution: retirement is **not** the time to start experimenting with your investments. To that end, I am much more in favor of leaving a little extra gain on the table if that is the cost of reducing the risk that you may lose more of your hard-earned money. *What you have when you start retirement is all you have, and it needs to last.* If you intend for stocks to be the majority of your retirement savings, you need to start well before you expect to retire, or you need to hire people to help you. If your retirement plan is fully funded and secure, go ahead and take the risks—and reap those big returns when a stock hits big—with your everyday savings, but do not risk your retirement on something new and untested.

Asset Allocation and Diversification

If you go this route, be sure to diversify your portfolio, and be especially careful with the amount of risk you carry. Investing in a couple of "can't-miss" tech or biotech stocks that go bust can really hurt when you are supposed to be living off that portfolio for the next 30 years. Remember, you are no longer in the business of hitting home runs. Success in retirement is about tirelessly cranking out singles and getting on base, and it is about leaving the big all-or-nothing swings to the younger crowd.

To learn more about how to structure your portfolio, you can model it after a mutual fund that has a great track record investing in stocks. Look at the prospectus for a moderate allocation mutual fund such as Vanguard Wellington (ticker symbol: VWELX). This is an excellent fund. Consider how the fund managers decide on the "portion sizes"—the proportion of stocks, bonds, and so on—in their allocations. If you want to own 25 stocks, you may want to put 3 percent in each stock so that your portfolio consists of 75 percent stocks. The remaining 25 percent can be put in laddered bonds. Studying professionally managed mutual funds is a very instructive way to see how other managers do it—and you can do it too! You may want to use industry sectors, such as pharmaceuticals, in which case you would choose a percentage for each sector and then buy several quality stocks in each sector. You will find most mutual funds and individual money managers manage their portfolios that way.

At retirement, your stock and bond portfolio should be made up primarily of dividend producing stocks and a bond portfolio that is laddered over 10 years. With good dividend paying stocks and bonds, you will find it easy to withdraw the dividends. Dividends can always be reinvested, but after you retire, they are perfect sources of cash to fund your annual expenses.

Doing It Yourself

Choosing individual stocks and bonds on your own is not as easy as it would seem, **but** you can do it! There is quite a bit of pressure to own stocks—brokerage firms are constantly advertising their services, advisers boast of their ability to build market-beating portfolios, and financial news programs are full of "buy, sell, or hold" on individual stocks. Try to find a TV program that routinely focuses on mutual funds, and you'll be searching in vain. Stocks and bonds are, on the whole, good investment vehicles. However, the question to ask yourself is this: "Are these particular stocks and bonds good investments for **my retirement**?"

With careful management, a portfolio of individual stocks and bonds certainly can produce the same results as a portfolio of mutual funds. I am less certain, though, that those results are really all "essentially the same" when you consider everything that goes into a portfolio of individual securities.

Holding individual securities takes more time and more work. It may expose you to more risk, and it can be more expensive. I would argue that a portfolio of individual securities needs to do **better** than a similar portfolio of mutual funds to make up for that additional work. After all, you will be investing a significant amount of your time to manage your portfolio appropriately. You are not really trying to "beat the market," but you want your hard work to produce a good, more or less consistent result. Investing can be a lot of fun, so don't be pessimistic and say, "I can't do it!" (Don't forget, retirement shouldn't end up being more work!)

Just a quick note about the "hold" philosophy. Holding a carefully chosen stock that performs well is a wonderful thing—and you can and should hold it indefinitely. On the other hand, if you (or a firm managing your money) can't make up your collective minds about a stock that is not performing, and its prospects are uncertain, but the idea is to "hold" it for a while longer to see what happens—you and the firm are nuts. If you don't like it and it is not performing, there are a lot of fish in the sea that can replace it.

Two books that will get you started are *Asset Allocation: Balancing Financial Risk* by Roger C. Gibson and *Essentials of Investments*, ninth edition, by Zvi Bodie, Alex Kane, and Alan J. Marcus (the latter is an excellent book used in undergraduate courses on investing).

Getting Started

How do you begin to invest in individual stocks and bonds? There is so much information available that it may seem mind-boggling. Once armed with a handful of good formulas, such as the P/E Ratio, the Quick Ratio, and others in this section, you can make as many right and wrong "guesses" as many professional managers. Let's keep it simple, and I think you will enjoy doing some of it yourself.

Remember, much of the investment advice you get from TV is mostly showmanship and hocus-pocus. That's why I like to stick with the numbers.

Essential (and Easy) Analytic Tools

There are a number of very useful and very easy-to-master analytic formulas that every stock investor should know. They are invaluable when making decisions.

Here's the main thing you want to ask yourself: "Is the **value** of a stock I am going to buy worth the price?" You wouldn't buy a quart of milk at a grocery store for $25, would you? Of course not! You are willing to pay a reasonable price, but you are not willing to throw your money away. Buying a stock also boils down to paying a reasonable price for the value of what you are buying.

Comparing your stock choice with the stock of similar companies is a great way to check out how reasonable the market price is. Ideally, you should compare four to eight other companies. You always should look at all the major stocks in a particular category. And you always have to be mindful that you are comparing oranges to oranges, not oranges to pistachio nuts. Don't try to compare Coca-Cola with Pfizer.

I use the ratios in Table 9.1 as my core formulas in head-to-head comparisons: Price-to-Earnings (P/E) Ratios, Price-to-Earnings Growth (PEG) Ratios, Earning per Share (EPS), Price-to-Sales (P/S) Ratios, Price-to-Book Value Ratios, and Beta. (I also look at the income-generating ability of the stocks by including dividend and yield amounts in my comparisons.) These ratios quickly weed out the not-so-good stocks from the ones under consideration in a particular category (such as soft drinks or pharmaceuticals). All of the reported data for these ratios is easily found on any financial reporting website like Morningstar or Value Line. I pulled the examples in Table 9.1 from Yahoo! Finance (http://finance .yahoo.com).

The *Price-to-Earnings* (P/E) *Ratio* is a very simple, very powerful formula. It is simply the current price of the stock divided by the company's annual earnings. This ratio is a useful bellwether for determining how a company compares with its peers and the overall market. The higher the

Table 9.1   Stock by Stock Ratio Comparison

Firm	Symbol	Price	P/E Ratio	PEG Ratio 5 Yr. Expected	Earnings per Share	Price-to-Sales Ratio	Price-to-Book Value Ratio	Beta	Dividend and Yield
Coca-Cola	KO	$41.97	22.43	3.00	1.87	4.00	5.68	0.34	2.90%
PepsiCo	PEP	$89.85	20.30	2.75	4.43	2.06	5.98	0.35	2.90%
Dr Pepper Snapple Group	DPS	$59.03	17.76	2.36	3.32	1.92	5.24	0.22	2.70%
Nestlé ADR	NSRGY	$76.92	21.92	5.91	3.51	2.37	3.50	N/A	2.64%

Source: Data from Yahoo! Finance (http://finance.yahoo.com), July 11, 2014.

ratio number, the more likely the stock is overvalued, but when you compare similar companies, you'll find overvalued is relative:

Price-to-Earnings (P/E) Ratio

$$\text{Price-to-earnings ratio} = \frac{\text{stock price}}{\text{annual earnings}}$$

The *PEG Ratio* is the *Price-to-Earnings Growth Ratio*—in this case, the growth in earnings expected over the next five years. It is a good ratio to use when determining whether a stock will grow its earnings going forward and whether the stock really has any value. In general, a PEG ratio of less than 1 means it is undervalued by the market. Over 1 means that the stock is overpriced. *Most* of the time, a PEG Ratio of 1 or less is considered good, and as it gets closer to 2, the company is believed to be expensive— relative to future growth in earnings of that stock. The PEG Ratio is a simple "tool," but it should not take the place of more diligent research:

Price-to-Earnings Growth (PEG) Ratio

$$\frac{\text{Price-to-earnings}}{\text{growth ratio}} = \frac{\text{P/E ratio}}{\text{annual earnings per share (EPS) growth}}$$

The *Price-to-Book Value Ratio* is the ratio of the current market value of the equity to the book value of the equity, which is the measure of the shareholders' equity on the balance sheet. It is written several ways, such as the market value of the equity divided by the book value of the equity or as shown below:

Price-to-Book Value Ratio

$$\text{Price-to-book value ratio} = \frac{\text{stock price per share}}{\text{shareholders' equity per share}}$$

where

Shareholders' equity per share = balance sheet divided by the number of common shares outstanding

The *Price-to-Sales* (P/S) *Ratio* is another good way to compare stock values. Take the share price and multiply it by the number of shares, and you have the numerator. Once you have that number, divide it by the total sales over the last 12 months. In those cases in which you are comparing different stocks in a category, the lower the debt is also important. This formula is similar to the price-to-earnings (P/E) formula:

Price-to-Sales (P/S) Ratio

$$\text{Price-to-sales ratio} = \frac{\text{share price}}{\text{revenue per share}}$$

It is important to compare the companies in the same industry; otherwise you are just wasting your time. The comparison of stocks in the same industry gives you a wider view of the company as it stacks up in the industry.

Beta and Dividend Yield are easily found on http://finance.yahoo.com under Key Statistics. Look on the right under Trading Information for Beta and further down the same column for Dividends. These are also found on Moringstar.com and in Value Line Investment Survey sheets in your library.

Table 9.2 shows a comparison of the competitors of Coca-Cola (ticker symbol: KO) and the averages of the soft drink industry. Each soft drink company may have other competitors, so it is best to look at them all. This table contains more data than we have discussed, but you can look up these

Table 9.2   Direct Competitor Comparison as of July 11, 2014

	Coca-Cola KO	Dr Pepper Snapple Group/DPS	Nestlé ADR	PepsiCo PEP	Industry
Market Cap.:	$184.47B	$11.59B	$245.34B	$136.22B	$2.88B
Employees:	130,600	19,000	333,000	274,000	11.75K
Qtrly. Rev. Growth (yoy):	−0.04	0.01	0.00	0.00	0.14
Revenue (ttm):	$46.40B	$6.02B	$103.46B	$66.46B	$2.06B
Gross Margin (ttm):	0.61	0.59	0.48	0.53	0.47
EBITDA (ttm):	$13.08B	$1.38B	$19.37B	$12.56B	$187.60M
Operating Margin (ttm):	0.24	0.19	0.16	0.15	0.09
Net Income (ttm):	$8.45B	$673.00M	$11.22B	$6.87B	N/A
EPS (ttm):	1.87	3.32	3.51	4.43	0.93
P/E (ttm):	22.43	17.76	21.92	20.30	26.88
PEG (5-yr. expected):	3.00	2.36	5.91	2.75	1.75
P/S (ttm):	4.00	1.92	2.37	2.06	1.63

Note: B means billions; M means millions; yoy means year over year; ttm means trailing twelve months; EBITDA means earnings before interest, taxes, depreciation, and amortization.

terms on http://www.investopedia.com (a great online information source) and use them also if you'd like. The more you know about a company, the better you will feel about choosing that company's stock.

Another ratio I use frequently is the Quick Ratio (or Acid Test Ratio). The *Quick Ratio* is the result of taking the sum of the cash and cash equivalents, plus the short-term or easily marketable investments and the accounts receivable, and dividing that by the current liabilities of the company:

Quick Ratio

$$\text{Quick (Acid Test) Ratio} = \frac{\text{cash and cash equivalents} + \text{marketable securities} + \text{accounts receivable}}{\text{current liabilities}}$$

The Quick Ratio is an easy way to see how a company is run, and it also tells investors if a company can meet its short-term obligations. The simplest way to find the information and do the math at Yahoo! Finance (http://finance.yahoo.com) is to enter the company symbol or name. On the left side of the screen, scroll down until you see the heading "Financials." Under "Financials" is "Balance Sheet." The higher the Quick Ratio, the better prepared the stock is to meet its immediate obligations.

Are these all the ideas and formulas I use? **No**. These ideas are a good place to start. They are easy to find and look at while I am looking for a stock in a particular category. Once I do the quick comparison, I put the ones that make the first cut to a stronger test.

Testing for High-Quality Stocks

The importance of investing in high-quality companies cannot be overemphasized. High-quality companies have long-term track records for consistent earnings growth, uninterrupted and increasing dividends, institutional sponsorship, and liquidity. There are a lot of mistakes being made currently by investors chasing high dividend yields. Sometimes companies who don't have very good balance sheets (or they have other problems) choose high dividend payouts to attract money. The unaware investor chooses that stock, only to learn later that the company is a failing enterprise.

High-quality companies tend to have the widest "moats." The wider the moat, the more difficult it is to have some company mimic your product—just like holding off the invaders trying to get into your castle.

When you have a set of potential stock candidates after running the ratio tests above, look at Value Line (http://www.valueline.com) and the *Investment Quality Trends* newsletter (http://www.iqtrends.com). Value

Line is more in-depth than a newsletter could possibly be, but the IQT newsletter is really good for serious stock investors.

If you decide to use Value Line (get a trial subscription or visit the library to decide if you'd like using this reference material), here is a Value Line checklist of things to consider before you buy a stock. Only a select few stocks pass this test, but when it comes to your retirement, you should hold any stock you consider for your portfolio to high standards:

1. It has a Value Line safety rating of **1 or 2**.
2. Earnings have improved in **7 of the last 12 years**.
3. Dividends have been paid **for at least 20 years**.
4. Dividends have been **increased in at least 5 of the last 12 years**.
   - There are over 92 companies that have increased dividends over the last 25 years, and some have increased them over 50 years.
5. It has a financial stability rating of **A or higher** and an earnings predictability of over **65 percent**.
   - This data can be found at the bottom of a Value Line sheet describing the stock.
6. There are at least **8 to 10 million shares** outstanding for this company.
   - There are over 4,309 companies who have 8 million shares outstanding, and there are 4,179 companies who have 10 million shares outstanding.
7. Of the stocks outstanding for this company, **75 to 80 percent** are owned by institutional investors.
   - There are over 1,676 companies with institutional ownership of 75 percent or higher. Of those, 1,409 have over 80 percent institutional investors.

I use Value Line in conjunction with the other tools I mentioned above, so I feel that I have a good handle on the stock that I am researching. But in investing, there is never "too much of a good thing" when it comes to stock analysis!

A good example of a value identification system is the "Criteria for Select Blue Chips" used by *Investment Quality Trends*. IQT uses this simple set of "The Six Rules" to identify high-quality, dividend paying stocks:

1. Dividends have increased at least five times in the last 12 years.
2. The S&P quality ranking puts the company in the A category.
3. There are at least 5 million shares outstanding.
4. At least 80 percent of the outstanding shares are with institutional investors.

5.   There have been at least 25 years of uninterrupted dividends.
6.   Earnings have improved in at least 7 of the last 12 years.

The IQT newsletter sorts through stocks for you, and I think it is terrific for the novice. I stumbled across the *Investment Quality Trends* newsletter at a meeting in the early 1980s. Geraldine Weiss started writing it in 1966. I have spoken with her from time to time, and I can tell you that she is one terrific human being. The IQT is one of the oldest continuing newsletters in the investment world, and it is first-rate. There are so many letters that just hype stocks and products and don't teach you how to take care of your portfolio. In contrast, the IQT is truly informative. It continues today under the capable leadership of Kelley Wright and Michael Minney. Ask for a free newsletter at http://www.iqtrends.com.

"The Six Rules" are in each issue of the *Investment Quality Trends* newsletter, and they are more adequately explained in Weiss's first book, *Dividends Don't Lie*, which she wrote in 1988 along with Janet Lowe. The book was updated and published in 2010 as *Dividends Still Don't Lie* by Kelley Wright.

These rules seem simple, but they can be tough to follow if you don't keep your mind on the ball. The data you need to follow the rules is fairly easy to find online from resources like Yahoo! Finance or Value Line. You may have to put some time into research at the beginning to get the hang of it, but it is well worth the effort to find the stocks that work.

Using the previous guidelines can get you quality stocks with great results. There are more ways to screen and select stocks than you could ever imagine, but these work! And that is important.

Owning Stocks for Income

Can a portfolio of dividend paying stocks provide you with the income you need in retirement? My answer to that question is "Yes, but . . . ," and that "but . . ." is very important indeed. Although a portfolio of companies that pay healthy dividends can produce solid income, like everything in the investment world, you have to keep up with your stocks' dividend status. If an investment manager (or a mutual fund) is doing this for you, they keep up with the stocks and any problems that might arise.

Individual companies can, and do, run into trouble, and sometimes they have to cut their dividend. Highly regarded bank stocks like JPMorgan were long considered reliable sources of very generous dividends. However, the housing bubble and credit crisis forced banks to significantly cut those dividends. If you were depending on a quarterly dividend check to support your retirement income needs, you'd be facing a huge cash flow problem (not to mention a massive drop in market valuation that could take years to rebuild).

Dividends are not the only way to create income from a stock portfolio. Many individual investors become quite good at writing *covered calls*. I know a few retirees who keep a small portfolio for themselves on which they write covered calls. One of my friends said that this way he is forced to "keep up with the market," and he can better make decisions about the rest of his portfolio that is either in managed accounts or mutual funds.

Covered-call writing is a slightly risky strategy that can produce good income. *Writing a covered call* means that you sell somebody the right to buy a stock you own at a fixed price for a specific period of time (typically less than a year). You get a small premium for doing this, but if the stock goes above the agreed-upon price, you have to sell your shares to the other person for that agreed-upon price. You don't exactly lose money, but you do have to sell those shares for less than you could in the open market. Of course, there is a chance that the stock price won't go as high as that price, in which case you get to keep your shares and the premium—this is the "income" that you get in covered-call writing.

There are some catches to covered calls. First, you can find yourself forced to sell a stock that you would have preferred to keep, and you may have to pay capital gains taxes if the proceeds are in a personal account. Second, options contracts often carry higher commissions than stocks, and you have to be relatively active as a call writer to make significant income from this strategy. Also, the premium you receive is not treated like a dividend by the IRS. Instead, it is treated as a capital gain.

What to Look For in Bonds

Bonds are popular go-to investments for folks looking to generate predictable income from their portfolio. Unfortunately, it can be pretty expensive to build a proper portfolio of individual bonds if you are not careful about fees, but it *is* doable.

Let's limit our discussion to bonds that are rated AAA through BBB by Standard & Poor's and rated Aaa through Baa by Moody's (Table 9.3). Let me give you an easy way to remember whether a bond you are considering is rated by S&P or by Moody's. If the rating is all capital letters, it is an S&P rating because their ratings are in all capital letters. If you are looking at a Moody's rating, well, the first letter in the rating is capitalized, and the rest of the letters are lowercase. There is another rating agency, Fitch, but you will probably not see those ratings as frequently.

Table 9.3   Major Bond Rating Agencies, Grades, and Risk

Moody's	S&P	Grade	Long-Term Ratings	Risk
Aaa	AAA	Investment	Minimal credit risk	High quality
Aa	AA	Investment	Very low credit risk	High quality
A	A	Investment	Low credit risk	Upper medium grade
Baa	BBB	Investment	Can be speculative	Medium grade
Ba and B	BB and B	Junk	Substantial credit risk	Speculative
Caa, Ca, and C	CCC, CC, and C	Junk	High credit risk	Very speculative
C	D	Junk	Typically in default	Usually in default

The biggest three risk concerns we are going to have with bonds are the *default risk*, the *inflation risk*, and of course, *taxes*. There are very few companies that are rated AAA or Aaa, so most of the bonds we will consider are rated Aa or AA through Baa and BBB. Anything below those ratings is considered a junk bond, and they are risky investments that don't belong in most retirement portfolios. If you are going to own any junk bonds, those bonds should be a small part of a well-diversified mutual fund or ETF. The default rate is high on individual junk bonds, so why take the chance?

Designing a Bond Portfolio

What's the best way to plan and hold a bond portfolio? Without a doubt, it is a portfolio of *laddered bonds*. As I mentioned in Chapter 7, *laddering* is a method that diversifies your portfolio, protects you from interest rate fluctuations, and generates post-retirement cash flow (Table 9.4).

Let's say you want to put $100,000 into fixed-income investments (a.k.a. bonds) and that you are going to use the tried-and-true laddering technique. In this case, you would buy 10 bonds—each due to mature in a succeeding year for 10 years. After you've set it up, all you have to do is look for a bond each year to replace the one that matured. This way you are not tying up all of your bond money in one security. That helps reduce interest rate risk, and it helps increase your liquidity—that is, your ability to get to your money if you should need it quickly such as for an emergency. It also helps with what is known as *duration*, which will be discussed in the next

Table 9.4   10-Year Bond Ladder

Bond Name	Maturity Date	Recommended Action at Maturity
Bond 1	Dec. 1, 2015	Reinvest with a Dec. 2025 maturity
Bond 2	Dec. 1, 2016	Reinvest with a Dec. 2026 maturity
Bond 3	Dec. 1, 2017	Reinvest with a Dec. 2027 maturity
Bond 4	Dec. 1, 2018	Reinvest with a Dec. 2028 maturity
Bond 5	Dec. 1, 2019	Reinvest with a Dec. 2029 maturity
Bond 6	Dec. 1, 2020	Reinvest with a Dec. 2030 maturity
Bond 7	Dec. 1, 2021	Reinvest with a Dec. 2031 maturity
Bond 8	Dec. 1, 2022	Reinvest with a Dec. 2032 maturity
Bond 9	Dec. 1, 2023	Reinvest with a Dec. 2033 maturity
Bond 10	Dec. 1, 2024	Reinvest with a Dec. 2034 maturity

section. (If you hold individual bonds to maturity, you don't have to worry about duration.)

You can and should diversify when you build a bond portfolio. That means a little more work with research, record keeping, and tracking performance, but in the end, once you get the hang of it, it is easy. Be sure that you space the maturity dates evenly so that you are reinvesting your proceeds at regular intervals.

Investing in Bonds

By going to http://www.treasurydirect.gov, private investors can buy Treasury Bills, Treasury Notes, and Treasury Inflation-Protected Securities (TIPS) directly from the Treasury without paying a commission. The instructions on the website are very easy to understand. It is sometimes possible to buy municipal bonds straight from an issuer also. However, you must use a broker (and pay brokerage fees) to buy corporate bonds and many municipal bonds or bonds issued by foreign governments. Those fees will have an impact on your return, so be sure and ask about them. There is not nearly as much competition for bond brokerage services, and commissions can be relatively high when compared to stocks. You can buy and sell bonds online from some brokerage firms today. Just be sure you talk to someone at the firm before you start, so you know the "rules of the road."

Owning any individual bond except those with the higher ratings (no lower than Baa or BBB) means that you will have an individual risk with each bond. Now, the U.S. government is not going bankrupt any time soon (despite our politicians' best efforts), but companies and even cities **can** go bankrupt. If 5 to 10 percent of your expected retirement income was going to come from a particular company's bonds and that company ran into serious difficulties, your retirement plans could be in danger.

Owning individual bonds can also make your tax return a little more complicated if those bonds aren't held within a retirement plan or an IRA. If you buy a bond that is selling for more (or less) than its face value, you have to adjust the taxable amount of interest by that premium (or discount). It is not an impossible task to do the math yourself, but if this is a personal account, let your accountant help you the first time, and then you'll understand what records you need to keep for taxes.

The one possible exception to any headaches that individual bonds might cause could be *municipal bonds*. Municipal bonds (often referred to as *munis*) typically have some significant tax advantages for residents of the same state as the issuer. Better yet, these bonds are often backed either by a revenue-generating asset (like an airport) or the tax-assessing authority of a state or local government. Many bonds are issued with insurance that is designed to pay off the bond if the issuer runs into financial difficulty. Considering all of those attractive details, they are a pretty popular option for some folks in retirement.

Of course, you don't have to buy individual munis to enjoy these advantages. If you live in a large state like New York or California, it is not too difficult to find a selection of mutual funds or ETFs that invest in municipal bonds issued within that state. In those cases, then, it may be appropriate to own a few individual bonds and particularly if you can use the tax benefits. If you live in a smaller state though, you might not find the same kinds of options.

If you do want to own bonds, there are a number of factors to consider. It is dangerous to simply look for the highest yields (or yields to maturity) that you can find. If a borrower has to pay a high rate, there are probably some real issues with the creditworthiness of that borrower. Bonds aren't supposed to be high-yield instruments. They are supposed to be stable, and stable investments just don't pay out big yields. Likewise, it is important to own a mix of different types of issuers (governments, corporations, and so on) and different maturities.

Understanding the duration of a bond is very important, so make sure to review it when you are researching and buying a bond. Duration is the measure of the sensitivity of the principal to changing interest rates. The longer the maturity, the higher the duration. It is a fairly complicated

Table 9.5   Bond Duration

Name	Average Duration
Long-term government average	15.54
Long-term bond average	10.00
Inflation-protected bond average	6.61
Intermediate-term bond average	4.88
Intermediate-term government average	4.88
Short-term government average	2.09
Short-term bond average	2.02

calculation, but thankfully, the duration of bonds and bond funds is found just for the asking. Table 9.5 is for mutual funds specializing in bonds, but each individual bond has a duration.

To understand the chart, keep in mind that each 1 percent rise in interest rates would make a long-term government bond lose 15.54 percent of its value. Conversely, each 1 percent drop in interest rates would create a gain of 15.54 percent. Having a low duration does **not** mean that the bond is risk free.

Table 9.6 shows examples of bond funds and their durations as of January 2014. Vanguard has good bond funds, and while you don't have to own only Vanguard funds, you should certainly consider some of their funds for your portfolio.

Bonds to Avoid

As with any investment going into your retirement portfolio, you want high-quality and minimal- to moderate-risk instruments. It's even more important to evaluate the risk associated with particular bonds because

Table 9.6   Vanguard Bond Fund Durations

Fund	Symbol	Duration
Vanguard Short-Term Bond Index	VBISX	2.68
Vanguard Intermediate Bond Index	VFICX	6.50
Vanguard Long-Term Bond Index	VBLTX	14.03

Source: Data from Steele Mutual Fund Expert, January 2014.

you should be buying them as conservative, rather than speculative, investments. As such, retirement-minded investors should avoid *individual* junk
bonds, trust certificates, many zero-coupon bonds, and finally also the "BS
bonds" like mortgage-backed securities (MBS), asset-backed securities
(ABS), and commercial mortgage-backed securities (CMBS).

Mortgage-backed securities are usually pools of mortgage loans such
as first mortgages on residential properties. Asset-backed securities might
be assets like credit card receivables, and commercial mortgage-backed
securities are mortgage-backed securities secured by loans on commercial
property.

Individual Bonds Versus Mutual Funds

Owning individual bonds can be expensive and a lot of work. Setting up a
diversified portfolio, laddering maturity dates, and tracking performance
starts to take a toll. So, as I told you in Chapter 7, owning mutual funds
with bonds in their portfolios offers you all of the benefits of owning bonds
(income generation, stability, and so on) while being much easier (and
more affordable) to research, buy, and manage.

If you don't have at least $200,000 to $300,000 to put in a bond portfolio, you may want to consider using mutual funds with a significant concentration of bonds (Conservative Allocation Funds) or even bond funds.
Why? I want to be sure you are well diversified. There is nothing wrong
with owning some of both. Many clients own several bond funds even if
they have a portfolio of individual bonds, and some of these clients also
own a few individual bonds when they count their bond fund holdings as
their "bonds."

Owning a high-quality bond fund frees you from having to worry
about those details, and it puts your money in the hands of people who
focus on those markets every day (and who can probably calculate duration in their head while brushing their teeth). With a bond fund, you not
only have a team of professionals managing a large portfolio but you also
have the advantage of easy one-step diversification. You might consider
Bullet Bonds and BulletShares, which are bond-based ETFs that can't be
redeemed until the maturity date. These instruments lack the liquidity that
traditional bonds possess—but they are sold with a clear end date, which is
good for forecasting retirement income. Bond funds can also simplify your
taxes because you will get a regular statement at the end of the year, and you
do not have to worry about the individual calculations. Best of all, there are
plenty of funds that do not charge you very much at all. Considering all of

the risks, costs, and inconveniences, I think it is much easier for investors to own bond *funds* or bond-based ETFs, but if you do opt to buy individual bonds yourself, make sure you've got all those bases covered.

The Costs of Owning Stocks and Bonds

If you decide to own individual stocks and bonds, you need to actively manage your portfolio. Accordingly, you will need to make changes more often than you would if you owned a mutual fund—and those changes cost money. Whether you are tweaking your stock holdings every so often, adjusting your bond ladders, or making a massive overhaul of the whole portfolio, these changes can be much more expensive than the occasional rebalancing of a portfolio of mutual funds. Yes, the fees at online brokerage firms are nice and low, but if you are making a lot of changes, those expenses can really add up over the years and take a lot of the wind out of your sails.

Worse still, because stocks can move much further much faster than diversified mutual funds, you will probably need to rebalance a portfolio of dividend paying stocks more often than a portfolio of income producing mutual funds. As long as you can hold your total costs of owning individual stocks to what a mutual fund would cost (around 1 percent or less), that's fine.

Don't forget that you are also responsible for dealing with capital gains and losses, and the tax issues that result from trading, if the portfolio is not in an IRA or a retirement account.

Most people will find that trying to own a portfolio of individual bonds is more work and hassle than they want or need—and the rewards (in terms of outperformance) are often quite small. That may not necessarily be the case for stocks, but here too there is a lot of work, commitment, and potential risk.

Unless you really have a passion (and skill) for building your own portfolio out of individual securities, I would advise you to either stick with mutual funds or work with a professional asset manager who can help you build a portfolio that is suitable for your goals, needs, and risk tolerance.

Hiring a Money Manager

You *don't* have to be running the portfolio yourself in order to own a portfolio of individual stocks and bonds. This is perhaps where the right financial advice can really pay for itself. I don't think that you need to pay an outside professional to pick half a dozen high-quality mutual funds and then hold them for years at a time, but when it comes to individual stocks, good advice can be a lot more valuable.

As I have become increasingly busy since I elected to continue to work, I now have my individual stocks and bonds managed by the same invest-ment management firms that we use for clients. Even in gloomy times they have done well. I have always believed that I should eat my own cooking, and my own money is invested right alongside the clients'.

Because dividends are so useful for a retirement portfolio, I have cho-sen value- and dividend-oriented money managers for my portfolio. These managers are skilled in selecting stocks that generate healthy dividends, so I can use the dividends and let the stocks continue to grow.

It is certainly not necessary for you to use professional management if you have the desire, the time, and the ability to actively manage your stock and bond portfolio. I urge you to at least start trying it yourself, even if you are a real novice. Just approach it slowly and carefully. The total fees for a well-selected and diversified mutual fund portfolio should be no more than 1 percent.

If you decide you don't want to manage your money yourself, you should not pay an investment management firm more than 1 percent per year in management fees to manage it for you. The amount of 1 percent is reasonable for accounts under $1 million in almost all cases. And that 1 percent should include what is paid to your financial adviser who helps you choose and oversee management of your money. (That is usually a 75/25 split.) Trading fees such as those related to buying and selling stocks, mutual funds, and ETFs are not included in either of the 1 percent bench-marks I've mentioned. Once the portfolio is set up and running, fees should be negligible if you have chosen the right funds or ETFs—or managers.

Managing and Rebalancing Your Portfolio

We've discussed the need to track your stock portfolio actively, monthly if not more frequently, but that is merely dealing with the performance and other timely issues of individual holdings.

You also need to conduct a regular assessment of how your portfolio is supporting your retirement goals. Are you generating enough income? Are you beating inflation? Is your portfolio stable enough? Is it growing? If you have researched the stock well enough to know how it did in the last recession, don't have a knee-jerk reaction if the stock market goes down. Holding steady with good stocks is a great way to make money. Just don't expect every stock to go up every year. Bonds don't require the same monthly scrutiny as stocks, but you will need to manage your ladder annually.

As with mutual funds (as we discussed in Chapter 8), you will need to rebalance your portfolio on a regular basis. Because individual stocks can move much further much faster than diversified mutual funds, you will probably find that you need to rebalance a portfolio of dividend paying stocks more often than a portfolio of income producing mutual funds. I recommend rebalancing your mutual fund portfolio every four years. With a portfolio full of individual stocks, you may need to rebalance your portfolio annually—or more often if there is an unanticipated change.

Conclusion

Stocks and bonds are going to be the central holdings of your portfolio throughout your retirement. I just happen to think that it's easier and more cost-effective to hold those through a small number of well-chosen mutual funds or ETFs. But I might add that everyone is not like me. If you can actively and successfully manage a well-diversified portfolio of stocks and bonds—and if you enjoy it—go for it!

10

Other Investment Options

There is no shortage of places to put your hard-earned money. Between stocks, bonds, mutual funds, real estate, commodities, and other instruments, there is an almost uncountable number of options. Clearly, we can't talk about all of them, but let's highlight some of the advantages and drawbacks of the most common alternatives. Many of these ideas sound better than they actually are, so ultimately I believe stocks, bonds, mutual funds, and exchange-traded funds (ETFs) should make up the bulk of your holdings into and throughout retirement.

Real Estate

Real estate is one of the hardest topics in personal finance. When you are planning for retirement and your portfolio needs stability and predictability, it is even harder to master. On one hand, real estate has proven itself over time as a top-notch investment category and as a better hedge against inflation than gold. On the other hand, the words *real estate* and *bubble* go together a little too often for comfort now.

We do know that it is no longer the golden egg it was from the 1980s through the mid-2000s, when it was a "can't lose" proposition. Owning a home does not automatically make someone a very savvy real estate investor. Keep that in mind as you decide which is best for you.

Real estate also often takes quite a bit more work to manage and maintain than other investments. Worse still, it is a perfect example of an investment for which your knowledge really matters. With real estate, the success (or failure) of an investment sometimes comes down to whichever side at the table knows the most.

As a general rule, the large amounts of capital, risk, and know-how that go into developing real estate and speculating in raw land mean that they really are not appropriate for regular investors, especially investors focusing on retirement. Flipping houses or any other real estate can be a risky way to earn a return, and it requires quite a bit of effort. Although a lot of people made money flipping properties in the hot housing market of the early to mid-2000s, many of them lost all that they had gained—and more—when the bottom fell out of the market and they were stuck with properties they couldn't sell and loans they couldn't refinance or afford. I don't recommend flipping real estate as a part of your retirement *investment strategy*, but it can be a part of your post-retirement *life* as long as you are using non-retirement capital to invest. In other words, some of your "if you lose it, so what" money.

For most people, investing in real estate while planning for retirement comes down to *rentals*, *Real Estate Investment Trusts* (REITs), and *Master Limited Partnerships* (MLPs). Investing in rental property can be as simple as owning a house down the street or owning a few houses or condos around your community, or it can be as complicated as owning shares in multiple apartment buildings in several cities. REITs are publicly traded shares (stocks) of companies that buy, hold, develop, and operate properties. The particular rules governing REITs means that they avoid taxation on much of their earnings as long as they pay the earnings out as dividends. Because REIT shares trade like any other stock, they are an accessible option for investors who want exposure to real estate. MLPs function about the same from an investment standpoint, and I think either one would be acceptable in your portfolio once you have researched them. Most people think of MLPs in the oil, natural gas, and propane industries, but they are in all sectors, and some of the really good MLP units are in real estate.

Because real estate is more complex and slower to generate a positive income, you don't want to have more than 5 percent of your retirement money in it, whether your investment is in REITs and MLPs directly or it is in ETFs or mutual funds that invest in real estate holdings. (Your home is not a retirement investment as long as you are living in it!)

Rentals and Direct Ownership

Properly handled, rental properties can be an excellent source of income in retirement. You do have to ask yourself some critical questions: Are you experienced in identifying quality properties and spotting those problems that sellers might conceal? Are you adept at assessing the value of properties? Do you want to deal with people (your renters) and their problems?

More than anything else, what you really need to determine before you get involved in real estate is your staying power. *Staying power* depends on having the following in adequate amounts:

- Liquidity: freely available cash
- An asset base: your total wealth—including retirement and non-retirement savings
- Time to be patient

Good real estate investors will wait patiently for years to find the right properties, and they won't be rushed into paying too much just to get involved. These investors have the financial means (and the asset base) to hold onto a property and pay for its upkeep even if it doesn't rent out as quickly as expected. Finally, they also have sufficient resources on hand (liquidity) to pay both the scheduled bills on their investment properties and any unexpected or emergency costs that pop up, without having to sell any assets or raise money in a hurry.

If you don't have staying power, directly investing in individual pieces of land or buildings is a very dangerous idea. If any of your retirement savings are tied up in real estate when a market bubble pops (or when property taxes spike or a natural disaster occurs, or something else happens), that money might be gone for years or longer. Are you able to take that risk?

Running rental properties can be a hassle. You have to worry about the maintenance and upkeep, particularly if you manage your properties yourself—angry tenants can call you at midnight and tell you that the heating or plumbing is not working, and you'll have to solve the problem. And you also have to worry about whether the rent will come in on time. If the thought that you might have to sue tenants or evict them for nonpayment of rent unsettles your stomach, being a landlord is probably not for you. Ultimately, you have to assess whether the benefits of receiving rent outweigh the costs and hassles of property management and maintenance. Everybody's threshold for hassles is different, but when it comes to retirement, your top priority is to protect your wealth.

On the positive side, rental properties *can* provide solid monthly income. Ideally, if you are managing your properties correctly and the market is healthy, you will earn a good spread on each property. (The *spread* is the difference between the cost of the property, including taxes and mortgage payments, and the rent you get.) A healthy spread means the properties will pay for themselves fairly quickly. Every market is different, but it is not uncommon to earn annual returns in the range of the high single digits—a level of return that is competitive with the stock market.

If you find yourself asking "Is investing in real estate a good idea for me?" then common wisdom suggests the answer is almost certainly no. Since that may seem a little too cut-and-dried, let me explain in a little more detail. If you are not already experienced in buying and holding properties with the intent of developing them, rehabilitating them, or renting them out, then retirement is almost certainly **not** the time to start.

I am certainly not going to tell you not to do it, but some of our clients have grown older, slower, or sick, and they could no longer manage the rental real estate part of their portfolio. It began to be a burden instead of an asset. Their investments were making reasonable returns when they were actively managing their properties, but when things had to be turned over to a real estate firm to take care of the properties, fees made it a less attractive investment.

REITs and MLPs

Unfortunately, it can be very difficult and cost prohibitive to invest directly in the most lucrative real estate. Farmland and timberland, for instance, are some of the best performing investment categories that anybody's money can buy. The trouble is that there are so few ways to successfully invest in them. You can go out and buy a farm or a stand of trees, but you will have to manage that land yourself, and you will find that the costs of running a small parcel of land suck away a lot of the gains. It is difficult to really do well with less than 1,000 acres of timberland. With timberland selling for about $1,200 an acre these days, you can see the scale of the problem. There are partnerships that invest in all types of land and real estate, but they tend to be almost exclusively for wealthier investors, and the partnerships impose high minimum investments and rigorous net worth requirements.

There are numerous individual REITs and mutual funds and ETFs that include REITs that you could consider investing in. Put in the "10 best REITs" (or mutual funds) in your search engine. You'll see a wide variety of lists from different sources. Once you have a short list, you can research the companies just as you would a stock or mutual fund by using Value Line, Morningstar, or Yahoo! Finance.

Each fund has a slightly different twist. Some offer income from real estate and some from growth. Many have been around over 10 years, and some for more than 15 years. You can see how well they did in good times and bad, and that information will help you make your investment deci-sions. Not to beat a dead horse, but the rules that apply to finding good mutual funds apply just as readily to finding good real estate mutual funds. Look for consistent, team-oriented management and a long-term track record of success.

There are also many ETFs available in the real estate space. Although I would typically prefer a top-notch real estate mutual fund over a pas-sive ETF, there is probably an exception or two. The number of real estate mutual funds with significant overseas exposure is quite small, and ETFs that are indexed to global or international real estate indexes may give investors a hard-to-duplicate diversification option.

I'll explore MLPs later in the chapter since they exist in many areas, not just real estate.

Annuities

It's impossible to talk about retirement and not talk about annuities. They are such a popular option for retirement that the top five provid-ers (which are all insurance companies) in the United States hold close to $700 billion in annuity fund assets alone. Millions of Americans have pur-chased annuities. This section is not an attempt to cover everything about annuities. It is intended to give you enough information to help you decide whether annuities are for you or not.

In the simplest terms, an *annuity* is a contract that provides for a regu-lar stream of payments over a fixed or indefinite period of time. The buyer of an annuity gives his or her money to the annuity provider, either as a series of regular payments or a lump sum fixed payment. Those funds build over time, and when the agreed-upon time comes, the annuity pro-vider makes payments back to the buyer.

Annuities are actually rather unusual financial instruments because they share characteristics of both life insurance and other types of invest-ments. Moreover, even though they can be issued only by life insurance companies, they are regulated by the Securities and Exchange Commission. Annuities have two phases—one phase in which the customer contributes money and that money builds up, and a second phase in which the cus-tomer gets that money back from the insurance company.

Annuities differ in how those payments are structured. An *immediate annuity* begins making payments immediately, while still taking advan-tage of the tax-deferred growth of the principal. Some annuities make payments over a set period of time, while others will pay out over the life of the recipient. It is also possible to get *life annuities* with a benefit rider that will allow another person (like a spouse or other family member) to continue collecting those payments. There are also various hybrids available—some life annuities, for instance, will also contain a *period certain clause* that guarantees payments for a certain minimum number of years no matter when the annuitant dies.

Tax-deferred annuities came into being during the 1970s, and like retirement accounts—such as IRAs or 401(k)s—they are a way of building savings in a tax-deferred fashion. There are two major types of tax-deferred annuities. A *fixed tax-deferred annuity* grows almost exclusively due to interest income. A *variable annuity* allows for money to be invested in mutual funds, but many critics say the cost is too high compared to the fees you might incur by investing in mutual funds yourself.

Let me go on record as saying I don't like variable annuities. If you put $300,000 in one, you are giving a salesperson 7 to 8 percent, which he or she splits with the company. That's about $12,000 in the salesperson's pocket. No wonder the salespeople like annuities! There is a great article in *Forbes* about variable annuities. Search for Carolyn T. Geer's "The Great Annuity Rip-Off" at http://www.forbes.com.

A third variety came into the market in the 1990s—the *fixed indexed annuity*. This hybrid product carries a guaranteed minimum return from the issuing insurance company (provided that the customer does not cancel it early), but it has the potential for growth in excess of that amount. Perhaps not surprisingly, these annuities often carry higher fees.

Everything about annuities makes them look and sound like regular investment products, but they are not. An annuity is an insurance contract. Annuities are ultimately underwritten by insurance companies, but they have very little in common with your insurance policy. The annuity focuses on paying money over the owner's lifetime—or over a defined period of time. It does not focus on death benefits as an insurance policy does. In most cases, the proceeds from an insurance policy are tax free, whereas earnings on an annuity are taxed. You can buy an annuity from just about any firm that offers money management products—even banks, brokerage firms, and financial planners—not just insurance agents.

Why are annuities so popular? There are many reasons. The death of defined benefits pension plans almost certainly has to have something to do with it. In the past, retirees knew pretty much what they could expect to get each month in retirement benefits. But with defined contribution pension plans, such as IRAs and 401(k)s, there are no such guarantees.

To some extent, an annuity is a way for a person to convert a defined contribution plan into a defined benefit plan.

Longer lifespans also have something to do with the popularity of annuities. Although it is possible to buy annuities that will continue to pay benefits for the life of the surviving spouse (or some other recipient) or annuities that pay out a guaranteed minimum total amount, there is still a basic risk that you will meet your demise before you earn a fair return on the money you spent to buy that annuity. As a matter of fact, the insurance company that underwrites the annuity is *counting on it*! The whole annuity "system" relies on the fact that some people will die relatively soon after buying the annuity—these people basically subsidize the folks who end up living exceptionally long lives.

On first look, annuities seem like such a perfect idea for retirement. You take your life savings as a lump sum (or at least a big piece of it), and you use that money to buy an annuity. Then you collect a check every month that covers your expenses and financial needs. In principle, you have none of the risk, hassle, or time commitment of managing your investments on a month-to-month or year-to-year basis.

If this book has taught you anything, nothing is ever quite that simple. Annuities can be quite expensive, and many types will not perform any better than they advertise (and may actually do worse when the fees and costs are factored in). What's more, the money is not necessarily guaranteed. These companies can go out of business, as can the insurers who back their commitments. Even if the money is recoverable, that process can take time, and you may find yourself short of funds to meet your day-to-day needs while waiting to get your money back on a failed annuity.

Think about buying an annuity like buying a car. Every option that you want on your car raises the price. On your "plain vanilla" annuity, the options you choose (commonly called *riders*) are just like getting an optional piece of equipment on an automobile. The more riders, the more it costs you. That means you either get less money with each payment, or you end up spending more for the annuity up front. Check the options carefully!

Despite their problems, annuities may yet be appropriate for some people. One advantage of an annuity is that it is a "mindless" investment in the sense that you do not need to do anything yourself to keep the check arriving every month. While I do believe you can do just as well (if not better) than an annuity with a portfolio of mutual funds, there may be situations in which that is not a viable option. As unpleasant as it is to think about, if you receive a diagnosis that suggests you may face significant declines in your mental capabilities, it may be a prudent move to put *some* money into an annuity.

Annuities can also be appealing to people who have maxed out their other retirement savings options. There are annual limits on how much you can contribute to a 401(k) or an IRA, but there are no limits on buying an annuity. Annuities are typically bought with after-tax dollars, but the value of the annuity builds over time without incurring any taxes along the way. So if you are already saving as much as you can in tax-shielded accounts, buying an annuity with any "extra" cash gives you another option for building up retirement savings in a tax-advantaged way.

All in all, whether you go with mutual funds or a stock and bond portfolio, there are better (and more affordable) options (mutual funds or stocks and bonds) than annuities in almost every situation.

What Are the Costs of Annuities?

Annuities happen to be incredible "honeypots" for the companies that sell them. Commissions that take 6 to 7 percent off the top are not uncommon, and there are ongoing fees that further whittle away your hard-earned money. (All of a sudden, mutual fund loads and brokerage fees seem small!) You'll notice that they never seem to mention commissions on the TV ads.

If you are interested in buying an annuity, you are probably better off ignoring the pleas and pitches of your local insurance agent until you find out as much as you can. Instead, start with http://www.immediateannuities .com, and find out what "retail" companies charge. Not everyone charges the same thing. Then go to an online brokerage firm like Vanguard or Fidelity, and check the cost of annuities as part of their offering a "complete" investment package to people.

Shop around. There is a huge amount of competition in this market, and you can save a lot of money (or get more for your money) with a little bit of work on your part. While you're at it, pay attention to the details, and make sure you're comparing the same sorts of annuities—some annuities, for instance, have lower fees because they do not offer features like guaranteed minimum death benefits.

What Are the Drawbacks of Annuities?

Annuities take time to build value if you are *not* buying an *immediate annuity*. While you can certainly buy *immediate annuities* that begin paying the month after you buy them, other annuities require a build-up period.

To enforce this, most annuity contracts limit the amount that can be withdrawn without incurring a fee, and that fee disappears over time (typically 7 to 12 years). As a result, if you will need regular payments in a fairly short period of time, annuities may not be a great option because you will pay for that privilege of early access.

Annuities may also limit your liquidity to some extent. If you agree to make payments into your annuity over time, that will be a contractual obligation that you must maintain if you wish to preserve the value of that annuity. What's more, you generally cannot tap annuity assets before age 59½ without incurring a 10 percent tax penalty from the IRS. Annuities also are restrictive in that they pay what they promise to pay, not necessarily what you need. If you find that one year's spending needs are significantly different from what you had planned, you can sell some of your mutual funds or bonds or other investments. But with an annuity, you are much more limited in that respect.

And there's that matter of expenses. While the customer buying the annuity will not necessarily (or even often) pay that commission directly, the insurance company more than recaptures the money from the high fees and expenses that it charges the customer. The tax-deferred growth is certainly a perk, but investors who make sure to fully invest in retirement programs can gain the same benefits.

Many people like that annuities do not ask them or require them to have any ongoing responsibility or input in the investing process. The problem is that people just pay too much for the dubious convenience that annuities offer. A competent fee-based financial manager can move your money between equities and bonds, and he or she probably will charge you quite a bit less. Likewise, remember that your annuity funds are being invested in the same stock and bond markets that mutual funds **can and do** access. If a mutual fund beats its target, you get to keep the difference; if an annuity does better than its target, the company keeps the money!

I also do not like how often annuity products are included in 401(k) or other retirement plans. Sometimes, they are the only options that are offered. These retirement plans are already shielded from taxes during the contribution and growth phases, so the tax-deferred growth benefit of annuities is totally wasted in these accounts. What that means is that investors stuck with these options are basically forced into overpaying for investment performance on a par with (or inferior to) cheaper mutual fund options. Why would a company do this? Like most things, it comes down to money—many companies want to find the cheapest retirement benefits provider, not necessarily the best.

Investors considering annuities also need to remember that there is no federal guarantee or insurance for them like the Federal Deposit Insurance Corporation (FDIC) guarantees. Since annuities are treated as insurance products, they fall under the jurisdiction of state insurance commissions, and the rules that govern insurance, guarantees, and investor recoveries vary from state to state. Some states require only that annuities be guaranteed up to $100,000, and the process of recovering your money can be difficult and expensive. There are guarantee and insurance programs for annuities (and the companies that back them), but investors need to check into this protection before buying to see just how much they can get.

Some people have used annuities for the "bond" part of their portfolio. When annuities were paying 7 to 8 percent, that practice might have had some merit, but today, I think it would be a terrible mistake. You can do better using a 10-year laddered bond portfolio or a few well-chosen mutual funds that own fixed-income investments like bonds.

Although I do not typically endorse annuities, I can see how they are appropriate in certain circumstances. If you simply do not want to be responsible for your retirement income or you have reason to believe you may not be able to carry out these responsibilities, an annuity may be the better option. Likewise, annuities can offer a "ground level" amount of income every year that you do not have to worry about, no matter what the economy or stock market does.

Gold

Gold is one of those timeless investments that still manages to go through bouts of timeliness. During the worst periods of the Great Recession beginning in 2008, we saw one of those periodic bull markets in gold. Whenever there are worries about government solvency, inflation, and whether politicians really have the willpower to make the tough decisions that are necessary to keep an economy healthy, there is typically a run on gold.

Since my focus is on preserving your wealth and making it last through a long and satisfying retirement, should soon-to-be-retired people look to gold as a way to protect themselves from the twin specters of inflation and poor governance? I don't think so.

Gold really is not as good an investment as the goldbugs brag. It actually has a pretty erratic history when it comes to serving as a hedge against inflation. On a year-to-year basis, the moves in gold prices have a very low correlation to inflation, and gold can underperform for decades at a stretch. What actually seems to be more common is for gold to lag for years, catch up in a sudden burst, overshoot, and then decline again.

Gold produces no income of any kind. A bond will pay you a coupon twice a year, a high-yield savings account will pay you interest every month, and a dividend paying stock (or mutual fund) will typically pay you four times a year. What does gold do? It just sits there and shines. In fact, gold can actually cost you money—you may have to pay cash every year for the safekeeping of your gold.

The worst problem with gold is that it guarantees mediocrity. Putting 2 or 3 percent of your wealth in gold won't hurt you much . . . but it also won't help you if things get really bad. If you buy enough gold to really hedge your money—something in the order of 30 percent or more—then you risk significant underperformance if the bad times **don't** come! Plus, you'll have to sell off some of your holdings any time you need cash (reducing your ability to achieve long-term growth).

There are ways to gain exposure to most (if not all) of the benefits of gold without actually owning bullion, although there are plenty of risks and costs involved. Several exchange-traded funds are available in which the shares represent ownership claims to actual gold held in vaults. Investors can also buy stock in the companies that mine gold. As gold prices rise, the share prices of mining companies rise as well.

Mutual funds may once again be the best option. Funds that buy the shares of mining companies can produce income (unlike gold itself) because some of these companies do pay dividends. That is not a trivial detail for investors who want the comfort of holding gold but cannot forgo interest-producing investments.

My usual rules apply here: look for funds with team-based management and long-term records of excellence. Consider a broad, diversified resources fund—one that has exposure to metals other than just gold, as well as perhaps other commodities like timber and agriculture. Of the more than 40 mutual funds that invest in gold and that have been around over 10 years, many have had lousy returns, compared to the market in general. I don't understand why people would want to own something that they could not use in retirement.

That said, if gold is what it takes for you to sleep at night, then you need to own some gold. As part of your overall asset allocation, I think that you should **never** own more than 2 or 3 percent of your wealth in gold. If you do buy gold, buy it from reputable people and in the most cost-effective ways.

Target-Date Funds

Target-date funds are another example of a financial product that sounds great when you're talking about it over lunch but looks worse and worse the more you investigate it. In theory, a target-date fund eliminates the need for investors to worry about how to allocate their money between stocks and bonds (and different types of stocks and bonds) as they age and approach retirement. Alas, there are some thorn bushes between theory and reality.

Target-date funds are designed as hands-off, long-term investments that will hold a shifting mix of risk and stock and/or bond exposure over time. Specifically, the funds will invest more conservatively as time goes on. Supposedly, they do pretty much what you would expect a full-time personalized financial planner to do for you. These funds have fast become one of the most popular retirement products available, approaching almost $2 trillion in assets under management.

In principle, you find a target-date fund whose date matches your anticipated date of retirement. The fund invests in a fashion that the financial manager believes is consistent for a portfolio with that amount of time left. Along the way, the manager will shift between stocks and bonds, between growth and income, and between risk and conservatism in a fashion that would be consistent with the conventional wisdom on retirement investing—that is, less stock and less risk as the retirement date approaches.

I think the conventional wisdom is largely too conservative—leading people away from holding enough equity and enough riskier equity (like foreign stocks) and short-changing their ability to grow their portfolio and stay ahead of inflation. Likewise, I see signs that target-date funds are being bullied by regulators and outside observers into holding less equity so that the funds are less volatile for the owners. Here, then, is another reason to keep your investments in your own hands—you have the freedom to invest (and take risks) as you think best.

Are all the plans alike? At random, I picked eight funds from eight different companies, which were listed as target-date funds for 2021 to 2025. The U.S. stock allocation for these funds ranged from 34.39 to 52.25 percent. The objectives ran from Growth to Growth and Income to Asset Allocation. The returns for the last five years for these eight funds ran from 12.72 to 16.40 percent—and the worst of these funds was down 33.48 percent in 2008. (The S&P 500 was down 37 percent.) Target-date funds are not all equal—not by a long shot!

In practice, the only real "target" with these funds is your money—the fees and expenses they can deduct from your account every year and whatever principal amounts they can convince you to keep in their hands.

If you do want to think about adding target-date funds to your portfolio, here are some important questions you must ask.

Question 1. What Is the Glide Path?

The term *glide path* refers to how a fund allocates its money—specifically, how much of the fund's assets are invested in equities and how that allocation is expected to change over the life of the fund. Target-date funds have taken a lot of criticism for being too heavily invested in equities for too long—leading to a lot more near-term volatility. While some of this criticism is misguided (equities are vital for outpacing inflation), many investors are fleeing faster than anybody had planned for, making the equity exposure more problematic.

If nothing else, examine the glide path to see how it fits in with your spending plans. Not every fund targets the same explicit level of income replacement, so you need to know where a fund's objectives and plans stand relative to your needs. You also want to know how the company arrived at that intended path and what sorts of things could lead them to change it.

Question 2. Is This Fund Designed to Get Me to *Retirement* or Through *Retirement*?

This is one of my biggest complaints about target-date funds. Most companies started off by offering funds that were intended to build assets up *to* the targeted date of the buyer's retirement. Those companies realized that they would prefer to keep your money in their hands longer, so many of these funds quietly morphed into instruments with much longer time horizons.

This matters because it significantly alters the point at which you can expect the fund to reach its most conservative allocations. A fund that is structured on the through-retirement basis may not reach its most conservative allocations until 10 or 20 years after you retire, and you may find that some funds are still invested as much as 80 percent in equities at the actual date of your retirement.

None of this is a deal breaker, but you need to know what you are agreeing to when you buy a particular fund.

Question 3. How Much Will It Cost?

Frankly, you should ask this question about every investment you consider, but it can be even more important in the case of these funds. The typically high fees of these funds are a big negative for me.

Question 4. Does the Fund Use Strategic or Tactical Allocation Analysis?

Every fund will have targeted allocations. Some will follow a strategic allocation model, others will follow a tactical allocation model. (I introduced those allocation approaches back in Chapter 6.) Many will give their managers the authority to deviate from those targets to some extent. That "to some extent" part is the real kicker, and you need to know just how much discretion an individual fund manager (or team) may have. Individual discretion is one of those things that's good right up until the point where it isn't—fund managers should have some flexibility but not so much that they could make wildly unexpected moves and produce large losses.

Question 5. How Diversified Is the Fund?

This question is also fairly straightforward. In short, you need to know how the fund manager invests the money. Ideally, there will be a good mix of stocks across multiple industries, multiple size categories (large-cap, mid-cap, and so on), and diverse regions. Likewise, the bond holdings should be spread around government, corporate, and other types of debt. It is also important to investigate how the diversification of the target-date fund fits into your other holdings—you do not want to own multiple funds that hold more or less the same stocks and bonds.

There is no doubt that target-date funds serve a very real and understandable need. Unfortunately, they don't do that very effectively if you have invested in the "wrong" one. They have been relatively successful products for Wall Street, but it is not so clear that they have been very successful for the regular people who buy them.

Limited Partnerships

If you can pardon the pun, I think limited partnerships have only limited value for most investors. The attractive part of limited partnerships is that they are a legal way of organizing a company in such a way that the business minimizes its taxes while simultaneously producing income for its owners that is itself tax shielded. Given that most retired people find themselves in lower tax brackets anyway, I am not sure that the benefits are worth the hassles. They can be expensive (in price and in commissions), and they can be hard to sell.

Master Limited Partnerships are a different matter. Many MLPs trade publicly like any other stock. These partnerships tend to be involved in real estate or in resource-related businesses like mining, energy production, or energy transportation (such as pipelines), and they often pay a dividend that works out to a yield between 5 and 8 percent a year.

If you do decide to include these in your portfolio, make sure that you do not buy them in tax-deferred accounts like IRAs. Because MLPs do not pay taxes on their earnings, the government frowns on investors trying to take what amounts to a double tax deferral, and the IRS will apply something called "unrelated business taxable income" to you if you own them in an IRA and earn more than $1,000 from them.

On the whole, these assets fit best outside the realm of retirement planning, so you might want to limit your investments in MLPs to your non-retirement funds.

Conclusion

As we wrap up our look at the different types of investments for your retirement portfolio, you'll notice that the complexity of the instruments **and** my cautions about them have increased greatly. While all of these investments have some merits, it's important to ask yourself, "Are these appropriate for my *retirement*?" If your goals are growth with controlled risk and liquidity when you need the money, you'll find that many of these investments don't pass muster for your retirement portfolio. So tread wisely here—and give a little more thought to mutual funds, stocks, and bonds.

11

Social Security

In 2012, the average Social Security check was $1,229 per month, which is $14,748 a year. That average is the same as working for $7.37 per hour for 2,000 hours (50 weeks times a 40-hour week). This is before the Medicare monthly premium is taken out, which reduces the amount by about $300 per month. So the average recipient is really getting roughly **$929 per month**.

By some estimates, *one-quarter* of retirees depend on Social Security for *90 percent or more* of their retirement income, and more than half of retirees get 50 percent of their retirement income from the program. Considering that even high earners may get as much as 20 percent of their annual retirement income from Social Security, it is a topic that affects every retiree and *everyone planning their retirement.*

There are plenty of criticisms about Social Security, but it does have at least two solid positives in its favor. First, it is really the only source of income that I can reliably say will be guaranteed for the life of anyone currently in sight of retirement—regardless of the rhetoric that comes out of Washington. Second, Social Security attempts to keep pace with inflation—the "official" rate of inflation that is used to adjust payments may not be the best or most accurate measure of real inflation, but it is better than nothing.

The big question is this: How long can you survive on your monthly Social Security payments? Too many people allow themselves to think that Social Security is the core of their retirement plan—and everything else is a supplement. Those people end up on the short end of the stick after retirement, often coming up short when bills come due.

My philosophy is exactly the opposite. Your own retirement investments are the heart of your plan. Social Security should be the supplement.

That's why I've placed this chapter deep in Part Three, "Retirement Tools and Resources," after mutual funds, stocks, bonds, and the other essential parts of your portfolio. Social Security is the "icing on the cake" and nothing more.

Yes, Social Security is also your money too. It just needs to be regarded as a smaller slice of the pie. While it is sometimes talked about as an entitlement program, that really is not entirely true. An entitlement is a guaranteed benefit that the government chooses to provide without an offsetting contribution, typically out of the general budget and with the amounts determined largely by political processes. In comparison, Social Security is much more like a mix of mandatory insurance and an inflation-protected bond—you paid for it (through direct taxes), and your benefits are determined by established mathematical formulas. So, while political debates roil, you can expect to keep receiving those benefits.

How Much Will I Get from It?

Earlier, you established your goals and a plan to get you there. Now that we've folded your investment portfolio into your plan as a source of cash flow and capital growth, let's begin to factor Social Security in by determining how much you will take out.

Social Security is set up such that the benefits you get upon retirement are tied to how long you worked, how much you earned, and when you choose to start receiving benefits. Put simply, the more you make, the longer you work, and the longer you wait to take benefits, the larger your monthly check will be (as long as you worked for a total of 10 years). Of course, these benefits are subject to taxation, so your net benefits will be impacted by your other sources of income.

The Social Security Administration sends periodic statements that outline your past earnings history and the sort of payments you can expect upon retirement. These are just rough estimates, however, and a lot of important details can change in the meantime. Your earnings, the rate of inflation, and when you choose to take benefits will have significant impacts on the actual amount you receive. It is, however, a credible ballpark estimate that you can use as part of your overall planning process.

Instead of immediately tossing these reports into the "circular file cabinet," take a moment to read through them. Make sure you check the earnings history for any errors—not only is it a lot easier to fix (or get an explanation for) any inaccuracies before you put in for benefits, but it gets harder to remember your earnings as time goes on. (Quick quiz: Do you know what your annual earnings were 15 years ago? See what I mean?)

You can get some general answers to your questions about retirement benefits at Social Security's website (http://www.ssa.gov), but you won't find many specifics about your own payments there. That's why the statements are important planning tools.

How Can I Get the Greatest Benefits out of the System?

There are so many different ways that you can get Social Security other than the plain vanilla way of working all of your life and then applying to get it at 62 or at the age when you can get your full benefits. It's up to you, however, to explore them. The best place to begin is at the Benefits section of http://www.ssa.gov. This can be a confusing and convoluted experience, but you might find some opportunities to maximize your benefits.

For instance, one spouse might want to draw on his or her own benefits starting at 65 and then switch to the higher payout when he or she goes to take his or her payment from the other spouse at age 70. Social Security benefits also offer a good example of the potentially high costs of early retirement. Although people are eligible to receive Social Security benefits at age 62, doing so permanently reduces the payments they will receive by 20 percent or more. In contrast, those who hold off until age 70 to start collecting can get **increased** benefits above what they would have received if they had started collecting at age 66. There is a very definite advantage in waiting as long as possible before receiving benefits. The best way to get that nice bonus is by either working until 70 and accruing additional benefits—or by treating Social Security as a supplement to your primary retirement plan and waiting to tap into it at 70.

If you request benefits early but end up regretting the decision, the Social Security Administration gives you a limited chance (within 12 months of your original benefits claim) to change your mind. You must pay back what you have been paid without any interest. (You may be able to obtain a refund on any taxes you paid on those benefits.) You can then refile your benefits claim later and get the better (higher) payout rate. This is a very valuable option if you decide to return to work after a brief "experiment" of retirement or if you find that you just do not need the extra income.

Marital status also affects your potential Social Security payments, and in almost uniformly positive ways. First, spouses are entitled to payments worth up to 50 percent of the higher earner's benefits (assuming those would be higher than the benefits they would receive otherwise), although a low-earning spouse does have to wait until the official "full retirement age" to collect that 50 percent. Better still, it does not affect the payments to the other spouse in any way (the payments are not reduced because of the spouse's decision to receive 50 percent).

Next, although a spouse cannot receive payments until the other files, the higher-earning spouse can "file and suspend"—that is, he or she can file for full benefits but have the payments suspended, and he or she can continue working or simply wait until the maximum benefit level is reached. Last, widows and widowers can receive the higher earner's full benefits, and they can actually receive those benefits starting at age 60 (though not at the full level). These rules also apply to divorcees as long as you were married for at least 10 years and as long as you do not remarry. It is possible, then, for two (or more) ex-spouses to collect up to 50 percent of the benefits of a single earner as long as they meet that 10-year minimum and do not remarry.

Waiting for these extra benefits does come with a catch: you have to be alive to collect them. Grim as it is to contemplate, if you have not yet put in for benefits and you have received a grievous medical prognosis, you may want to consider changing your plans and collecting as much of your payments as possible.

As much as I recommend waiting for benefits (and thereby increasing the amount you will receive), please remember that Social Security and Medicare are **not** the same program. There is no improvement in benefits if you delay filing for Medicare and no advantage in doing so. So even if you do not plan to take any Social Security for many years, be sure to get your Medicare filings in promptly ahead of your sixty-fifth birthday.

While there are many Social Security calculators that you can use online, you should make an appointment and sit down with a Social Security representative and discuss the pros and cons of the different ways you can receive payments. Visit http://www.ssa.gov and read all of the material before you go talk with someone at the Social Security office. It pays to have read everything so that you can enter into a good discussion and be sure that everything is being covered. There are some ways that you can "tweak" the system that will astound you.

Will Social Security Be There?

Social Security seems to be the subject of a lot of fear mongering among politicians, journalists, and assorted social commentators. It is a huge part of the federal budget: Social Security payments amount to more than

$500 billion a year and represent more than 20 percent of the federal budget, and there is a very real likelihood that the taxes coming in from workers will not be sufficient to cover the payouts to benefit recipients if things do not change. But that does not mean there is any imminent danger.

There are never any guarantees when it comes to government programs, but it is difficult to imagine that Social Security will ever go away entirely. A long-term program like Social Security is a lot like quicksand—it is so much easier to get into it than to get out. Even if it were legal for the federal government to essentially renege on a multigenerational promise, the reality is that the government depends upon the "tax now, pay later" mechanism of Social Security, so it is not likely to go away.

First of all, the government has several alternatives to bridge the gap. A more open policy toward immigration could bring in larger numbers of younger workers, workers whose taxes could help pay for those benefits and who would not necessarily be eligible for benefits themselves. Of course, the government can also increase the tax rates on the income of those who work, and this is the system that much of Western Europe uses to pay for its extensive social spending programs.

Along similar lines, it is probable that inflation and taxation will reduce the value of whatever benefits Social Security pays out in the future. The government has tinkered with the *cost-of-living adjustment* (also known as COLA) before, and artificially suppressing that below the real rate of inflation can help plug the gap. Likewise, the government can always either increase the tax rates paid by Social Security recipients or change the dollar amounts where those taxes begin to apply.

It also seems like a pretty good bet that the government will push up the age at which somebody can collect full benefits—so your kids or grandkids may learn to think of 70 as the "normal" retirement age. That not only pushes up the day of reckoning but it also creates the possibility of collecting more taxes in the interim (assuming those people keep working).

Another possibility is that the government may introduce something called *means testing*—essentially cutting or restricting benefits to wealthier people. There is some chance that the government could eventually declare some people ineligible for Social Security benefits because they already have too much money. Given the questionable legality of this move, it would be more likely that the government would just find a way to increase taxes on these people (taking back with one hand what they give with the other).

The biggest potential change to Social Security could be the partial privatization of the system. Politicians have periodically floated the idea of either investing part of the trust fund in the stocks and bonds of U.S. companies or giving individual workers the right (and responsibility) to invest the money for themselves. If that sounds similar to what has happened in the world of corporate retirement policies, you are on to something: moving Social Security into the hands of individual workers would be another example of transferring still more responsibility for retirement savings and planning onto individuals. For most people, though, this would be a significant increase in the risk that goes with retirement planning.

Luckily, although these options are always "on the table," they are unpopular enough that no swift changes will be made. If the changes ever come, you will likely have years of warning. However, because Social Security *can* change, it's a good time to remind you once again . . .

Conclusion: Try to Make Social Security the Dessert, Not the Main Course

There is no question that the importance of Social Security to your retirement plan is going to be a function of your particular circumstances. If you were an above average saver throughout your working life, you might find that you can meet most (if not all) of your retirement spending needs even if you never really made a large salary. Likewise, a couple who earned a lot during their careers could find that Social Security is vital to their ongoing spending needs if they neglected to save and invest before retirement.

If you are still young enough to have a choice, I suggest you choose to save as much as you can and rely on Social Security as little as possible (and wait as long as you can to begin taking the benefits)—ideally targeting less than one-third of your retirement income needs as coming from Social Security. The more you have to depend on Social Security, the more you have to depend on politicians and their decisions about the federal budget when it comes to the quality of your own retirement.

12

Finding the Right Financial Adviser and Investment Manager

Everyone reading this book is capable of fully outlining his or her goals, dreams, and wishes for retirement. That is why I wrote this book—as a guide to creating and implementing your own personal plan. By the same token, I realize that your career and financial success may take a lot of your time, and you may not have the space on your calendar that you can dedicate to the full management of your retirement plan. If so, then as you start to build your plan for managing and investing your retirement savings, you need to consider whether you want to hire professionals to help you with some (or most) of the job.

You may have attempted the hands-on approach and found you just weren't up to the task. You may have decided that you simply do not want the burden of doing this and would like to lean on a professional instead.

First things first, you should understand the difference between *financial advisers* and *investment managers*.

You may encounter financial professionals of many stripes—and titles. As in every field, there will be some great ones and some not-so-great ones. Some financial advisers are fee-only Financial Planners who charge you a flat rate for setting up a plan. You may only meet with that planner once a year after that for an annual progress review. Some are sales-driven Financial Planners who sell loaded mutual funds, insurance, and other products "off their shelf." Personally, I prefer the former because I like to put a plan together without the pressure of a sales pitch.

The best Certified Financial Planner I knew only needed a legal pad and two three-hour meetings to get his clients organized. Once a basic plan was in place, he recommended different professionals in the community: an attorney for legal needs, an insurance agent that specialized in long-term care (a vital topic you'll learn more about in Chapter 15), a firm to help manage some of the client's money, and so on. He was only interested in being sure that his clients got the best help for whatever they needed in an efficient and professional manner. He would meet with each of his clients once a year to review and adjust their plans.

What's the difference between a Financial Planner and a Certified Financial Planner (CFP)? A CFP undergoes more formal training and certification to attain that title. Even if a planner lacks that certificate, you may find that you will get great advice and dedicated service. As always, check out any potential planner's qualifications and references!

An investment manager may have an MBA degree or a CFA (Certified Financial Analyst) designation. They generally only manage personal and/or retirement accounts, moving money in and out of investments that are appropriate for a client's existing plan. Some investment managers *do* have a CFP designation as well. That allows the manager to better understand the client's total financial picture to help properly position the client's investments.

There are numerous good independent investment managers, so you do not need to employ a broker with a big brokerage firm just to access an investment manager. You will pay more than you should, and you may just be getting what the bosses in the fancy headquarters have decided is the most profitable flavor of the month. You always want to be able to talk with the person directly who manages your money and understands your goals. You do not want a broker who hands you off to a salesperson who knows every excuse in the book.

I have always believed in that philosophy, and that is why I became involved in financial planning and investment management for my clients back in the 1980s. Most of the brokerage people I knew thought I was insane. The most frequent comment I heard was, "Just look at how much more money you could be making." To me, the most important thing is taking care of people in a fair way. My parents always felt that way, and maybe I got it through osmosis. If you love your money, you owe it to yourself to find a financial adviser who is able to help you with all aspects of planning—and who can help you access professional management with the same philosophy of being available to work with you directly.

You may already have people working for you (on retirement questions or just general finances), and now would be a good time to evaluate whether they are still the right choices for your needs. Of course, there are plenty of potential candidates ready to jump in and serve you (and claim their new fee revenue!). In fact, as a professional in your line of work, you probably get regular solicitations from people who want to be your financial adviser. That's because you are, in all likelihood, listed in a database of potential high-net-worth individuals. Thanks to that, there will be no shortage of salespeople (good *and* bad) looking for you. The trick is for you to find the right people for you, your family, your plan, and your money.

The following are some of the things I believe you ought to consider and evaluate when thinking about finding the best professionals for your situation.

Goals First

Before you have any conversations with others, you need a clear vision of your retirement goals. (That's the work we did in Chapter 3.) If you don't set your goals in place early, you run the risk of falling into that cookie-cutter retirement package. You don't need a plan in hand. A good adviser and investment manager can help you build and execute a plan. But you do need to have honest, clear, and personal goals established if you want to hire the right people to help you reach them.

Reputation Matters

The overwhelming majority of people working in the securities business are honest people, but there *are* a number of bad apples in the barrel. Given how much damage a shady character can do to your financial future, it definitely makes sense to spend some time establishing that you are not dealing with the next Bernie Madoff. Too many people just gave everything to Madoff and did not investigate his returns. Never put all of your eggs in one basket! You need diversification!

For beginners, ask around within your circle of friends and professional acquaintances—people are usually pretty eager to recommend people they have liked or warn you about people who didn't live up to their standards. But let me caution you. When I was a young practitioner, I got a lot of calls on the weekends from parents whose children were having problems. When I asked a few questions, it became apparent that they had used the advice of their next door neighbor or a new friend living nearby. More often than not, they did not share the same values. They were obsessed with either "convenient or cheap"—not necessarily quality. You get the picture. Carefully check out the referrals before you go.

Remember, we are talking about retirement. Just because someone's done a good job managing a colleague's stock portfolio, it doesn't mean that he or she is going to be adept at navigating the intricacies of understanding *your* goals and implementing *your* plan. As I've said before, investing *for* retirement is very different than investing *in* retirement.

Likewise, you should check any potential adviser or manager through the Financial Industry Regulatory Authority (FINRA) database. The financial services industry is largely self-regulating, and FINRA is the organization that establishes the rules, standards, and enforcement policies for financial firms and their employees. FINRA has a free database (http://www.finra.org/Investors/ToolsCalculators/BrokerCheck/) that the public can use to investigate brokers, advisers, and other professionals. If financial services professionals have ever been sanctioned or if they have been a party to an arbitration proceeding, that information will be in the database.

Costs

Have a serious talk about costs. Table 12.1 shows you four simple scenarios, each starting with the same investment: $500,000. We assumed that each investment would grow at 8 percent a year over 10 years. But you'll see each initial investment *is* different. That's because fees would eat away at the money going into the mutual fund with a load and the money handled by a manager before it was even invested. If all else were equal, you'd be better off using a no-load fund that charged 1 percent a year or an investment manager. As Table 12.1 shows, you would be behind using a loaded fund.

Table 12.1 The Cost of Money Management

Investment Approach	Amount to Invest	5.75% Load Funds	Annual Management Fee	Growth at 8% for 10 Years
Loaded fund	$500,000	$471,250	1.00%	$929,406
High management fee	$500,000	—	1.25%	$963,921
Mutual fund	$500,000	—	1.00%	**$986,108**
Investment manager	$500,000	—	1.00%	**$986,108**

The same holds true with higher-priced private investment management. Remember, trading costs are *not* included in fees charged to a client. Plan on those costs as well. Keep this in mind when evaluating expenses: fees are important, but results matter more.

There are many different ways that you can pay for financial services, so it is important to have a frank conversation with your would-be adviser about how he will charge you and how he is compensated for his efforts. Our firm believes in a 1 percent total fee arrangement for clients using investment managers. When we manage ETF portfolios and other hands-on investments, the fee is much lower because these are handled in-house for 401(k) plans and other accounts. You do not have to pay a fortune to get good service and management. There are quality companies available to you around the country.

There are four primary ways that financial service providers will get paid. But before we get into these, remember, adding another fee on top of these fees is going to seriously limit your returns.

These approaches—commissions, percentage-of-assets models, flat fees, and hourly rates—are all pretty straightforward, and it is not uncommon for some firms to use a combination. There is no simple answer as to which approach is best because they all have their advantages and drawbacks.

Commissions may be the most perilous in that they create the incentives for the advisers to recommend more trades and/or products that bring the advisers larger payouts. Honest professionals will not overtrade your account—and you don't want to be dealing with less-than-honest people no matter how they get paid! If the professional you hire gets a cut of the products he sells to you, you need to know this—it does not necessarily invalidate the advice, but it at least creates the possibility of a conflict of interest.

The *percentage-of-assets model* is often seen as the most "customer friendly." If you are paying 1 percent on your portfolio, then you know what you are getting. The more you make, naturally the more you pay—and that is worth it. That goes in the opposite direction too. If your portfolio declines, then you pay less. The idea is that the professional makes more money only if you make more money—if your assets grow, the adviser's percentage is worth more. (Additionally, in theory, if you are pleased with the service you are getting, you will send your adviser more money.)

Sometimes, clients with smaller portfolios worry that they are not getting the same amount of care and attention or that the better ideas go to the larger clients first. Most firms have a minimum account size they work with. That may seem unfair if you don't reach that minimum, but the existence of the minimum account level should keep you from worrying that your portfolio is not getting the same care that a larger portfolio is getting.

Financial advisers who use the *flat-fee model* (which is usually an annual billing) won't tend to push unwanted investments on you, but they may lack the incentive to work on your account constantly. It is nice to have a predictable expense and a lack of the aggressive salesperson mentality, but you've got to keep an eye on performance.

Hourly rates are fine, once you reach maintenance mode, but when you are implementing a retirement plan for the first time, it's hard to predict how long it will take, and therefore, you might end up with higher than expected expenses.

No matter what approach you agree to, make sure you get your money's worth if you decide to hire someone else to help you look after your portfolio. There's no hard-and-fast rule about what makes for a fair price or a bargain when it comes to financial services. You may find that a $150 newsletter subscription meets all of your needs so that you can do it all yourself, or you may find that a full-service adviser and manager who charges 1.5 percent of your assets each year more than earns his keep (by outearning the market averages consistently). The bottom line is that you need to be getting real value.

Be careful not to fixate on price—or performance—as the sole factor. After all, this isn't all about dollars and cents. You can't put a price on confidence and peace of mind. If you worry that your helpers take on too much risk or don't really listen to you, it doesn't matter how little they charge—they are not the right people for you. By the same token, a good night's sleep is a must-have if you are going to really enjoy retirement. Don't beat yourself up about choosing someone who may not be the absolute top performer (as long as they perform reasonably well) if he or she makes you feel more secure.

Rational Expectations

When evaluating an investment manager, make sure that you have rational expectations in mind. If you want someone to double the value of your portfolio in three years with little to no risk, you are asking the impossible. Likewise, there are very few managers who can completely steer their clients around the inevitable bear markets. It is perfectly reasonable to look for managers and advisers who have fared better than most during down markets, but no honest financial services professional will ever guarantee performance or make a promise that you will not lose money no matter what.

So, what's rational?

It *is* entirely reasonable to expect advisers and/or investment managers to help you achieve long-term returns in excess of the rate of inflation and then some (after expenses, of course). This will not necessarily be true on a year-by-year basis. (Even the best professionals will have down years.) But when you evaluate their track record over a longer timespan (at least five to eight years or more), the positive results need to be there. There is no reason to stick with managers who cannot at least do better than inflation.

Beyond that, "reasonable" becomes more tied to the details of your personal situation and your plan. You should expect that the equity and bond components of your portfolio do as well as the average comparable mutual fund. If a professional cannot outperform the same mutual funds that you could buy on your own, there must be other services in play to justify whatever you are paying.

It is also rational to expect someone to periodically set aside the time to talk at length about your goals, resources, and concerns. Likewise, it is reasonable to expect candid feedback from your professional. If your goals are out of line or if you are likely to outlive your assets based on your current spending plans, he needs to say so.

That is a good segue to another important point. There is more to good financial advisory firms and investment managers than just the annual returns that their recommendations produce. You need to also have a meeting of the minds in terms of how you will interact. A brilliant financial adviser who does not return your calls on a timely basis or who is not concerned about your own individual needs is just not going to be a good match. Likewise, you may decide that you do not need (or want) the hand-holding that a more proactive professional wants to offer.

When interviewing a potential steward of your money, make sure to establish how often you will meet as part of an ongoing relationship. You also want to know how often your portfolio will be examined and adjusted and how often you should reexamine your needs and goals. Remember, these are your goals, so you need to feel 100 percent comfortable with your manager's approach to them—and your money!

Finding an Adviser Who Understands You and Your Business

With so many people putting out a shingle as a financial adviser, there are a lot of styles and approaches to choose from out there. Make sure you find a professional whose goals and skills line up with yours. More important, find someone who has had significant experience in either money management or financial planning. I would not consider someone who has not had at least 10 years' experience in financial advising, and I would want to use an investment manager who has at least $200 million under management. *You want experience, not promises.*

Above all, make sure that your prospective adviser focuses on the kinds of investments that are right for you. An adviser who focuses on a niche investment area like private placements (nonpublic stock offerings) may be brilliant at that, and those skills may be a real boon for wealthy, risk-tolerant investors, but it is unlikely that those investments would be very appropriate for retirement accounts. Likewise, some folks will be whizzes with growth stocks or options strategies, and those could be fine approaches when you are a younger worker able to take some additional risks. In retirement, though, those strategies are not nearly as useful. What this means for you is that you really need to quiz the person across the desk. Ask the adviser to discuss his or her strongest areas of advice and performance. If retirement management is not a primary focus for that adviser, you should probably keep looking.

Don't go to an adviser and ask the easy question: "Can you help me reach my goals?" The answer 99 percent of the time is going to be, "Yes, come into my den," said the big bad wolf, hungry for fees! There are many questions you can ask, but the following ones will let you know if you are in the right place:

1. What are your credentials?
2. How long have you been in business?
3. How do you charge for your time and or services?
4. What investment products do you use? Are these loaded or no-load funds? Do you get any 12b-1 fees?
5. When we finish discussing my needs and portfolio, I would like to have a reasonable discussion about fees.
6. Do you specialize in a specific type of client?
7. What service can I expect after starting? Will I be working with you directly, or will I be working with a team or with an assistant of yours?

While matching your personal retirement goals with an adviser's talents and experience is a top priority, it's also important to find someone who understands your business situation. In all likelihood, you might have trouble finding an exact match. (Trust me, I don't know of many other dentists who are also CFPs who have a lot of dentists as clients.) But you should insist on finding someone who has had experience with clients who are:

- Holding a large chunk of wealth that is tied up in an illiquid asset (that is, your practice)
- High-net-worth individuals
- Business or practice owners

The last one is important, but it's a tricky one to navigate. All the brokers and CFPs you meet are going to claim that they work with wealthy people because everyone in this business wants to be working with wealthy people. So focus on the first two bullet points. Ask for examples of how the adviser serves clients with complex, illiquid wealth. Get recommendations on how to streamline your portfolio into simpler, more liquid, and safer retirement savings. For example, when a great deal of wealth is tied up in a business or practice, how can it best be converted to a liquid investment suited for retirement?

Ask about the adviser's communication model. For example, when does he or she reach out to clients? You are a busy person. You probably don't need the distraction of trivial check-ins from your adviser (and you definitely don't have time for sales calls if the callers are pushing investments). But you sure need to be able to reach the adviser when you've got a pressing question.

While it's important that you find someone who understands your business, ultimately, you need someone whose work matches your personal retirement goals, and you need someone with an impeccable reputation, great endorsements, and a strong history of results.

Deciding Whether You Should Work with Your Current Adviser

What if you already have been working with a financial professional and you have benefited from that relationship? It might surprise you that you still need to ask whether or not that person is prepared to transition you into and through retirement. Almost every financial professional will attempt to answer your questions about retirement, but working with someone who lacks experience in the retirement planning world could be disastrous. Request detailed recommendations about retirement plans, ask tough questions about the adviser's abilities and experience, and ask for references from the adviser's clients. *No adviser* is equally good at every aspect of financial planning. If an adviser is honest enough to tell you that he is not especially proficient with retirement planning, you should certainly look elsewhere. There's no reason that you can't retain your current adviser to handle your everyday investment portfolio, but there's also no reason for you to have to limp along toward your retirement goals because this person isn't experienced enough.

One additional caution: no adviser likes to lose business. This is something of a common problem with company-sponsored retirement plans (as well as those target-date funds discussed earlier in Chapter 10). Once your retirement date arrives, the sponsors of these plans and investments often do not have much in the way of retirement planning to offer, but they want to keep your money in their hands. Consequently, they may encourage you to transfer your assets into "safer" investments like annuities—investments that generate large fees for them but that may not be appropriate for you.

Remember, no one loves your money like you do, so you need to find the right people and right place for your money, even if that means changing advisers at critical times.

Measuring Investment Performance

At some level, all investors want to know is how well they can expect their portfolio to perform if they hire someone to help them manage it. Measuring investment performance is not quite as simple as it may seem. Sure, it is easy enough to calculate how each stock, bond, or fund in a portfolio has performed and how the total portfolio has performed, but that is not always a useful measure of performance.

Looking only at raw numbers, a portfolio that earned 12 percent would seem better than one that earned 10 percent. But if that 12 percent portfolio was twice as risky, that extra 2 percent of performance does not look as good anymore. Likewise, if a manager makes frequent trades, you may find that the extra transaction costs and tax liabilities erode those simple raw returns. Managers should make it clear to you whether they are offering performance reports that include or exclude fees. (In fact, if they are following regulatory rules, they have to.) Along similar lines, financial services professionals should be able to give you a general sense of the tax efficiency of their investment approach, as well as the liquidity of the investments they choose. If your would-be adviser is going to recommend tying up a piece of your savings in investments that are difficult to sell quickly, this is definitely information you need to know!

Part of measuring performance also includes comparisons and benchmarks. A manager who routinely delivers 8 percent a year is doing a fine job if the target is 6 percent, but not if the stated benchmark is going up 10 percent a year. There are many benchmarks that a manager can choose, but the important point is whether the benchmark is a fair comparison for the portfolio—an investor who typically buys the stocks of small companies but who compares his performance to the Dow Jones Industrial Average (which contains huge, well-known companies such as GE and Coca-Cola) is going to give a misleading impression of how good he is at picking stocks.

The Holistic Approach to Offering Financial Services

There is a huge range of services that you can get from a financial services professional. Advisers can help you create your investment plan, provide tax advice, manage your portfolio, assist you in establishing personal budgets, help you formulate investment strategies, establish retirement and estate plans, and even evaluate your insurance needs and coverage. Very few individuals attempt to do all of these things at once, but many large companies do.

Throughout the 1990s, more and more financial services firms tried to adopt a "financial supermarket" business model by which they tried to offer as many services under one roof as possible. In my view, that's a classic example of a "good news, bad news" situation. A supermarket is really convenient, and it may sound like a great idea to get all of your financial needs taken care of at one stop. But the problem with the supermarket model is that it tends to focus on the bestselling and most profitable products, sometimes at the expense of quality. Just as most supermarkets won't carry prime filet of beef or really fine wine, a financial supermarket may try to sell you the investment equivalent of "Chateau Screwtop" instead of the best financial products.

Some advisers can help you with a wide range of needs—investing, cash management, insurance, and so on. In other cases, firms will put entire teams at your disposal, even estate planning attorneys. By the same token, don't dismiss a good adviser or manager simply because he or she won't try to do everything. Advisers who have been in practice for a while typically have built up a network of friends, colleagues, and contacts who can help you with any additional services you might need. What you really need is good, cost-effective advice—not necessarily the most convenient advice.

Dear Adviser: How Do You Invest Your Own Money?

When I first started my dental practice in 1964, I was as gullible as they come! I didn't know the right questions, so I got steamrolled by a broker. He had been in the business for about 10 years, and he used all the right buzzwords like "grow for your retirement." I was in seventh heaven; I *knew* I had found the right person. Then one day, I happened to be at a large cocktail party, and I was standing right behind him. I heard him tell one of his colleagues that he liked a particular product (the one he had sold to me) because the payout was so good for the broker. I almost choked on my drink.

If I have the opportunity to talk to a broker now, I bluntly ask if he owns the stock, mutual fund, or whatever it is that he is selling to clients. After my early experience, though, I go out of my way to avoid brokers. I fully realize that some are great people doing a great job for their clients, but you and I know that they are few and far between. Some of those Wall Street movies are closer to the truth than you and I would like to think.

You need to have a clear understanding of the investment philosophy that guides your adviser's actions and what that means for your portfolio. A *market timer*, for instance, will believe that he can accurately forecast the twists and turns of the market and position the portfolio accordingly. Market timers do very well when they are right, but most evidence suggests that "successful" market timing is more a question of luck ... and when that lucks runs out, the losses can be painful.

Likewise, a *value investor* will often buy overlooked or underperforming stocks with the idea that things are better than they seem and the market will eventually wake up to that and send the shares higher. Value investors do not tend to lose very much when they are wrong, but they can be left behind in bull markets. Buying value is a safe way to do very well. Ask Warren Buffett! Value investing is hard to beat.

The debates over the "best" style of investing have gone on for decades and will never end. Almost every approach has its merits and can work in the right circumstances, but it is important that the style fits *your* goals and *your* comfort level. There are some pretty exotic and sophisticated products and strategies out there, and a lot of them are wholly inappropriate for a retirement portfolio. If an idea sounds a little strange to you (cattle ranching in Patagonia, adjustable mortgages from Portugal), it probably isn't right for you.

It is also worth asking a potential adviser just where and how he gets his ideas. If your candidate works at a large, nationally known brokerage, the odds are pretty good that a lot of his "ideas" will be coming down from the analysts and strategy teams in New York. A small independent adviser may be relying on her own research skills, or she may supplement them with various newsletters or subscription services. Again, there is no automatic right or wrong here, but it is your money, and you have a right to know where the ideas that are going to influence *your* results are coming from!

I always jokingly tell clients now that I want to know everything about them, except the last time they had sex! We all laugh a minute, and then they realize that my joke is closer to the truth than not. They *should* want us to know everything we can about them so that we can better advise them on their investments. While many of our clients use the same investment management firms or mutual fund portfolios as our other clients, the amounts allocated and invested vary with each client's individual needs, age, risk tolerance, total portfolio size, and other unique factors.

Conclusion

Like picking a family physician or an attorney, selecting and hiring a financial professional is an inexact science, and every investor has different needs, concerns, and priorities. Clearly, you want a qualified professional. (True, new talent needs someone to take a chance on them, but retirement isn't the right time for you to do that!) You also want someone with whom you have a good personal rapport. You need a professional whose interests and expertise align with your needs. You probably wouldn't want to go to a criminal attorney for estate planning or a neurosurgeon for a flu shot, so make sure your financial services candidates focus on the needs of clients in retirement and that you are within the normal range of their clients in terms of assets, sophistication, and so on.

Above all, don't be afraid to ask tough questions or to take your time gathering information and mulling over your decision. Remember, it is up to you to love your money. *Do not compromise on what is right for you by settling for what is convenient for them.*

PART FOUR

LIVING THE GOOD LIFE:
LIFE AFTER RETIREMENT

13

Using Your Savings for the Rest of Your Life

You'll be happy to know that we've finally reached the point in the book where you can spend the money you've earned, invested, and grown. If no one loves your money like you do, perhaps this is the time when you'll love it the most. However, you've got to continue to give it the care, attention, and love it needs to see you all the way through retirement.

There is a reason why this Part Four on using your retirement savings appears so far into the book. You first had to begin with goals, a plan, and a budget (as discussed in Part Two). Without those things, you would have been challenged to have any idea about how much you would need to have saved and invested. Once you had a plan, you needed to make your money work for you with a thorough and active set of investments (as featured in Part Three). In order to reach your retirement goals and to comfortably fund your desired retirement living expenses, you need a portfolio that grows and thrives.

Now that you have your money for retirement, what are you supposed to do with it? How do you actually live off a collection of stocks, bonds, mutual funds, ETFs, and savings accounts? After all, it's all well and good to successfully invest the money, but drawing it down in the right way also is important. The accumulation phase is much different than the post-retirement spending phase. You need to make that money last for the rest of your life, which means you need to minimize your risk and get the most out of it. My approach is not only simple but it should also help protect your near-term spending needs from the vagaries of the market.

How Much Can You Withdraw? The 4 Percent Rule

Retirement is just like the rest of your life. Ideally, you should earn more than you spend. That's sounds a little wacky, doesn't it? It's a little bit trickier when your income streams aren't as plentiful. But if you are following my plan, you should be well positioned to stay in the black. The key is the amount of money you draw from your investment portfolio each year. Remember, it is how you have your money invested and how you are taking it out of your personal savings and your IRAs.

You have to start somewhere, so that's where the 4 Percent Rule comes into play. I recommend that you draw no more than 4 percent of your total investment funds each year. In fact, you'd be better off if you took out a maximum of 3.5 percent for the first year or so. Some experts will tell you that you shouldn't take out more than that each year. Others will go as high as 6 percent. There is no right answer, but there is one very important factor that will influence the amount: *the quality of your portfolio.*

As you will recall, your portfolio has two objectives: to beat inflation and to grow. A healthy, diversified portfolio should be growing at 8 percent per year or more. Inflation has averaged about 3.5 percent per year over time, so that leaves you about 4.5 percent growth after inflation. That's why I believe you can target a 4 percent annual withdrawal rate. If your portfolio is performing extraordinarily well, you *can* take more than 4 percent out of it, but again it is how the portfolio is set up that makes the difference. I would recommend that you still limit your withdrawals and let those earnings keep growing. When the market dips, and it will someday, you'll have a little extra cushion in your portfolio. My total portfolio does not take on the risk of the marketplace, and neither should yours.

You may have grand plans for retirement, but you also have financial obligations like a mortgage, utility bills, groceries, and insurance premiums. Make sure your annual budget needs fall under the 4 percent mark. When you are earning more, you can fund those big plans, but you need to make sure you've got a portfolio that's healthy enough to pay the bills.

Most of you will start taking money from your savings and retirement plans before 70, and if you do, I would recommend that you start removing a little less the first year than you would like so that you won't get into trouble thinking you have a whole bowlful of candy! Some people get a little crazy when they see all that money that they've never had their hands on before.

While there's certainly room for debate and disagreement about the "right" way to withdraw your savings, I can tell you one approach that does

not work. You may run into some people who say, "Take whatever you need. After all, you earned it!" If you find those people, back away slowly and then run. A healthy retirement savings account balance is not a wishing well. It's a fixed and finite resource that must be carefully tended. The last thing you want to do is throw out a careful plan and start spending on the basis of a whim.

How to Withdraw Money Wisely

We are going to begin to look at different ideas for removing money from your personal savings and retirement plans. You have been saving for such a long time that you now have to shift gears. I want you to spend time looking at this carefully so that, as we progress and build on ideas, you understand exactly what you're doing. I also want you to understand the difference between **accumulating** money and **removing** money to live from your savings. They must be approached differently.

In the next chapter, I'll show you how to manage the withdrawals so that it becomes easy to get your "check" every month and gradually increase your "allowance" based on last year's inflation rate. I'll also show you how to put those budgeted funds in safe places, so that if the market does tank, it won't hurt your lifestyle or your long-term retirement plan. This model gives the rest of your portfolio the opportunity to continue to grow (or at least break even) when inflation and market dips eat away at it. A portfolio that grows even after you retire means that you and your loved ones can live out a happy life free from financial worry.

Structured Withdrawals

Structured withdrawals is a formal-sounding name for the way you will remove money from your retirement plans, but trust me, this works very easily.

With structured withdrawals, you decide before retirement how you will work down your retirement savings. You create a budget of annual expenses that allows you to take enough each year to live comfortably but not so much that you start digging into the principal too early and risk coming up short if you outlive your expectations.

Naturally, when your money is performing well, there's a greater temptation to spend it too. But remember, you are in this for the long term. Being able to take money out in excess of your usual amount requires a good portfolio. That is something many investors just don't have because they have not stopped to figure out how to set one up that works over a long period of time.

Table 13.1   The Duration of Major Economic Downturns

Downturn	Duration	Cause
Panic of 1901	3 years	Assassination of President McKinley and drought
Wall Street Crash of 1929	4 years	Speculation
The Dot-Com debacle 2000–2001	2 years	Enron, the bursting of the initial Internet bubble, and accounting scandals
U.S. bear market 2007–2009	2 years	Housing bubble, Lehman Brothers bankruptcy, global credit freeze (greater than 20% decline in U.S. markets)

A structured withdrawal system (along with the Three Pots system in the next chapter) helps you deal with inevitable market downturns with very little effort. By planning your withdrawals in advance, you will be able to store three years' worth of withdrawals in very conservative investments. These investments rarely lose value even during huge market downturns.

Why three years' worth of money? Over the last 100-plus years, the markets have been down 3 years in a row only twice (see Table 13.1). Once was the Great Depression. There have been plenty of shorter downturns that caused havoc for the average investor, but the structured withdrawal system keeps the money for your immediate needs safe, while allowing the rest of your portfolio to recover and grow again.

Many of the investors who took a big hit during a long downturn were not properly diversified. They didn't have enough money in safe havens, and they were forced to sell their holdings at a big loss just to stay afloat.

Do you have to religiously adhere to your structured withdrawal amount? No. If your portfolio has been doing extraordinarily well over a long run, you could treat yourself to something out of the ordinary—a trip to a foreign country, for example—once every four to five years or so. (Of course, you could have built those "treats" into your original budget too.)

Remember, the accumulation phase is very different from the removing, spending, and using phases of retirement savings. When you were a child and saved money to buy a bike or something equally important to you, it seemed like saving the money took forever. Then, within the moment you made the purchase, the money was gone. As you've grown older and you've had more choices—or needs—to spend your money on, things are different. Once you spend your retirement money, it's not coming back, so you can't make exceptions to your structured withdrawals an every-year affair.

Required Minimum Distributions (RMDs)

Here's an interesting twist on the 4 Percent Rule. Once you reach the age of 70½, you are required to withdraw a certain percentage of your IRA each year. This is what's known as a *required minimum distribution* (RMD). As you can see in Table 13.2, the number jumps over 4 percent by the time you turn 73. A mandatory withdrawal doesn't mean mandatory spending. You can stash the money you don't need in a savings account or reinvest it in a

Table 13.2   IRA Withdrawals: Required Minimum Distributions for 2014

Your Age	Annual Payout
70	3.65%
71	3.77%
72	3.90%
73	4.05%
74	4.20%
75	4.37%
76	4.55%
77	4.71%
78	4.93%
79	5.13%
80	5.35%
81	5.59%
82	5.85%
83	6.14%
84	6.45%
85	6.76%
86	7.09%
87	7.46%
88	7.87%
89	8.33%
90	9.52%
91	10.10%
92	10.64%

(Continued)

Table 13.2   (*Continued*)

Your Age	Annual Payout
93	11.37%
94	12.05%
95	12.82%
96	13.70%
97	14.50%
98	15.38%
99	16.40%
100	15.87%

Note: For example: Dick is 71 years old. His year-end IRA
balance is $1 million. How much does he need to take out?
Answer: $1 million times 3.77 percent, which equals $37,700.

non-retirement investment account. You do have to pay taxes on the with-drawals so you should factor that into your budgeting.

Most of you are going to find that the amount you have to take out, and other information about your RMDs, can be found in IRS Publication 590 and the Uniform Lifetime Table. This table applies to three types of people: (a) unmarried owners, (b) married owners whose spouses are not more than 10 years younger, and (c) married owners whose spouses are not the sole beneficiaries of their IRAs. For updated data, or if you have any different requirements for removal at 70½ (if you don't fit those three criteria), visit http://www.irs.gov and search for "Required Minimum Distributions" to access Publication 590 and to find the table that covers your situation.

Alternative Approaches

There are other thoughts and theories and plans for moving money from investment accounts and using it to meet your day-to-day needs. Some of these ideas get rather complicated—scenarios that have you withdrawing (and spending) more money in the earlier years of retirement, when you are presumably healthier and more active, and withdrawing less in the later years. I can understand the appeal of these approaches, but what happens if you live a longer, healthier life than you expect? Let's take a look at some of these other models.

The Dividends and Interest-Only Approach

This can work well if the interest and dividends exceed what you need. But look at the interest rates on bonds and money market funds today. The bond market has been going down for the last 30 years. What we remember as a great source of interest payments is not what is happening today. As I mentioned previously, I use moderate allocation money management firms and mutual funds to achieve my goals. This allows me to take the dividends from my managed accounts. Because my mutual fund portfolios are in IRAs, I take principal and interest, and it is not a big deal to do that. I know the target percentage that I should withdraw from the whole portfolio, and I go from there.

You can set up a moderate allocation portfolio of stocks and bonds, if you have enough in the way of funds to live off the dividends, without needing to dip into the principal too often. For me, taking the time to research the stocks seemed too exhausting, so I decided to use first-class money management firms to do the job for me. Again, it just depends on whose management firms and investments you are using.

An investment plan based on interest and dividends will not ignore the risk of inflation **if** it is invested in good stocks that continue to raise their dividends over time. There are many great companies who continue to raise their dividends for their stockholders, but there are **no** guarantees that any company will do so—or even pay them at all. If you follow the dividend-as-income route, make sure you have a backup plan if your stocks' dividends dry up. Therefore, you'll need a bond component in your portfolio, as I mentioned in Chapter 9. A 10-year laddered portfolio of bonds will help you plan how much interest income you are going to get paid.

Time-Based Withdrawals

Time-based withdrawal plans call for a person to set up separate "pools" of funds and work through those funds in sequence. There will be a pool that you will use up in the first three to five years, another pool for the five after that, and so on. The idea is that each pool is invested appropriately to that length of time (the further off it is, the more risky assets like stocks it can hold) and "consumed" in turn. To a large extent, this is the strategy that a lot of annuity sales reps will recommend—setting up tiered or staggered annuities to establish those pools. I don't think it works as well as my Three Pots approach (featured in the next chapter), even though the annuity companies can scare you into thinking they are right.

My Three Pots approach is a modified version of a time-based withdrawal strategy. Where I differ from some time-based approaches is that I believe in actively managing the pools and moving money among them as time goes on. In a more traditional time-based system, you might first exhaust your near-term pool (which would hold very safe and secure investments like money market funds), then your intermediate-term pool (which would include Treasury Bonds and CDs), and then your long-term pool (which would have stocks and other investments).

I believe in active and dynamic management—"refreshing" the Holding and Spending Pots by moving money when necessary. In my experience, my approach minimizes the year-to-year risk and volatility of the markets, and in fact, it is actually easier to keep the Three Pots in sync or balanced this way.

Essential Versus Discretionary Spending

Some people believe in separating investment funds between "discretionary" and "essential" pools. The idea is that the essential pool will be invested in safe and predictable instruments, and it will be used to meet your essential year-to-year needs. The discretionary pool can be invested in higher-risk ideas and can be used to supplement your year-to-year living expenses.

I love this approach in theory, but I find the details make it a very difficult strategy to follow in practice. It is hard enough to come up with a budget as it is, and then you're supposed to figure out what is an essential expense and what is discretionary? Some of my friends think a trip to Europe each year is *essential* and not discretionary! How do you figure out how much of your gasoline usage is essential, or how much of your grocery bill is discretionary?

I do like borrowing part of this approach: creating a separate account for a special discretionary expenditure like a big trip and using that account to build up the money to pay for it. If the savings and investments work out, you can enjoy an even better trip than you planned, and if they don't work out and you can't take the trip you planned, at least your long-term savings position won't have been hurt.

Why Your Portfolio Should Continue to Grow After Retirement

We've talked a lot about how much you should spend annually after you retire—and how to safely withdraw money. But as I stressed earlier, the quality and strength of your portfolio are very important to funding your budget. Your portfolio needs to keep growing to beat inflation, to provide money for your living expenses, and to provide a cushion for unexpected expenses.

That's why you need to keep managing your portfolio carefully after you retire. Although you need to protect your short-term spending needs with conservative investments, I think the majority of your money should be invested in instruments that will grow. Don't let your entire portfolio get too conservative!

Here is a quick study in which type of portfolio you would rather have.

The Six Fund Portfolio Versus a 60/40 Portfolio: The Growth over 15 Years

As you saw in Part Three, the Six Fund Portfolio is allocated roughly between 70 percent stocks and 30 percent bonds. The stocks continue to grow my asset base, and the bonds keep me safe from market fluctuations. Many people move their entire portfolio toward safer ground as they age— closer to a mix of 60 percent stocks and 40 percent bonds. Even though I've passed retirement age myself, I've kept my 70/30 allocation. Why? Because I have three years of short-term investments protected, and I want the rest of my money to grow.

As an example, let's build a portfolio composed of 60 percent of the S&P 500 Index and 40 percent of the Barclay's U.S. Intermediate Government Bond Index. The combined return of this 60/40 portfolio would have averaged 4.63 percent per year from 1999 through 2013.Using the Six Fund Portfolio with a 70/30 split, though, I have been earning more than twice that average return: 10.6 percent. That is a difference of 5.97 percent per year! I'm beating inflation, I'm fully funding my annual budget, and I have money to both reinvest *and/or* splurge on a big purchase every few years. Having a well-diversified portfolio—mutual funds, ETFs, individual stocks and bonds—makes a very big difference in your long-term results.

One of the first lessons I learned was to be careful about fees and expenses but not to lose sight of the fact that while fees matter, **results matter more!** Of course, you and I both would rather make a higher return each year on our investments. That's why I wanted to use this simple exercise to show you that the funds' returns *net of fees* are more important than the *actual fees*.

Withdrawing Money in the Worst of Times

Let's look at two different scenarios for removing money from your savings and retirement plan. I have deliberately chosen the *January 2007 through December 2009* time period because it includes the so-called Great Recession. I wanted to show you how a retirement plan fared at the very worst economic period in recent times—and how investing in a good portfolio will make the difference in how much you have.

In Table 13.3, let's look at the 60/40 Portfolio with a planned withdrawal of 4 percent of the initial $100,000 balance each year. That works out to be $333.33 a month in the first year, with an inflationary adjustment based on the Consumer Price Index (CPI) each January. You can see how you would have fared over the "Great Recession." Now, take a look at the Six Fund Portfolio over the same time period in Table 13.4. What a difference a well-diversified portfolio makes!

Almost without saying, this was the worst time period to start showing anyone how this works, **but** too many people in the financial world want to show you only the sunny side of things—and that is not life!

Neither portfolio was "fireproof." Both lost some money, but it is obvious that having a mix of different types of stocks and bonds is better than using just a few indexed parts to your investment mix. Diversification matters! (In the next chapter, I'll talk about how to withdraw money without dipping into principal when the markets are going down.)

Table 13.3   Withdrawals 2007 to 2009: 60/40 Allocation

60% S&P 500/40% Barclay's U.S. Government Intermediate Bond Index				$100,000.00
Removed 4% a Year, Inflated with CPI, 1 Year Behind				
Month	% Return	New Balance	Withdrawal	Final Balance
Jan-07	0.88%	$100,884.62	$333.33	$100,551.29
Feb-07	−0.65%	$99,900.42	$333.33	$99,567.09
Mar-07	0.73%	$100,294.19	$333.33	$99,960.86
↓				↓
Oct-09	−0.89%	$82,548.43	$347.35	$82,201.08
Nov-09	4.11%	$85,580.07	$347.35	$85,232.72
Dec-09	0.48%	$85,644.70	$347.35	**$85,297.35**

Table 13.4   Withdrawals 2007 to 2009: Six Fund Portfolio

The Six Fund Portfolio				$100,000.00
Removed 4% a Year, Inflated with CPI, 1 Year Behind				
Month	**% Return**	**New Balance**	**Withdrawal**	**Final Balance**
Jan-07	0.98%	$100,984.60	$333.33	$100,651.27
Feb-07	0.05%	$100,701.19	$333.33	$100,367.86
Mar-07	1.36%	$101,731.96	$333.33	$101,398.63
↓				↓
Oct-09	−0.95%	$93,287.06	$347.35	$92,939.71
Nov-09	3.72%	$96,392.52	$347.35	$96,045.17
Dec-09	1.29%	$97,279.73	$347.35	**$96,932.38**

Note: To see month-by-month versions of both charts, visit the Inside the Book section at http://www.940financialconsulting.com.

There are two points that I don't want you to forget:

- **First:** You have to have a well-planned, diversified portfolio that will keep growing as you remove money. It's all about setting up your portfolio correctly in the beginning, and it's about making any corrections as soon as you learn more to protect your retirement.
- **Second:** If the portfolio is set up correctly, it can run for years with just minor (and sometimes *no*) changes. Certainly, if the unforeseen comes along, you may need to make some corrections as you steer your retirement boat, but they are not as many as you may think if you set it up correctly to begin with. Don't let someone tell you that you have to keep making changes, and don't believe everything you read that says you "have to have this or that" kind of portfolio after you retire or you won't make it.

Withdrawing Money Throughout Your Whole Retirement

In order to show you an apples-to-apples comparison over a longer length of time, Tables 13.5 and 13.6 show the two portfolios over a longer period—from January 2001 through December 2013. Each began with $100,000. I used the same annual withdrawal amount of 4 percent and the same adjustment for inflation each January. The 60/40 Portfolio after 13 years

Table 13.5   Withdrawals 2001 to 2013: 60/40 Allocation

60% S&P 500/40% Barclay's U.S. Government Intermediate Bond Index		$100,000.00
Removed 4% a Year, Inflated with CPI, 1 Year Behind		
Year	Monthly Withdrawal Amount	End of Year Balance
2001	$333.33	$90,289.65
2002	$338.66	$79,717.42
2003	$346.79	$89,579.18
2004	$353.38	$94,072.91
2005	$365.04	$95,385.97
2006	$377.45	$99,858.15
2007	$386.89	$102,465.32
2008	$402.75	$81,682.96
2009	$403.15	$83,637.76
2010	$414.15	$90,224.39
2011	$420.36	$96,868.39
2012	$432.97	$102,585.89
2013	$440.33	**$110,011.64**

ended up with a value of $110,011.64. The Six Fund Portfolio ended up with **$248,677.56**.

After 13 years of ups and (very big) downs, look at the difference in the final amount of money in each of the accounts. The 60/40 Portfolio performed decently, but it doesn't have a lot of margin for error. One expensive set of medical bills (or one splurge on a kitchen remodel) could have eaten up the little bit of gain this portfolio squeaked out. The Six Fund Portfolio used a diversified portfolio that mitigated risk and encouraged growth. Using well-diversified portfolios makes a huge difference today. The world is not the way it was 25 years ago. It is more complex, and by having a diversified portfolio, you can keep up with the entire market.

At the end of the 15-year period, each portfolio was using up an extra $100 a month for the same set of expenses that were incurred on day one. (I made my inflationary adjustments by using the previous year's Urban Consumer Price Index, also known as the CPI-U.)

Table 13.6 Withdrawals 2001 to 2013: Six Fund Portfolio

The Six Fund Portfolio		$100,000.00
Removed 4% a Year, Inflated with CPI, 1 Year Behind		
Year	Monthly Withdrawal Amount	End of Year Balance
2001	$333.33	$108,951.95
2002	$338.66	$107,001.47
2003	$346.79	$131,177.02
2004	$353.38	$144,442.51
2005	$365.04	$144,442.51
2006	$377.45	$175,402.64
2007	$386.89	$191,860.01
2008	$402.75	$146,298.25
2009	$403.15	$177,984.40
2010	$414.15	$194,969.03
2011	$420.36	$190,452.97
2012	$432.97	$208,339.82
2013	$440.33	**$248,677.56**

Note: To see month-by-month versions of both charts, visit the Inside the Book section at http://www.940financialconsulting.com.

By showing you these charts, I want to emphasize that setting up a good portfolio is easier than some would have you believe, and it works!

Resources for Managing Your Money Through Retirement

In this chapter, we've talked about the importance of a strong, quality portfolio to get you through retirement—and how to wisely draw down your money. I've also warned you about the so-called experts out there, and I think you should learn about your investments. So why would I want you to read others' opinions if they may be confusing to you? Because I want you to understand enough about how things work so that you can feel comfortable you are doing the right thing.

The people working in the investment field, unfortunately, are not always as sharp as they ought to be, and you are going to need to be able to work with them (or work around them). I've already mentioned Fred Schwed's *Where Are the Customers' Yachts? A Good Hard Look at Wall Street* in Chapter 6. It was written in 1940, but it still, unfortunately, tells the truth about the financial industry.

If you have read enough articles that have confused you and scared you that you are going to run out of money in retirement, you are not alone. I understand exactly how you feel. Reading some of the articles preparing for this book was enough to scare me too!

Back in 1994, author William Bengen created a landmark work, *The Four Percent Drawdown Rule*, which was published in the Financial Planning Association's *Journal of Financial Planning*, showing that a 4 percent withdrawal rate would give investors the best chances of having their money last for 30 years. That number became fixed in financial planners' minds as the only way to do it. However, a lot has transpired since then. Most important, we know that we don't all invest the same way. Many early studies were predicated on investors using only the S&P 500 and long- or intermediate-term government bonds. Not many people invest their money that way anymore. Instead, we can invest in REITs, MLPs, dividend producing stocks, mutual funds, ETFs, and so on. Investing has changed.

One final caution as you do your research: the *Monte Carlo simulation* is a concept you'll probably run across. It's something you should know about but **not** use. It is known as a *return-sequence risk program* that has as many detractors as it has supporters. I tried it out for a while, and I was not, and still am not, impressed at all. I would never suggest you let someone use that in planning your future. It gives you a *probability* of success—but **only** if you put in the right numbers to begin with. I have never found two programs using this methodology that give you the same answer. My vote is to stay away from anyone trying to use this with your hard-earned and saved money.

Ultimately, it all boils down to this: the most important thing you can do is to set up your portfolio correctly. If there is anything I recommend that you can do yourself and you need more information to do it, or if you're uncertain about something, I will be happy to stop and help you. You can find me at http://www.940financialconsulting.com.

Conclusion

With the knowledge that you should withdraw your money wisely and let the bulk of it continue to grow, let's move to the next chapter. I'll introduce the Three Pots system that keeps your short-term and intermediate-term money safe—and your long-term investments working hard. In my opinion, this system makes life easier for those who worry that the world is going to come crashing down on them, as well as for those who are just looking for an easy method to do what we have to do.

I have used the Three Pots system with clients for a long time. At first, I must admit while the markets were going up, they thought I was crazy. They wanted to keep their money invested in the surging market. After the decade of 2001 to 2010, though, I now have a group of real "believers"!

14

The Three Pots

If you have been following this book in a step-by-step fashion, you have already done a lot of the work. Now that you have figured out how much you need, want, and can afford to spend on a yearly basis—following the 4 Percent Rule featured in the previous chapter, it's time to manage and withdraw that money.

When you are two years from your planned retirement age, I believe you should sort your money into three pots—which you will see displayed throughout this chapter:

- Pot 1: Total Investments Pot
- Pot 2: Holding Pot
- Pot 3: Spending Pot

The first pot, the Total Investments Pot, is where the bulk of your money will be, and this is where you want to try to continue to achieve moderate growth. The second pot, the Holding Pot, is an intermediate step between your long-term investments and your short-term spending needs. The third pot, the Spending Pot, is where you will keep the money you expect to need over the next 12 months.

Setting up these pots two years before retirement gives you some time to set up new accounts if needed, to make a smooth transition, and to avoid the temptation of market-timing decisions. Until then, keep your money solely in the Total Investments Pot so that your savings continue to grow. This system is easy to master, and it doesn't require much effort, once you get the hang of it!

Getting Started

You'll notice that I'll be addressing your *total investments pool*. Until now, we've focused solely on retirement savings, but you have wealth outside of your retirement portfolio too. By the time you reach retirement age, it's time to bring all of your investments together to understand what you have. I recommend that you aim for holding roughly two-thirds of your money in a retirement plan and holding one-third in personal accounts, outside of a retirement plan. Why? When you pay the taxes on your withdrawals from your retirement plans or IRAs, you are going to see that the final balance really amounts to about 50 percent from those retirement plans and IRAs and 50 percent from your personal accounts. Remember, the money that has gone into your non-retirement accounts has already been taxed before you've invested it. You will still have capital gains taxes when you sell personal investments and dividend income taxes on any income-generating investments.

For those of you who may have retirement income from a pension that you receive directly from the company you worked for, visit http://www.940financialconsulting.com. The Three Pots will need to be configured slightly differently, but the information I've posted online will help you understand how this system will work for you, and it will clarify any concerns you might have. And guess what? The results will be the same.

Don't get concerned about the amount of money or the mix of investments I use as an example. Once you grasp the idea, it doesn't matter how much you have—it works.

Let's take a closer look at each of the Three Pots.

The Total Investments Pot: For Long-Term
(over Three Years and Beyond) Investments

- **Goal**: Moderate growth and beating inflation
- **Allocation**: Roughly 80 to 85 percent of your combined personal and retirement accounts
- **Primary investments**: Mutual funds, exchange-traded funds (ETFs), and stocks, bonds, and bond funds

On the day you established your retirement portfolio, you created the Total Investments Pot. Pre-retirement, this is where **all** of your retirement investments reside until you get to about two years away from retirement age. Post-retirement, this is where the bulk of your money (including non-retirement savings and investments) will reside.

This is the portfolio that is designed to produce the growth and gains you need to make your money last throughout retirement. It includes the full range of investments that you selected in Part Three, and it carries the same goals that you had when you set it up: (a) growth to increase wealth balanced with conservative investments and (b) staying ahead of inflation *and* your planned drawdowns for living expenses.

When you approach retirement age and beyond, this portfolio is where you will have the vast majority of your equity holdings along with your current allocation of bond investments. (Since you'll be adding personal non-retirement savings, you may be mixing in some riskier investment products. Make sure you don't upset your planned allocation model too much. You want to keep risk in check, so you may need to liquidate those riskier elements.) Money in this portfolio will always be invested with a long-term horizon no matter how far along you are in retirement.

The Total Investments Pot is what is going to keep your stake growing with (or ideally better than) inflation. Likewise, this is where you may be able to grow your money faster than you need to spend it. (Go back to Tables 13.5 and 13.6 in Chapter 13 to see how a diversified portfolio grew at a pace ahead of inflation **and** scheduled withdrawals.) This is the part of your portfolio that should do well enough that it outlives you . . . which is good just in case you end up outliving everyone else. After all, if you spend 4 percent of your money every year, if inflation runs at 3 percent, and if your Total Investments Pot can produce returns of 8 percent or better, you will have a much more comfortable retirement.

I know some readers will be nervous about their Total Investments Pot because of the potential risk that a big drop in the market will wipe out their life savings. I completely understand where you are coming from with this concern. My response is this: remember that the market rarely declines three years in a row and that large declines are pretty rare—and in fact, markets also tend to rebound fairly quickly. More important, because of the way the other two pots are structured, you should never need a dollar of these investment funds for your living expenses for at least three years. That allows ample time for the markets to recover (at least partially), and it helps ensure that you won't have to sell much (if anything) at the bottom of the market.

Let's start our example.

In the first pot, the Total Investments Pot, we have combined personal investments *and* retirement accounts like IRAs, and so on (Figure 14.1). The total is $2 million. We *have not changed any of the investments* in any of the accounts at this point. These investments are still held separately in

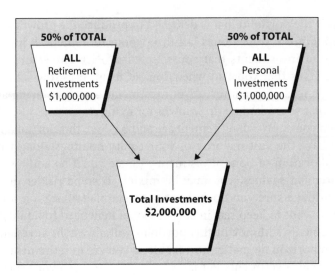

Figure 14.1   Creating the Total Investments Pot

IRA accounts, bank accounts, or personal investment accounts. This is just a virtual "get it all together" moment. This can be easier than you think. Don't include your house or physical possessions. This is about *cold, hard cash* (and investments that can be converted to cash) to live on and to enjoy the rest of your life. If you can't turn it into cash in a short time, forget adding it to the Total Investments Pot.

Now, that was easy—or at least easier than you thought.

To beat inflation and to keep your portfolio growing, you need to make it work for you. That's why the Total Investments Pot needs to stay stocked with equities—and why it should be the biggest piece of the Three Pots.

The Holding Pot: Short-Term Safe Haven for Two to Three Years of Living Expenses

- **Goal:** Keep your money safe from market volatility with conservative instruments
- **Allocation**: Roughly 10 to 15 percent of your investment portfolio
- **Primary investments**: Cash, fixed maturity bond funds (bullet funds), bank CDs, conservative mutual funds

The Holding Pot is a buffer zone between your long-term investment assets (the Total Investments Pot) and your short-term spending needs (the Spending Pot). You should plan to have roughly three years' worth of your planned living expenses held here.

The Holding Pot is designed to smooth out some of the volatility that comes with the equity holdings (and riskier bond holdings) in the Total Investments Pot. The Holding Pot will be conservatively invested in instruments like short-term bond funds, Treasury Bills, very conservative allocation funds, and cash in savings and money market accounts. As you'll see when the Spending Pot is set up, the first year's allotment of money should be turned completely into cash. Many people will say "I don't want to do that," but if the market hiccups when you are withdrawing your monthly "allowance," you want to be happy, and you want your money. Trust me: make the first year cash. The second and third years will be very conservatively invested.

How much should you put in the Holding Pot? Put it this way: *How much can you really live on?* Go back to your plan that you established in Part Two. You laid out the annual living expenses you will need to retire happily and/or comfortably. That's the target amount you'll need to have in the Spending Pot. Hopefully, that number is under 4 percent of your total portfolio because that's the withdrawal level you should aim for. (If it is not under 4 percent, you and your spouse need to have some meaningful discussions regarding how much you need each year. You might want to revisit your plan and your budget for living expenses. Make your long-term plans support your annual needs.)

Let's go back to our example. Let's just say that you and your spouse have decided that you can live on $100,000 a year. Of that, $20,000 is going to come from Social Security. (Social Security is not an investment, so you should consider it as income outside of the Total Investments Pot.) You'll therefore need to pull $80,000 annually from your investments. So far, so good.

The Holding Pot should be stocked with three years of annual expenses. You will need to take $240,000 from the Total Investments Pot and move it to the Holding Pot. Now you have a Total Investments Pot of $1,760,000 and a Holding Pot of $240,000 (see Figure 14.2).

Since the Holding Pot is the money you are going to spend for the next three years, you need to protect it from market volatility. You'll move $80,000 (one year's worth of budgeted expenses) of this $240,000 into the Spending Pot. The remaining $160,000 is going to be used to buy conservative investments to eventually turn into cash each year as needed to live on. You are not looking for high rates of return here. You are looking for safety—and when possible, a guarantee like FDIC protection or a government bond. You'll want to consider these safe options:

- Treasury Bills and Bonds
- Bank CDs

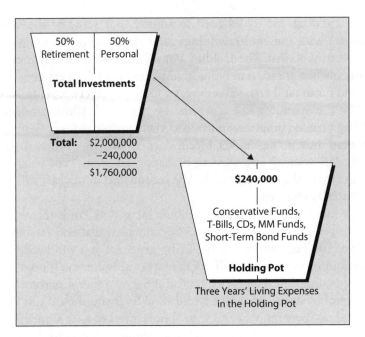

Figure 14.2   Stocking the Holding Pot

- Money market funds
- Short-term bonds, short-term bond funds, or Bullet Bond ETFs
- Conservative mutual funds or ETFs

The money remaining in the Total Investments Pot is still actively invested. Much of it will stay in the same instruments you've owned up until now, but depending on your goals, you may elect to shift some of that money into a more conservative allocation for the long run. (Before you change your allocation drastically, revisit the 60/40 Portfolio versus the Six Fund Portfolio examples—Tables 13.3 through 13.6—in the last chapter.)

How does the Holding Pot keep you safe? The stock market can drop for a year or two at a time, but it very rarely drops three years in a row. By always having three years of spending money in the Holding Pot, you can be confident that declines in the market will not impact your near-term spending for at least three years, and you will not have to sell very much of your portfolio at those unattractively low bear market prices.

In some respects, the Holding Pot might be the hardest pot for people to grasp. It is helpful to look at it this way: as a transition between your long-term investment portfolio and your short-term spending cash, this pot is a rotating chunk of capital that needs to be invested with a two- to three-year horizon. That means investments that are safe but not necessarily totally risk free. The Holding Pot should largely immunize you to the impact of stock market swings, and you should typically not have very much (if any) exposure to equities in this pot.

This is a pot that you should plan to update once a year. As you transfer one year's worth of planned living expenses into the Spending Pot, you need to make a similar transfer from the Total Investments Pot into the Holding Pot. Because you have a buffer of two to three years' worth of expenses here, you might skip one of those transfers if the market is truly tanking. But remember, your Total Investments Pot is the account designed to recover from market fluctuations, so there's no need to get too creative here. Use the Holding Pot as a buffer, not an active investment portfolio.

The Spending Pot: One Year's Expenses Invested in High-Yield Cash Accounts

- **Goal**: Having your immediate financial needs in a safe, liquid, easy-to-access place
- **Primary investments**: Interest-bearing checking, savings, and money market accounts, plus some bank CDs

The Spending Pot might be the simplest one of all. As the name suggests, this is the pot that funds your everyday spending needs (as well as the planned big-ticket items), but that is no reason to miss the chance to make the most of it. Even if it is simple, the Spending Pot deserves your attention and care.

This money has to be quickly available and convenient to access, and that will limit how much you can earn with it. That means cash equivalent accounts like checking, savings, and money market accounts, and possibly very short-term CDs.

Back to our example: The $80,000 in the Spending Pot is now held in cash or cash equivalents (Figure 14.3). You can now draw down the $80,000 on a monthly basis. This money will have had the taxes paid on it if it was previously held in a retirement plan, so that the $80,000 is essentially tax free. (Any interest earned after you withdraw it from your retirement account and put it into a regular CD or money market account would be taxable.)

Although safety and liquidity are your priorities, you can still make this money work for you. With a little bit of hunting around, you will find that there are online savings accounts with check-writing privileges and credit

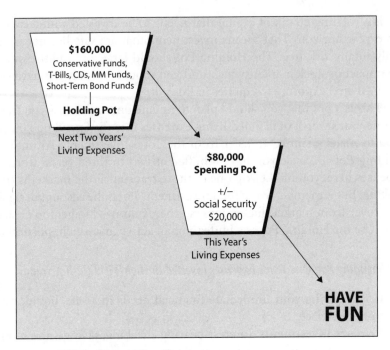

Figure 14.3   Filling the Spending Pot

unions that will pay you a higher rate of interest than most regular banks will pay. While you're at it, remember that it is usually easy to move money electronically from one account to another. Some transfers are instant, and others will take only a few days to be processed. That allows you to keep a relatively low balance in your checking account (which probably will earn you next to nothing), while keeping the bulk of your spending money in a higher-rate savings account.

Does this sound like a bit of a bother? I suppose it might. But let's look at that annual spending budget of $80,000. If you keep just one month's allocation in a regular checking account and the rest in an interest-bearing money market or savings account, you can make a few hundred bucks a year in extra interest. (Even if it's paying just 1 percent!)

Managing Your Three Pots

Managing the Three Pots is a dynamic process. It doesn't seem necessary to me to move money from the Total Investments Pot to the Holding Pot more than once a year, and if the stock market has a down year, you can transfer some of the two years of money that is still in the Holding Pot into the Spending Pot. Likewise, you may find that you do not always need to move the same amount every time. If the funds in your Holding Pot have performed unexpectedly well or if you are spending less than you had planned, you may find that you need to take less out of the Total Investments Pot.

Conclusion

Taking your regular "allowance" from the Spending Pot, which is essentially a cash account, and spending it while watching the market fall may make you a little uneasy. (After all, watching the market tumble makes most retirees uneasy.) But given the alternative of selling stocks at a loss to make ends meet, you can easily see that you are much better off. The markets have always recovered, sometimes not as quickly as you'd like, but they do come back.

Because you have a diversified portfolio of quality investments in the Total Investments Pot—and three years of very secure money in the Holding and Spending Pots, you can rest assured that you really haven't lost any money—just maybe a little sleep! But by this age, you have lost a little sleep over a few things in life.

Creating the Three Pots is a convenient and intuitive way of transitioning money from an investment portfolio to a day-to-day spending account, while maximizing growth potential and protecting yourself from the ups and downs of the market. Using this approach, you will minimize the odds that you are taking significant sums of money out of the market when it is at its lowest points, and you will also have a clear sense of how your actual spending requirements are matching up to your plans.

15

Long-Term Care, Healthcare, and Other Needs

Retirement isn't all exotic trips, fancy dinners, and extra time with friends and family. There will be some trying times after you retire, especially when it comes to your health and the health of your family members. Like it or not, healthcare—and long-term care—needs to be a part of your retirement planning and budgeting. This chapter is meant to be sobering, to make you think, and to help you "get your act together." We humans often put off thinking about things that aren't pleasant.

We have moved from family members taking care of the elderly, because they lived nearby, to moving the elderly into long-term care facilities because often the children are miles, or continents, away.

Long-term care is an idea that has been around for ages. It has simply evolved from the family doing the work to the family hiring professional caregivers in organized living situations. Like many things we have discussed in this book, long-term care is being radically changed by our lengthening lifespans.

Since you have a higher chance of living longer, you have a higher likelihood of needing more expensive care over time. You need to budget for it, and you need to make some important investments in insurance now to offset higher costs later.

How likely is it that you will need long-term care? It's impossible to give a one-size-fits-all answer, but the likelihood is going to keep increasing. The Department of Health and Human Services estimates that 70 percent of people over 65 will need long-term care at some point in their lives. Medicine can keep our bodies running better for longer than ever before, but it does not guarantee a particular quality of life, nor does it guarantee the ability to fully take care of ourselves for all of that time.

What if it turned out that you did not need this care? That's how the "cookie crumbles" sometimes. All insurance, whether it is your home or your automobile or yourself, is about trading the risk of a potentially very expensive loss for the certainty of a smaller loss. In this case, you would have paid a relatively small amount of money early in life to eliminate the risk (and worry) that you would have a much bigger bill to pay down the road. Besides, look at the bright side: not needing your long-term care insurance probably means that you lived a very long and healthy life and died at home in your sleep. That's not such a bad thing, all things considered.

The Cost of Long-Term Care

Long-term care is potentially one of the most expensive and least planned-for aspects of retirement. Early planning and investing in long-term care insurance, though, can significantly reduce the costs and give you better options when the time comes to go into long-term care. The American Association for Long-Term Care Insurance suggests that you begin to plan between the ages of 52 and 64. If you haven't begun to think about it, and you are between those ages, I suggest you do. As they get older, more applicants are turned down because of health issues. Currently in the 60- to 69-years age bracket, 24 percent are turned down, and that number soars in older age brackets.

Statistically, the length of time an average person spends in a nursing home is 2.4 years. Of those who enter nursing homes, 55 percent stay at least one year, and 21 percent stay longer than five years, according to http://www.GuidetoLongTermCare.com. Sadly, the average length of time from an Alzheimer's diagnosis to death is eight to ten years. Insurance company Genworth stated in its 2013 cost survey that half of their payment claims are from dementia patients, including Alzheimer's.

How much does a long-term care facility stay cost? A private room in a nursing home averages $230 a day (or nearly $84,000 a year), and the assisted living average is $3,450 a month (or approximately $41,500 a year). In New England, the rates per day currently are in the range of $200 to $550 a day. The prices vary by region, but that's a sobering sum. Look for the *Genworth 2013 Cost of Care Survey* online, and spend some time looking at the costs where you live.

With the average retired worker getting about $14,000 a year from Social Security, clearly the cost of long-term care is a problem. It is not hard to see how an unexpected stretch in a long-term care facility can devastate a previously sound retirement plan.

Unfortunately, contrary to many people's assumptions, Medicare does not cover very much of it. Following a 3-day hospital stay *and* when ordered by your doctor, Medicare pays for a nursing home in full for only 20 days, and after that, it pays a percentage of the cost up to 100 days. Beyond that, Medicare pays nothing at all, and in most states, Medicare currently does not pay for services like assisted living or adult daycare. The other major government program, Medicaid, helps those who are in really dire economic circumstances, and most people will not qualify. Since Medicare pays for relatively little, and a prolonged stretch of time in long-term care can devastate a savings plan, what can you do?

Investing in Long-Term Care Now

Ideally, you should buy long-term care insurance as early as possible. There are so many options available today that it is best to see someone who specializes in selling many types of policies so you can get a good cross section of what is being offered and the costs involved. Going to just your local insurance agent is a big mistake. Obviously, he or she is going to show you only what his or her company sells, so you may be unwittingly buying a policy that is not as good as another one.

These policies can be prepaid, and you will pay substantially less when you buy a policy as a healthy young person with many, many years to go before needing this care. Long-term care insurance may be prohibitively expensive (or unavailable entirely) if you are already in fragile health. My suggestion is to begin to look in your early fifties and buy soon after. The policy prices go up so that if you buy something at 50, you will pay less than if you wait until you are 60—and the way it works, you are going to pay the same amount (with premium increases over time) as you would waiting to 65. But it is easier to pay $1,000 a year at 50 than $3,000 a year at 60. By the time you retire, $1,000 a year will cut less into your retirement money than $3,000 a year.

Large insurance companies like Genworth and John Hancock offer this kind of coverage, but there are many others. The industry is changing, and some insurance companies have left the long-term care business. With people living longer, and nursing home prices going up, they have found that they cannot survive in this business.

Go online and look for long-term care insurance companies. Find a company rated A, A+, and AA+ by A.M. Best and Company and AAA or AA with Standard & Poor's. Both A.M. Best and Standard & Poor's have rated insurance companies for a long time—and these ratings are Superior or Excellent. Once you've found a couple of prospective insurers, evaluate their rates and special offers. Some companies will give discounts if you already have other policies in force with them. Once you've looked around, look for a company that deals in all types of long-term care policies.

What do I personally own? First, let me say as with the retirement portfolio I showed you in Part Three, just because I own it doesn't make it right for you! Second, I bought our insurance years ago when I was 60 and my wife was 57. I asked an agent to show me as many policies as we could find among companies rated Superior or Excellent. We bought lifetime policies with a 5 percent inflation rider from Genworth. Why lifetime? One child lives permanently overseas, another is out of state, and there's one nearby, so we need to be ready to provide for ourselves. The inflation rider and lifetime coverage made the policies 15 years ago more expensive at the time, but over the years, the premiums have gone up little, considering everything else. If either of us were to go to a nursing home and we *had not bought* long-term care insurance, our annual cost per year would be about what we have paid for the whole policy, so we are really light-years ahead.

Today, a long-term care insurance specialist here oversees our policies for us, and we feel very fortunate to have her and her extensive knowledge. Because new ideas such as "aging-in-place" instead of going to a care facility have become more of a reality, our long-term care insurance pays for help at home, and that is important to us and also cheaper for the insurance company.

Other Options

Of course, there are other options for funding anticipated long-term care needs. If you buy traditional long-term care insurance and don't need it, you probably won't get much (if any) of that money back. But what if you buy an *annuity* with the intention of using those payments to cover any care needs? On one hand, you may have to pay some fees, expenses, and commissions for the annuity. What's more, you cannot simply ask an annuity to start paying early because you need the money. You will begin receiving the annuity payments whenever the contract says you will, and that may or may not coincide with your needs. On the other hand, money put into an annuity is not at risk of going to waste—the annuity will pay you whether you are in long-term care or not, and you can spend the money however you wish. (For more on annuities, check out Chapter 10.)

However, companies have been designing policies that combine life insurance and annuities for long-term care. These new policies, commonly referred to as *hybrids*, have steadily gained in popularity. A hybrid policy has the benefit of blending two products into one. If you don't use the long-term care insurance, you can still benefit from the life insurance or the annuity. Put simply, this is not use-it-or-lose-it coverage. To many policyholders, this feature can add a great deal of value and peace of mind. These products are commonly funded with a single premium that can be reallocated from existing sources, like other annuities, CDs, qualified money, or even life insurance policies. *Cash value life insurance plans* taken out years earlier may be repositioned into a hybrid plan in order to provide long-term care benefits without giving up existing life insurance coverage. These hybrid policies are also specifically designed to receive special tax considerations when it comes to paying out the benefits.

There are also some *traditional (nonhybrid) life insurance* policies that are available. These policies include a rider that allows you to collect a cash advance against the death benefit of the policy. This is another option to consider when you are planning how to pay for long-term care. These clauses are usually very restrictive. For instance, to receive a payment, you may have to have a terminal diagnosis, permanent disability, or a long-term need for care. Odds are that you will pay more for policies with this feature, and you may not be able to get the full death benefit advanced to you. Because the details of these policies vary so much among carriers, I cannot emphasize enough the importance of working with a long-term care specialist.

Taking Care of Others

Many people will find themselves in a position in which they must help meet the long-term care needs of someone other than themselves and a spouse. More specifically, many couples find that they have to help with the long-term medical or financial needs of one or more aged parents. This is a difficult situation for everyone involved, but there are some options that can help the situation.

For starters, make sure you get as much information as you can. Parents may have a policy for long-term care that they have forgotten about, and there may be a rider in their life insurance policy (if they have one) that can help defray these costs. A reverse mortgage (which I address at length in Chapter 16) is also an option to consider. Failing that, you may need to consider helping a parent sell his or her home (if there will be no one living in it) and speaking to other siblings about sharing the costs of this care.

If you suspect that you will be in a position where you have to help out in the future, you could look into buying a long-term care insurance policy for the parents in question, though the odds are good that the cost will be very high by the time you realize long-term care is likely to be required. Alternatively, you can consider an annuity—either an immediate annuity or one that begins payments in relatively short order—as a way of covering those costs. These are not great options, but they can help mitigate some of the costs.

Healthcare Decisions

There are other financial details that you need to consider and plan around as part of a complete retirement plan. Taking care of your ongoing health-care needs is certainly a major concern. You also need to make preparations to cover situations in which you might be unable to make decisions on your own.

Health Insurance

Just because you may be approaching age 65 and eligibility for Medicare, that does not mean your health insurance needs are about to be taken care of completely. The Affordable Care Act is not totally comprehensive either. If you are over 65, Medicare is not all-encompassing. In order to cover those expenses that Medicare does not reimburse (or covers only partially), there are a host of Medicare *supplement* (or Medigap) insurance policies.

The Centers for Medicare & Medicaid Services have standardized these supplemental policies into 12 plans. They are designated A through L, and each has its own combination of benefits and premiums. Each state has a number of companies that offer these solutions. Log on to http://www.Medicare.gov, the official U.S. government Medicare website, and you may find answers to some of your questions.

Medicare supplemental insurance is sold by private companies, and it is known as *Medigap insurance*. It can help pay for services that Medicare doesn't pay for in some instances, and it also may help with deductibles.

The following "Eight Things to Know About Medigap Policies" is from http://www.Medicare.gov:

Eight Things to Know About Medigap Policies

1. You **must** have Medicare Part A and Part B.
2. If you have a Medicare Advantage Plan, you can apply for a Medigap policy, but make sure you can leave the Medicare Advantage Plan before your Medigap policy coverage begins.
3. You pay the private insurance company a monthly premium for your Medigap policy in addition to the monthly Part B premium that you pay to Medicare.
4. A Medigap policy covers only one person. If you and your spouse both want Medigap coverage, you'll each have to buy separate policies.
5. You can buy a Medigap policy from any insurance company that is licensed in your state to sell one.
6. Any standardized Medigap policy is guaranteed to be renewable even if you have health problems. This means the insurance company can't cancel your Medigap policy as long as you pay the premium.
7. Some Medigap policies sold in the past cover prescription drugs, but Medigap policies sold after January 1, 2006, aren't allowed to include prescription drug coverage. If you want prescription drug coverage, you can join a Medicare Prescription Drug Plan (Part D).
8. It's illegal for anyone to sell you a Medigap policy if you have a Medicare Medical Savings Account (MSA) Plan.

Medicare Advantage Plans

There is another choice to supplement your coverage: a Medicare Advantage Plan. A Medicare Advantage Plan is a type of Medicare health insurance plan offered by a private company, and most of these plans include prescription drug coverage. It contracts with Medicare to provide you with all of your Part A and Part B benefits. It can be a *health maintenance organization* (HMO), a *preferred provider organization* (PPO), a private *fee-for-service plan*, a *special needs plan*, or a *Medicare medical savings account* (MSA).

A Medicare Advantage Plan must follow the rules of Medicare. Each plan is different. Some Medicare Advantage Plans allow you to go to a specialist without a referral, and others require that you get a referral from your primary care doctor to see a specialist. Some of these plans require you to use a certain "set" of doctors. These rules are not carved in stone, and they may change from year to year. Just be sure as you review these plans that you look at a plan that will help you specifically. Your neighbor's plan isn't automatically the right plan for you.

Today, my wife and I personally have a Medicare Advantage Plan called Care Improvement Plus through UnitedHealthcare. This Advantage Plan is particularly good in the area of the state in which we live.

The following "Twelve Things to Know About Medicare Advantage Plans" is from http://www.Medicare.gov:

Twelve Things to Know About Medicare Advantage Plans

1. You're still in the Medicare program if you sign up for Medicare Advantage.
2. You still have Medicare rights and protections.
3. You still get complete Part A and Part B coverage through the plan.
4. You can join a plan at only certain times during the year. In most cases, you're enrolled in a plan for a year.
5. You can join a Medicare Advantage Plan even if you have a preexisting condition, except for end-stage renal disease (ESRD).
6. You can check with the plan before you get a service to find out if the preexisting condition is covered and what your costs may be.
7. You must follow plan rules, such as getting a referral to see a specialist to avoid higher costs if your plan requires it. The specialist you're referred to must also be in the plan's network. Check with the plan.
8. If you go to a physician, dentist, or other healthcare provider—or a facility or supplier—that doesn't belong to the plan, your services may not be covered, or your costs could be higher. In most cases, this applies to Medicare Advantage HMOs and PPOs.
9. If you join a clinical research study, some costs may be covered by your plan.
10. Medicare Advantage Plans can't charge more than Original Medicare for certain services like chemotherapy, dialysis, and skilled nursing facility care.
11. Medicare Advantage Plans have an annual cap on how much you pay for Part A and Part B services during the year. This annual maximum out-of-pocket amount can be different between Medicare Advantage Plans. You should consider this when you choose a plan.
12. If the plan decides to stop participating in Medicare, you'll have to join another Medicare health plan or return to Original Medicare.

Budgeting for Healthcare Costs After Retirement

As you plan and budget for your retirement, it is essential that you factor in health insurance and long-term care insurance. Make sure that you are considering things like deductibles and other costs like pharmaceuticals or equipment that might not be covered. It's a good idea to have money set aside in your annual budget for these expenses. If you don't need to use it, you can reinvest it or spend it as you see fit.

More Details That Matter: Legal Obligations

Retirement planning is more than just saving and spending. It's taking a long, hard look at your life and the steps you need to take to ensure that you can take care of yourself. But there are things that you **must** do so that your loved ones can take care of you too.

There are various types of authority you can grant to people—authority over your finances (or certain accounts), authority to make medical decisions for you, and so on. Not only is it important for you to pick people whom you trust and whom you can trust to execute your wishes but it is also important that the people you select want to be involved in the process. Giving someone the power of attorney means giving him or her lot of authority and a lot of responsibility.

Living Wills, Healthcare Powers of Attorney, and Making Your Care Wishes Known

It is vitally important that you think carefully about establishing a living will and healthcare power of attorney.

In most cases, a *living will* comes into play only when you are in a terminal condition (and some states actually specify that a certain number of physicians must determine that you are in a terminal condition). Moreover, living wills really pertain only to life-sustaining treatments. So in cases of Alzheimer's, dementia, and so on, a living will is of little use. It is also important to formulate a plan for managing a possible future decline in your mental faculties. As you might imagine, it is much better to address this matter when you are still in fine form.

A *healthcare power of attorney* should be discussed *thoroughly* with your attorney. This is a broader authority, coming into play not only when you may be terminal but also when you are not in a position to speak for yourself. With cases of Alzheimer's or prolonged mental incapacity, a medical power of attorney is not only useful but very important. You should be aware that some states do not allow you to use a universal form, and some states have special requirements for witnesses in certain care facilities.

The biggest advantage of having both a living will *and* a healthcare power of attorney is that the living will gives a clear expression of your wishes concerning life support procedures. A power of attorney can be a heavy responsibility for some people, and they may agonize over trying to decide what you would wish for them to do. A living will gives a little more clarity to the situation, and it may help ease any guilt that may go with making the decision to remove or prevent life support.

A nonprofit organization, Aging with Dignity, has gone a step further, and it created a document called "Five Wishes" (available at http://www .agingwithdignity.org/five-wishes.php). The first two wishes are basically a declaration of healthcare power of attorney and a living will—designating someone to make medical decisions for you if and when you cannot and detailing what sort of life support treatments you do (or do not) want.

The final three wishes are not legally enforceable documents, but they are important all the same. Wish 3 expresses your desires concerning pain management, grooming, and whether you wish to discuss hospice care. Wish 4 talks about even more personal preferences, including whether you would prefer to be cared for at home and whether you want religious attention at your bedside. The final wish is an opportunity for you to express how you want to be remembered, what sort of funeral arrangements you prefer, and other matters relating to tying up your personal affairs.

Financial Powers of Attorney

A *financial power of attorney* is another matter altogether. Simply put, a financial power of attorney gives someone of your choice the power to make financial decisions when you are not in a position to do so. This authority can extend to something as minor as allowing someone to pay your bills if you are stuck in the hospital for a few weeks, or it can extend to something as major as taking care of all your financial affairs if you become physically or mentally incapable of doing so yourself. A financial power of attorney does not give someone the authority to change your will, and like any other power of attorney, a financial power of attorney expires with you.

Estate Planning

Throughout the book, I've encouraged you to set up a portfolio that can sustain itself, even after inflation takes its bite and you withdraw your planned expenses. That means you're well positioned to have money left over when you pass away. Since you can't take it with you, you should also give thought to how you want to pass on your estate after you die and how you can do so in the most effective way possible. The following subjects are often complex. Since they fall outside of the realm of retirement planning, I want to address them briefly, but I encourage you to seek out more information and professional advice.

It is important to have a living will—and a *regular* will. Depending on your estate, you may need to add a trust or two to go along with your will, and the fees can range from a few hundred dollars to a few thousand or more if your estate is complex. If it is extremely complicated, a tax attorney should be used for planning and to create a valid and enforceable will. Moreover, attorneys can be helpful in making sure that you express your wishes on all relevant matters that pertain to your estate. You need to have at least a simple will. Don't put it off!

Write down your wishes for particular personal possessions (such as your golf clubs or your gold watch) that you would like to go to a specific child or grandchild. Put your written wishes in a safe place, and make sure you tell people where to look for it when you die. Some people like to include these instructions in their wills, but others just direct the executor to carry out their written wishes for distribution of personal property. Many people don't include personal articles in their will because they may change their mind about who should get a particular item. If the gift were included in the will, then they would have to alter the will (with additional legal expenses) in order to change things.

Dying without a will is just plain crazy. It can be disastrous for those left behind. The trouble and expense your heirs will go through may always color how they think of you in years to come. After almost 30 years of helping people with their finances, I can assure you that the easiest way to have a fight in the family is to not be specific about who gets what. Even at that, some children (or their spouses) are never satisfied. That being said, the only thing you really owe your family is the clarity that a will provides.

Tax Planning

Your savings in your retirement accounts are happily free from the headaches and hassles of the tax picture, at least until you retire and begin paying taxes on the money you withdraw. In all likelihood, you've got a fairly complex tax situation outside of your retirement portfolio. Tax planning becomes increasingly relevant and significant the more assets and wealth you have. The average couple may not need to worry too much about the tax ramifications of their decisions and their estate, but people who are in higher wealth brackets should certainly consult a qualified accountant and a tax attorney.

It is also an unfortunate reality that tax laws are perpetually in flux. Estate taxes, for instance, have become something of a political football in recent years, and nobody knows what the picture will be in five years.

Because of that, I would advise all readers to be careful about making financial decisions that cannot be easily reversed on the basis of taxes alone. It is all well and good to minimize your current taxes. (In fact, it makes all the sense in the world!) But you don't want to slip into "penny-wise, pound-foolish" thinking where you spend inordinate amounts of time and money just to send a few bucks less to the IRS every year.

Nevertheless, if there are substantial assets in your estate—particularly assets like businesses or real estate that you wish to pass on to the next generation—it is important to structure that transfer in a way that does not force your heirs to sell those same assets just to pay taxes. This is where a qualified team that includes your accountant and tax attorney really earns their fees.

Conclusion

Retirement should be a carefree, enjoyable time for you and your family. Planning carefully and investing wisely will help you get there. However, you must face facts when it comes to health-related, legal, and life issues that will be a part of your post-retirement world. Ignoring the challenges and realities of human life now will add to your burden later. You owe it to yourself—and to your spouse and other family members—to deal with your healthcare and legal obligations now. This investment in your future well-being is as important as any dollar you put into a retirement account.

16

Emergency Alternatives

Even if you follow every step in this book religiously, things may still go wrong. You know the old saying, "Even the best laid plans of mice and men . . ." Despite your best efforts and careful planning, something unexpected may happen in the markets or in your personal life. However, if you are diligent with your investing, most situations won't be severe enough to cause you to run out of money.

You *can* expect that the market will probably go down sometime during your retirement. After all, you are going to be retired for 20 or 30 years or more. You can bet the TV programs and the newspapers are going to scare you. But if you are careful and if your Holding and Spending Pots (discussed in Chapter 14) have three years of living expenses safely stashed away, you will be able to weather the storm.

When the Unexpected Occurs

Things may look bad, but now you have a **plan**. Most people don't. They just fly (and invest) by the seat of their pants. In your case, unless something unprecedented comes along, you can work through most problems if you stick to your plan.

Unexpected serious illness, legal problems, divorce, and the need to help out other family members can all seriously deplete your assets with little warning. But when you retire, you should let everyone know that, in most cases, other than taking care of yourselves, the checkbook is off the table.

Financial Triage

In extreme situations, you may need to consider financial triage. Think about how a serious accident involving many people is handled when those people reach the hospital emergency room. The emergency room personnel perform triage: they give top priority to the most serious treatable "injuries," while letting those with less serious conditions wait.

For financial triage, the first step is doing whatever you need to do to minimize any loss. It is hard to give precise advice on how to do this because no two emergencies are going to be the same. Nevertheless, try to get a sense of what the total cost is going to be, when you will have to pay, and what your cash flow needs are going to be as a result.

Reducing Expenses

The next step should be to eliminate any unnecessary expenses. Fixing an unexpected financial pothole is going to require some austerity, so you need to get comfortable with the idea of living a little lower on the hog for some time and using the surplus to repair your nest egg. If a fire seriously damages your home and you find that you are underinsured, it is probably not a good time to be heading for a ski vacation in Aspen. Likewise, even a simple change like switching from dining out to dining in could free up thousands of dollars that can go back into your retirement funds. Financial triage also requires that you reevaluate your goals and make them workable for you and your family.

Revisit Chapters 13 and 14. The 4 Percent Rule could be a great guide through tough times. Could you scale back your annual expenses to get them under 4 percent? If so, you could preserve your primary investments and give them a better chance to regain positive momentum when the market returns. Could you tweak the balances in the Three Pots to help out? You could move a little more money from the Holding Pot to the Spending Pot if you needed a safe haven from market volatility—or you could reduce your transfer into the Spending Pot if a market recovery were imminent. (You are gambling on the market when you make these kinds of moves, so proceed with the utmost of caution.) In many cases, you are going to find to your surprise that if you simply stay the course and keep following a steady, sustainable plan, you will quickly get back on track.

Other Options

If you find that going back to work is not an option and/or the deficit in your finances is too great to be healed by patient investing or cautious spending, there are some other strategies for raising money that you can consider. I will caution you that these methods can be complicated and expensive. None of them offer you a "great deal," but they are nevertheless reasonable approaches to dealing with a difficult situation.

Reverse Mortgage

I am not a fan of reverse mortgages in most cases. However, they can offer one solution to sudden money woes that can't be fixed by sticking with your plan and tightening your belt.

A reverse mortgage basically works like this: in exchange for the deed to your house when you die, the buyer agrees to make monthly payments to you for however long you are in the house. In some respects, a reverse mortgage is a lot like an annuity. You surrender an asset up front (in this case, your house), and in exchange, you get a stream of payments into the future.

In actual practice, a reverse mortgage is still a loan. The loan is underwritten with the understanding that the borrowed amount may exceed the value of the house (and the lender takes a loss), but it is a loan all the same. The money you can expect to get is critically tied to the location and condition of your property. If your house is in good condition and in a good location, you may get a decent value. But if your house is in less-than-pristine condition or it is in a less-than-desirable area, you may find it very hard to get a fair value.

Obviously, a reverse mortgage can be a good deal if you think you're going to live for a very long time and/or you have no one to leave your house to when you die. However, be careful about the fees and costs that often go with these plans, as well as the fine print. To qualify, you must be 62 years old. Also, any existing mortgage has to be paid off (though the proceeds from the reverse mortgage can be used for that purpose). Applicants will also be required to speak with an approved financial counselor with the Department of Housing and Urban Development (HUD) to make sure that they understand the process and its ramifications.

Potential users of a reverse mortgage should remember another detail: it is not just death that can trigger the transfer of the property to the lender. If you do not live in your house for a specified period of time (often one year), the house can be claimed by the lender if you cannot or do not repay the loan. This timing issue can become a big factor if you end up in a long-term care facility. Given that people who enter long-term care do not often go back to living independently, that may not be a problem, but it is worth remembering.

Entering into a reverse mortgage does not necessarily mean that your heirs cannot inherit that property. When you die and your estate is settled, there will be an option for your heirs to refinance (pay off) the reverse mortgage and keep the property. That does put a potential financial burden on your heirs, so it's a good idea to review the fine print *and* discuss it with your family.

The money you get in a reverse mortgage is *not* taxable income, so it will have no bearing on Medicare or Social Security. It does change the balance of your liquid assets, however, and that can impact eligibility for Medicaid, Supplemental Security Income (SSI), and other benefits.

In a financial emergency, a reverse mortgage may be a better option for you instead of trying to sell your current house, buying a smaller house, and then using the surplus to patch up those holes in your savings.

Selling a Business

If you've retained a share of your business or practice post-retirement, you can certainly consider selling those assets to plug a hole in your retirement savings. Keep in mind that selling a business is not like cashing in a savings bond or selling a stock. Not only might this be an emotional process but it is also neither fast nor simple.

Any way you slice it, selling a business should not be a response to a temporary or otherwise easily remedied problem. At a minimum, make sure to revisit your prior assumptions about income and expenses throughout retirement. If you had included regular dividends from your business as part of your retirement income, that income clearly has to be readjusted if you decide to sell that business.

If you do decide to sell your business, you will need to find a buyer, and you will need to value your business. Finding a buyer could be a simple matter of talking to a trusted employee or partner who has expressed interest in taking from you, or perhaps a competitor who has approached you in the past. Alternatively, you may run a franchise where the parent company has specific policies for transferring ownership (perhaps including the option for them to buy the business at some contractually determined price).

Beyond these options, you may want to talk to your peers, advisers, and even your banker. While bankers will not generally act as formal go-betweens, they may very well know people who run similar businesses and have an interest in expansion, or they may know those in the community who can broker a deal.

Ultimately, though, selling a business is like selling any other asset: it is a process of finding a common ground between you and the buyer. (See Chapter 5 for more on valuing and selling a business.)

Rethinking Your Business

Instead of selling a business, folks who can tolerate some extra risk may want to think about a radically different approach. If it is clear that you do not have enough savings for a comfortable retirement and if you are not likely to be able to build up those savings, you may want to think about using the money you have to *expand* your business. Let's say you have $40,000. You can either invest it in the market and make an 8 percent return, or you can use it to expand your business in order to earn a 10 percent return. In other words, it might actually make more sense to expand the business than to invest in the market. You have to be very realistic about these projections and the likelihood of earning a superior return by reinvesting in your business, but there certainly may be cases in which the returns would be superior.

Along similar lines, you can think about restructuring the business in a way that can continue to pay you after you are no longer able (or willing) to be involved in the day-to-day operations. Giving up authority and control can be difficult, but continuing to "work" as an absentee owner can give you a monthly income that basically replaces the income other people get from drawing down their retirement savings.

Borrowing Against or Selling Insurance Policies

If your financial problems look to be temporary or transitory, borrowing against the value of an insurance policy can be a reasonable approach. You are not going to get the best rate for this loan, but that's the way it goes when you need money and don't have a strong bargaining position. That said, the rates on these loans usually *are* quite reasonable and certainly preferable to the rates on credit cards and other unsecured loans.

Rules and laws about borrowing against policies vary among states, companies, and policies, but there are a few general points that are common. These loans do not necessarily have specific repayment terms. In fact, you may not need to ever repay the loan at all. Keep in mind, though, that any balance will reduce the eventual benefits that the policy pays out.

Holders of insurance policies can also elect to surrender those policies and receive the cash surrender value. This process is pretty straightforward, and the money received is treated by the IRS as ordinary income.

On the downside, you will never get as much from cash surrender as you will get from the death benefit, and you may get only a fraction of what you've put into the policy over the years (in the form of premiums).

Lately, another option for turning life insurance policies into cash has emerged: the selling or transfer of policies to investors in exchange for cash. There are investors out there who are attracted to the cash flow and diversification that insurance policies can provide. In principle, this is a win-win—the person holding the insurance policy gets cash, and an investor gets a nontraditional investment that can produce a return that has little to do with the stock market.

These sorts of transfers are usually handled through an intermediary, and as you might imagine, there are fees attached to that service. In cases in which policyholders have not been paying premiums for many years, these sales may produce more cash than a simple surrender to the insurance company.

This option can make even more sense after a spouse passes away and there is no one who needs the income replacement that life insurance policies are designed to provide. If the primary purpose of the policy was to make sure that the surviving spouse had enough to live on, it makes sense for the owner to get the best possible return from that asset.

Conclusion

When your retirement runs into rough waters, your first move still should be "Don't panic." You have planned carefully and saved diligently. It would be disastrous to throw out all of your hard work (and well-earned money!) just to fix a short-term hiccup.

Take a long-term view of the situation. Can you tighten your belt for a year or so to ensure smoother sailing in the future? More important, will your dramatic changes today have a permanent impact on the rest of your retirement? Take a deep breath, think carefully, and consider all of your options before taking action.

17

Life After Retirement for Professionals and Business Owners

As we wind down the discussion of planning for retirement and enjoying the fruits of your labor, I want to address a few things that my fellow professionals often ask. Funnily enough, they revolve around two opposite areas: "Can I retire early?" **and** "Can I keep working?"

Early Retirement

When you look around and see people who are retiring early, you may feel a little jealous. For many people, early retirement is a dream with an almost irresistible pull, and they work toward that goal almost from the day they start working. Whether it's leaving the rat race, traveling the world, spending time with kids, or pursuing charity work, there are a lot of people who really hope to stop working well before the "normal" retirement age.

It really isn't a fantasy, but retiring early is going to cost you. If you are going to retire at age 55, you'll need about one-third more money than you would if you retired at 65. You will have healthcare needs before you become eligible for Medicare, and you will have to pay for that care (and/or insurance) on your own. You will also have to fund your living expenses—you may not be able to tap into any of your tax-deferred accounts without incurring IRS penalties, and you may find that the capital gains taxes that go with selling stocks, bonds, and funds take a nasty bite as well.

The first thing to consider about early retirement is whether you **really** want to retire early. A number of people I know have taken a sabbatical of six months or longer, and that has allowed them to rethink early retirement. After their sabbatical, many went back to their old job or to their business or practice, having realized that they just needed an extensive break. By all means, it is never worth staying in a job that makes you miserable, but you also do not want to let a bad job push you into an early retirement that ends up significantly less than what you had hoped for earlier in life.

While many retirement programs (including Social Security and many corporate and government pension plans) have provisions that will let a worker retire many years before the statutory retirement age, there is always a catch. Retirement plans are set up and run according to certain assumptions, and two of the big ones are how long workers will remain in the workforce and how long they will spend in retirement. When you retire early, you basically break their assumptions, and the price for "breaking the rules" is a reduced benefit.

If you have been working for yourself, you have become aware of some of the problems that will arise with early retirement. If you have been working for others, those problems may not be as clear. So before you consider retiring early, you need to see what the ramifications will be for you.

For example, companies will offer early retirement benefits as a way of cutting the workforce without "firing" people, and sometimes they will sweeten the pot by reducing or eliminating some of those early retirement penalties. However, you really need to be careful in analyzing these offers. If you are lucky enough to still have a defined benefits plan with your employer, will you still get the same payments and for the same length of time? Will you still get healthcare coverage through your employer? These are vital questions you need to answer before signing on the bottom line. Ultimately, the decision has to be based at least in part on your financial means. If you are in your forties and you can divide your savings by your annual spending needs and come up with a rather large number (say, 50), then you are in good enough shape to retire early.

Staying Active in Your Field—by Choice or by Necessity

If you are a healthcare or legal professional or a business owner, you are a little bit different from the rest. You are dedicated to your career, you like the challenges of your work, and you like having control over your professional life. I can tell you right now that your retirement will also be a little bit different. Sure, a break seems like a nice idea, but you may have a hard time giving it all up. And that need to achieve may continue to work to your advantage. With your strong work ethic, you can continue to supplement your retirement savings—and in more uncertain periods, it can save the day if the market crashes or if unexpected expenses pop up.

Once you retire completely, everything changes. You may find that you miss the work—or that you miss the income. You might find that you miss having something to do. I'm not going to advise you on how to keep yourself entertained, but I can help with some thoughts on the business side of retirement. There are ways that you can remain active that positively impact your retirement plan.

Steps to Take Before Retirement

If you are the type who won't be able to quit working cold turkey, be honest with yourself, your partners, and your family. If you aren't honest with yourself about it, you might end up making a poor business decision (and therefore, a poor financial decision) when you reach the age of retirement. (In other words, don't sell your practice or your business if you really want to keep working there!)

If you know that you aren't going to be able to give up working, you might consider ways to have an ongoing role but downshift your responsibilities at your practice or business. For example, you could retain your partner or ownership status—and reduce your hours. Alternatively, you could sell your ownership stake in the business and rejoin it as an employee or a contractor.

These are personal decisions that will affect your happiness and well-being, but they will also have an impact on your retirement wealth.

If you continue on as a partner in your practice or business, you'll be keeping a large chunk of your wealth tied up in a very illiquid asset. It may well be worth retaining that ownership, but low liquidity is generally not a desirable thing in retirement. It may come back to bite you—and more important, it may be a complicated thorn in the side of your spouse or other heirs. Have an exit strategy in place.

If you are simply going to continue working (without the ownership factor coming into play), you should factor your ongoing income into your overall plan. Consult those goals, and figure out how to save (and/or spend) that money accordingly. If it's simply a supplement to your solid and successful retirement savings, it's okay to spend the money or to invest it in something more aggressive than the bulk of your assets.

Going Back to Work

Some people, it's sad but true, retire and then have to un-retire due to unexpected problems. Miscalculations. Unexpected expenses. Market volatility. Poor management. If any of these happen, double-check your plan and your goals. Do your best to figure out what went wrong, but if your plan fell apart, don't keep plugging money into it.

You do need to keep saving, as best you can. A permanent, stable retirement should still be your goal—and it can be achieved even after a rough first try.

When you reenter the workforce, refresh your retirement plan, and carve some money out of each paycheck to rebuild your nest egg. A steady stream of income is a budgeter's best friend, so try to work out a contract or a position where you are bringing home a reliable and predictable sum.

Of course, as a professional, you can't just waltz back into work if you are no longer qualified to do so. Make sure you keep your license and any needed certifications up to date. Take some continuing education courses. Keep your network and your industry connections up to speed.

The Effect of Going Back to Work on Social Security, Pensions, and Other Income Sources

If you earn money after you "retire," remember that you may be short-circuiting some other income sources, like Social Security. With Social Security, you can earn about $40,000 a year in wages or self-employment income after you reach full retirement age. (That's somewhere between 65 and 67, depending on the year you were born.) After you pass that earning level, your Social Security check will start to decrease (by $1 for every $3 you earn), so there's a point where you might be at a disadvantage between your paycheck and your Social Security check. (Remember, as we saw in Chapter 11, you can also benefit by waiting to claim Social Security benefits until age 70.)

Don't forget that you will have to start taking *required minimum distributions* (RMDs) from most of your retirement plans when you reach 70½. There may be exemptions if you are still working or if you have rejoined the workforce, so check with your plan administrator to be sure.

Your work status may also have an impact on other retirement income flows, like pensions. You should double-check the pension rules and regulations to make sure that your extended non-retirement or unanticipated reentry into the workforce is addressed.

Leveraging Your Talents to Create Income Streams Without "Working"

Most professionals love their jobs—and even more love the money they make doing the work they've dedicated their lives to. Let's take a brief look at other ways to continue making money for those of you who can't, won't, or don't want to "work" after retirement.

These paths can bolster your retirement nest egg and keep you active in your field while leveraging your years of education and hard work. It's a good idea to make the right connections sooner than later, but isn't it always a matter of investing for your future one way or another?

Consulting

Using your professional skills in a consulting role is a great way to leverage your knowledge into a post-retirement "career" of sorts. For medical professionals, one of the most likely consulting paths is as an adviser to attorneys dealing with medical cases, especially if you have specialized in a specific field. There might also be consulting roles with pharmaceutical and biotech companies, medical organizations and hospitals, universities, and local government agencies that are involved in your area of expertise.

Outside of the health fields, you might find advisory and consulting roles in similar places as well as with peer companies (and perhaps even competitors!).

Serving on a board of directors is another quasi-consulting role to consider, but make sure you understand the risks and liabilities of that kind of service. Some board members have been sued and fined when problems arose. There are forms of liability insurance for board members, but it's not always foolproof. You should be augmenting your nest egg, not risking it!

Contracting

Trying to differentiate between *contracting* and *consulting* may be splitting hairs for someone with a career's worth of experience, but I'm referring to the short-term work that is typically done under a work-for-hire contract. This kind of work is usually a little more hands on than consulting work. For dentists and physicians, contract work might include a fill-in or emergency backup role at a practice. For attorneys, it might be conducting research or interviews for a larger case.

Teaching

Of course, the classic option is to teach. In all likelihood, you'll find most opportunities here are unpaid—as a mentor, adviser, or speaker. But there may be ways to get involved as an instructor at a higher-learning institution, especially if you have cultivated those relationships early on. (You are probably already on a target donor list from your alma mater and your local university. This might be a favor you can call in later.)

Conclusion

Whether you want to (or have to) work after retirement, make sure you factor your decisions into your overall retirement goals, investment plan, and budget. Be honest with yourself and your loved ones. It's easier to keep working than to stop and start again. Don't make yourself miserable mentally after you've worked so hard to take care of yourself and your family financially.

Conclusion

Putting It All Together

Planning for retirement requires a significant investment. I'm not just talking about your money though. You need to commit your time and energy to it too. I hope you've seen that if you spend the time up front with your plan and your portfolio, you don't need to make retirement planning a full-time job.

Let's recap some of the most important ideas that will shape your retirement:

- It all starts with a plan. You need to establish your goals and a realistic budget for life after retirement. That plan will influence how you invest and how you withdraw your money post-retirement.
- You have to balance the joys of retirement with the realities of your healthcare and long-term care needs, especially when setting your goals.
- Before you start investing, you need to set up an asset allocation plan that supports your goals and keeps your investments diversified.
- With just six carefully chosen mutual funds, you can have a portfolio that outperforms the market and keeps you protected from extreme market volatility.
- Investing in individual stocks and bonds requires more time, more effort, and more attention to diversification, but you can be successful if you accept the challenge.
- Post-retirement, stick to your plan and budget. Keep your withdrawals consistent and under 4 percent.
- Use the Three Pots system to protect your money from volatility in the short term—and keep the rest of your money working hard.

In the end, I want to remind you about two things. First, *no one loves your money like you do.* You've got to watch out for it, protect it, and make it work for you. You don't have to do it all yourself, but no one will look out for your best interests as much as you will.

Second, you can do this. I've worked with hundreds of clients. While I'm happy to help them, I push them to define their personal goals for themselves and to understand what they need to do to be successful investors.

With a little work and a little guidance, you are going to have a great retirement.

Index

A

ABS (asset-backed securities), 151
Advisers, financial (*see* Financial advisers)
Affordable Care Act, 224
Aging with Dignity, 228
"Aging-in-place," 222
AIG, 111
Alzheimer's disease, 220
American Association for Long-Term Care, 220
Analytic assessment tools, 139–145
Annual reports, 128
Annuities, 159–164
  costs of, 162
  for covering long-term care costs, 222–223
  defined, 159
  drawbacks of, 162–164
  fixed indexed, 160
  fixed tax-deferred, 160
  immediate, 159–160, 163–164
  life, 160
  in personal finance inventory, 54–55
  popularity of, 159–160
  types of payments on, 159–160
  variable, 160
Assessment tools, 139–145
Asset allocation:
  with bonds, 112
  with mutual funds, 100–103, 112–113
  overview, 75–78
  with stocks, 137
  strategic, 76, 132, 168
  tactical, 76, 168
Asset Allocation: Balancing Financial Risk (Gibson), 91, 138
Asset Allocation Funds, 96, 101, 107–108
Asset-backed securities (ABS), 151
Assets, in personal finance inventory, 51–56

B

Back-end load funds, 113
Balanced Funds:
  investment objectives with, 101
  overview, 107–108
  in portfolio, 77, 95–96
Bank accounts, 50, 215–216

Bengen, William, 206
Berwyn Income Fund (BERIX),
    43–44, 82
Beta, 139
Biotech stocks, 137
Bismarck, Otto Von, 14
Bloomberg L.P., 90
Bodie, Zvi, 138
Bonds, 146–152
    and asset allocation, 112
    avoiding risky, 150–151
    costs of, 152
    designing portfolio of, 147–148
    domestic and international bond
        funds, 104–107
    government, 213
    hiring money managers for advice
        on, 152–153
    investing in, 148–150
    laddered, 147–148
    and living expenses, 212
    and managing your portfolio,
        153–154
    municipal, 149
    mutual funds vs., 151–152
    short-term, 214
    stocks vs., 104
    Treasury Inflation-Protected
        Securities, 46
Bottom-Up goal-setting method, 29–34
Broker fees, 89, 117
    (See also Load fees)
Budgeting, 39–40, 226–227
    (See also Goal setting)
Bullet Bond exchange-traded funds, 214
Business partners, 63
Businesses and practices, 59–68
    assets of, 56
    company retirement plans for, 59–60
    dealing with partners of, 63

debts stemming from, 58
restructuring of, 234–235
retaining shares of, 67–68
safeguarding savings from loss/
    liability of, 60–62
sale of, 65–66, 234–235
transferring ownership of, 66–67
valuation of, 62–68

C

C Corporations, 61
Capitalization, 83
Carroll, Lewis, 27
Cash and cash equivalents, 50
Cash value life insurance plans, 223
Centers for Medicare & Medicaid
    Services, 224
Certificates of deposit (CDs), 50,
    213, 215
Certified Financial Planners, 178
Checking accounts, 215
COLA (cost-of-living-adjustment),
    175
Commercial mortgage-backed
    securities (CMBS), 151
Commissions, financial adviser, 181
Company options, 53
Company retirement plans, 17, 59–60,
    186
Company-specific risk, 136
Compounding earnings, 73
Conservative portfolio allocation, 36, 37
Consulting services, 241
Consumer Price Index (CPI-U),
    41–43, 202
Consumer Price Index for the Elderly
    (CPI-E), 41
Contract work, 241–242
Cost-of-living-adjustment (COLA),
    175

Covered-call writing, 146
CPI-E (Consumer Price Index for the Elderly), 41
CPI-U (Consumer Price Index), 41–43, 202
Credit card debt, 57–58
Credit unions, 50

D
DCA (*see* Dollar Cost Averaging)
Debt, 57–58
Default risk, 147
Defined benefit pension plans, 160–161
Defined contribution pension plans, 161
Direct home ownership, 156–158
Discretionary spending, 200
Diversifiable risks, 79–80
Diversification:
  for avoiding investment problems, 179
  with bonds, 148
  of investments, 78–85, 87
  with stocks, 137
  with target-date funds, 168
Dividends Still Don't Lie (Wright and Lowe), 145
Dividends-as-income approach, 199
Dodge & Cox Stock Fund, 124–125
Dollar Cost Averaging (DCA), 74–75, 80, 127
Domestic bond funds, 104–107
Domestic stock funds, 103–104
Dow Jones 30 Index, 110
Duration (bond funds), 105, 147–148

E
Early retirement, 237–238
Earnings per Share (EPS), 139

Emergency situations, 231–236
  borrowing against insurance policies, 236
  expense reduction, 232
  financial triage, 232
  restructuring your business, 235
  reverse mortgages, 233–234
  selling insurance policies, 235–236
  selling your business, 234–235
EPS (Earnings per Share), 139
Essentials of Investments (Bodie, Kane, & Marcus), 138
Estate planning, 228–229
Exchange-traded funds (ETFs):
  Bullet Bond, 214
  in Holding Pot, 214
  overview, 108–111
  in real estate space, 159
Expense ratio, 116
Expenses:
  with annuities, 163
  assessing your, 39
  of fund companies, 113, 126, 127
  hidden, 116–117
  living, 212–215
  reducing your, 232
  in retirement planning, 7–8
  underestimation of, 44

F
Farmland, 158
Federal Deposit Insurance Corporation (FDIC), 164
Fee-for-service health plans, 225
Fidelity, 124–125, 162
Financial advisers:
  fees of, 18, 180–182
  investment managers vs., 177
  value of, 9
  (*See also* Financial professionals)

Financial calculators, 73–74
Financial Industry Regulatory
    Authority (FINRA), 180
Financial Planners, 177–178
Financial power of attorney, 227–228
Financial professionals, 177–189
    achieving goals with, 179, 183–185
    fees of, 180–182
    holistic approach offered by, 187
    and measuring investment
        performance, 186–187
    personal investment practices of,
        188–189
    qualifications of, 178
    realistic expectations for, 182–183
    reputation of, 179–180
    retirement planning expertise of,
        185–186
    types of, 178
Financial services industry, 6, 9,
    17–19
Financial triage, 232
FINRA (Financial Industry Regulatory
    Authority), 180
First Eagle Global A Fund, 114
Fitch, 146
Fixed indexed annuities, 160
Fixed tax-deferred annuities, 160
Flash Crash of May 6, 2010, 111
Flat-fee model (financial advisers), 182
Ford, Gerald, 41
The Four Percent Drawdown Rule
    (Bengen), 206
4 percent withdrawal rule, 194–198
401(k) plans:
    annuities in, 163
    in personal finance inventory, 51–52
FPA Crescent Fund, 37, 125
Front-end load funds, 113, 115
Future liabilities, 58

G

Geer, Carolyn T., 160
Genworth, 220–222
Gibson, Roger, 91, 138
Glide path, 167
Global Funds:
    investment objectives with, 101
    in portfolio, 77, 96
Goal setting, 27–47
    Bottom-Up Method for, 29–34
    and budgeting, 39–40
    creating list of goals for, 27–29,
        45–46
    and financial professionals, 179,
        183–185
    inflation as consideration for, 32–33,
        41–44
    and investment returns, 35–39
    top priorities in, 46–47
    Top-Down Method for, 34–35
Gold, 164–165
Google, 83
Government bonds, 213
Growth and Income Funds:
    investment objectives with, 102
    in portfolio, 77, 95
Growth Funds, 108

H

Health insurance, 224–226
    (See also Medicaid; Medicare)
Health maintenance organizations
        (HMOs), 225, 226
Healthcare, 224–228
    assessing costs of, 40
    budgeting for, 226–227
    Medicare and Medicaid, 174, 221,
        224–226
    power of attorney for decisions
        related to, 227–228

Healthcare power of attorney, 227–228
HMOs (health maintenance organizations), 225, 226
Holding Pot (Three Pots investment strategy), 212–215
Home ownership, direct, 156–158
Housing costs, 39

I

Idiosyncratic risk, 88
Immediate annuities, 159–160, 163–164
Immigration, 175
Independence, 22
Index funds, 108–109
Individual retirement accounts (IRAs), 51, 169
Inflation:
  and goal setting, 32–33, 41–44
  and Social Security, 175
  and withdrawals from savings, 202
Inflation risk, 147
Installment debt, 57–58
Insurance:
  borrowing against policies, 236
  health, 224–226
  (*See also* Medicaid; Medicare)
  liability, 62
  life, 223
  for long-term care, 221–224
  malpractice, 62
  in personal finance inventory, 54
  selling policies, 235–236
Interest rates, 105
Interest-only approach to savings withdrawal, 199
International bond funds, 104–107
International stock funds, 103–104
Investment Company Fact Book, 94

Investment managers, 177, 178
  (*See also* Financial professionals)
Investment portfolio:
  bonds in, 147–148
  growth of, 200–201
  increasing riskiness of, 45
  managing and rebalancing your, 153–154
  moderate vs. conservative allocation in, 36, 37
  mutual funds in (*see* Mutual funds)
  stocks in, 136–137
Investment Quality Trends newsletter, 143–145
Investments, 71–91
  analyzing returns on, 35–39
  asset allocation of, 75–78
  compounding earnings on, 73
  costs of, 89
  diversification of, 78–85, 87
  Dollar Cost Averaging model for assessing, 74–75, 80
  financial calculator for assessing, 73–74
  individualized nature of, 82–83
  resources for finding information on, 89–91
  and time value of money, 71–73
  (*See also specific types, e.g.:* Mutual funds)
IRAs (individual retirement accounts), 51, 169

J

John Hancock Insurance, 221
Journal of Financial Planning, 206

K

Kane, Alex, 138
Khan Academy, 90

L

Laddered bonds, 147–148
Legal obligations, 227–228
Lehman Brothers, 111
Leisure money, 40
Liabilities, 56–58
Liability insurance, 62
Libraries, resources from, 90, 122
Life annuities, 160
Life expectancy, 19
Life insurance, 223
Limited Liability Companies (LLCs), 61
Limited Liability Partnerships
    (LLPs), 61
Limited Partnerships, 169–170
Living expenses, 212–215
Living wills, 227–229
LLCs (Limited Liability Companies), 61
LLPs (Limited Liability
    Partnerships), 61
Load fees, 113–118
    gathering information on, 117–118
    and hidden expenses, 116–117
    overview, 113–114, 126, 127
    and performance, 114–116
Long-term care, 219–224
    cost of, 220–223
    history of, 219
    for others, 223–224
Long-term investments, 210–212
Lowe, Janet, 145

M

Madoff, Bernie, 179
Malpractice insurance, 62
Marcus, Alan J., 138
Marital status, 173–174
Market timing, 74–75, 188
Master Limited Partnerships (MLPs),
    156, 158–159, 169, 206

MBS (mortgage-backed securities), 151
Means testing (Social Security), 175
Medicaid, 221
Medical savings account (MSA), 225
Medicare, 174, 221, 224–226
Medigap insurance, 224–225
Micro-cap stocks, 83
Microsoft, 83
Minimum amounts (mutual
    funds), 128–129
Minney, Michael, 145
MLPs (Master Limited Partnerships),
    156, 158–159, 169, 206
Moderate portfolio allocation, 36, 37
Money:
    healthy relationships with, 14
    time value of, 71–73
Money managers, 152–153
    (*See also* Financial professionals)
Money market funds, 50, 214, 215
Monte Carlo simulation, 206
Moody's bond ratings, 146–147
Morningstar, Inc., 85, 90, 122, 158
Mortgage-backed securities (MBS),
    151
Mortgages:
    in personal finance inventory, 56–57
    reverse, 57, 233–234
MSA (medical savings account), 225
Municipal bonds, 149
Mutual funds, 93–108, 112–119,
    121–133
    analyzing returns on, 123–125
    asset allocation with, 100–103,
        112–113
    average performance of, 35–39
    benefits of investing in, 87
    bonds vs., 151–152
    composition of, 83
    conservative, 214

cost of, 113–118, 126, 127
exposures with, 125–126
fees associated with, 126, 127
gathering information on, 94, 103,
121–122, 128–129
managers of, 122–123
managing your, 129–132
number of, 95–103
objectives of, 86
overview, 93–94
prospectuses of, 128
purchasing, 126–128
risk and volatility of, 125, 129
selecting, 121–129
types of, 103–108, 118

N
Nasdaq, 94
National Registry of Unclaimed
Retirement Benefits, 52
Net asset value (NAV), 109
New Deal, 15
New York Stock Exchange, 94
No-load funds, 113, 115
Nondiversifiable risks, 79
Nonsystematic risks, 79–80

O
Opportunity cost, 72

P
Partners, business, 63
Partnerships, limited, 169–170
P/E (Price-to-Earnings) Ratio, 139, 141
PEG (Price-to-Earnings Growth)
Ratio, 139, 141
Pension plans:
changes in, 160
defined benefit, 160–161
defined contribution, 161

and going back to work, 240
income from, 210
in personal finance inventory, 51–52
Pentagon Federal Credit Union, 50
Percentage-of-assets model (financial
advisers), 181
Performance measurement (for
investments), 186–187
Personal finance inventory, 49–58
annuities in, 54–55
business assets in, 56
business liabilities in, 58
cash and cash equivalents in, 50
company options and stocks in, 53
credit card and other installment
debt in, 57–58
future liabilities in, 58
insurance policies in, 54
mortgages in, 56–57
property and real estate in, 53–56
retirement accounts in, 51–52
Power of attorney, 227–228
Practices (*see* Businesses and practices)
Preferred provider organizations
(PPOs), 225, 226
Price-to-Book Value Ratio, 139, 141–142
Price-to-Earnings Growth (PEG)
Ratio, 139, 141
Price-to-Earnings (P/E) Ratio, 139, 141
Price-to-Sales (P/S) Ratio, 139, 142–143
Private practices (*see* Businesses and
practices)
Profit sharing accounts, 51–52
Property, 53–54
(*See also* Real estate investments)
Prospectuses, 128
P/S (Price-to-Sales) Ratio, 139, 142–143

Q
Quick Ratio, 143

R

Real Estate Investment Trusts (REITs),
    156, 158–159, 206
Real estate investments, 155–159
    Master Limited Partnerships, 156,
        158–159, 169, 206
    in personal finance inventory, 55–56
    Real Estate Investment Trusts, 156,
        158–159, 206
    rentals and direct ownership, 156–158
    risk with, 155–156
Real estate market bubble, 55
Rebalancing, 131–132, 153–154
REITs (*see* Real Estate Investment
    Trusts)
Rentals, 156–158
Required minimum distributions
    (RMDs), 197–198, 240
Retirement accounts, 51–52
Retirement living, 237–242
    making money during retirement,
        241–242
    and retiring early, 237–238
    and returning to work, 240–241
    staying active in your field during,
        238–239
    steps to take prior to, 239–240
Retirement planning, 3–11, 13–23
    approach to, 9–11
    benefits of, 22
    changes in, 15–16
    common excuses for delaying, 19–21
    expenses in, 7–8
    financial professionals' knowledge
        of, 185–186
    and financial services industry, 6, 9,
        17–19
    finding time for, 13, 21–22
    getting started with, 5–6
    and loving your money, 14

mistakes made with, 8
    options for, 16–17
    and retirement as new
        phenomenon, 4
    Social Security in, 14–16, 171–172
    trends in, 5
    (*See also specific headings*)
Retirement savings, 193–207
    dividends and interest-only
        withdrawal approach to, 199
    essential vs. discretionary spending
        of, 200
    4 percent rule for withdrawal from,
        194–198
    and portfolio growth, 200–201
    resources for managing, 205–206
    safeguarding your, 60–62
    time-based withdrawals from, 199–200
    timing of withdrawals from, 202–205
Return-sequence risk program, 206
Reverse mortgages, 57, 233–234
Riders (annuities), 161
Risk(s):
    with bonds, 150–151
    company-specific, 136
    default, 147
    diversifiable (nonsystematic), 79–80
    idiosyncratic, 88
    inflation, 147
    with mutual funds, 125, 129
    nondiversifiable (systematic), 79
    with real estate investments, 155–156
Risk tolerance, 79
RMDs (required minimum
    distributions), 197–198, 240
Russell 1000 Index, 110

S

S Corporations, 61
Savings (*see* Retirement savings)

Schwab Institutional, 114
Schwed, Fred, Jr., 85, 206
SEC (*see* U.S. Securities and Exchange
    Commission)
Short-term bonds, 214
Small businesses (*see* Businesses and
    practices)
Social Security, 171–176
    determining amount of your,
        172–173
    and going back to work, 240
    history of, 14–16
    political challenges to, 21, 174–176
    privatization of, 175–176
    as supplementary part of retirement
        plan, 171–172
    waiting to collect, 173–174
S&P (Standard & Poor's), 146–147
    (*See also* Standard & Poor's 500)
S&P (Standard & Poor's) 500 Index
    Fund, 37
Special needs health plans, 225
Spending, discretionary vs. essential,
    200
Spending Pot (Three Pots investment
    strategy), 215–216
Staggered maturity dates, 105
Standard & Poor's (S&P), 146–147
Standard & Poor's (S&P) 500:
    comparing your mutual funds
        with, 96
    exchange-traded funds following,
        110
    overview, 80, 82, 97
Standard & Poor's (S&P) 500 Index
    Fund, 37
Statements of additional information,
    128
Statutory prospectus, 128
Steele Mutual Fund Expert, 90, 122

Stocks, 135–146
    analytic tools for assessing, 139–145
    asset allocation and diversification
        with, 137
    bonds vs., 104
    categorization of, 83, 84
    costs of, 152
    covered-call writing with, 146
    doing research on, 135, 138
    domestic and international stock
        funds, 103–104
    hiring money managers for advice
        on, 152–153
    income from, 145–146
    investing in individual, 87–89
    and managing your portfolio,
        153–154
    micro-cap, 83
    in personal finance inventory, 53
    portfolios of, 136–137
    technology, 80, 137
Strategic asset allocation, 76, 132, 168
Structured withdrawals, from savings,
    195–196
Student loan debt, 57–58
Summary prospectus, 128
Systematic risks, 79

T

T. Rowe Price, 123
Tactical asset allocation, 76, 168
Target-date funds, 166–169
Tax planning, 229–230
Tax-deferred annuities, 160
Tax-deferred growth benefit, 163
Taxes:
    with bonds, 147, 152
    with private businesses, 67
Teaching, during retirement, 242
Technology stocks, 80, 137

Third-party administrators (TPAs), 60
Three Pots investment strategy,
    209–217
    dynamic money management in,
        216–217
    Holding Pot in, 212–215
    Spending Pot in, 215–216
    time-based withdrawals vs.,
        199–200
    Total Investments Pot in, 210–212
Timberland, 158
Time horizon, 79, 80
Time value of money, 71–73
Time-based savings withdrawals,
    199–200
TIPS (*see* Treasury Inflation-Protected
    Securities)
Top-Down goal-setting method,
    34–35
Total Investments Pot (Three Pots
    investment strategy), 210–212
TPAs (third-party administrators), 60
Traditional life insurance plans, 223
Transportation costs, 40
Treasury Inflation-Protected Securities
    (TIPS), 46, 148, 213

U
U.S. Bureau of Labor Statistics, 41
U.S. Department of Health and
    Human Services, 219

U.S. Department of Labor, 52
U.S. Securities and Exchange
    Commission (SEC):
    asset allocation resources provided
        by, 90–91
    mutual fund resources provided by,
        117
    and prospectuses, 128
    registration with, 53
U.S. Treasury, 46

V
Value Funds, 108
Value investors, 188
Value Line for Mutual Funds:
    checking stocks on, 143–144
    information provided by, 90, 122
Vanguard, 111, 162
Vanguard Wellington fund, 100, 137
Variable annuities, 160

W
Weiss, Geraldine, 145
*Where Are the Customers' Yachts? or
    a Good Hard Look at Wall Street*
    (Schwed Jr.), 85, 206
Wills, 227–229
Wright, Kelley, 145

Y
Yahoo! Finance, 90, 122, 158

About the Author

Jim Jackson is a Certified Financial Planner, who in the late 1980s founded Jackson Financial Co., Inc., a financial planning and registered investment advisory firm. As a partner in the newly formed JBJ Investment Partners, LLC, he continues to advise clients on investments and retirement planning, overseeing and managing assets for clients from coast to coast.